CONTENTS

PREFACE: THE GOODWILL NEWSLETTER

Global events are the most heart-warming goodwill newsletter of modern times. Periodically, they burst into social consciousness as part of an established cycle of global festivity (the Olympics, the FIFA World Cup, the Rio Carnival, the Sydney Mardi Gras) or in response to an international emergency or incident (Live Aid, Tsunami Relief, the Benefit Concert for Hurricane Katrina). For the duration we are conscious of being part of an international community in which pre-ordained divisions of race, class, religion, sexual orientation, politics and the vulture logic of capitalism appear to magically vanish. Instead, the urge to do good, which is an entirely human and proper sentiment, is hot wired into disinterestedly celebrating the athletic prowess of Olympians or world class professionals in sport; feeding the hungry in Africa; ending torture in Darfur; providing relief from the misery and want that follows an earthquake or *tsunami*; saving the planet from pollution and corporate greed; or more prosaically, conveniently reminding ourselves at the company meeting that we are truly serving the customer and doing good, rather than merely maximising profit. The point about disinterest is revealing, because event logic is built on highly personal displays of emotional energy. Participation in events has become a mark of responsible citizenship, with all of the subsidiary implications for judgements of self-worth, validity and ethically acceptable behaviour that this implies.

Events are designer-built packages to boost publicity, symbolise fraternity and heighten awareness. Increasingly, global events employ celebrities to transfer glamour from the entertainment sector onto charitable and business undertakings.

The organisers and front men and women that present them see themselves as providing positive pedagogy (teaching us about third world inequality and injustice), enhancing social networking and contributing to cultural literacy.

Success in entertainment is redefined as honing a strong humanitarian, global perspective. For example, in Sydney (2011), the Global Leadership Forum brought George Clooney and Martha Stewart together with Muhammad Yunus, Russell Simmons, Michael Fertik and Jeff Taylor and put them on the stage of the Sydney Convention Centre to 'unwrap the concepts, vision and motivation' behind 'authentic leadership' and provide 'challenging new ways of thinking, working

EVENT POWER

HOW GLOBAL EVENTS MANAGE AND MANIPULATE

CHRIS ROJEK

Los Angeles | London | New Delhi
Singapore | Washington DC

Los Angeles | London | New Delhi
Singapore | Washington DC

SAGE Publications Ltd
1 Oliver's Yard
55 City Road
London EC1Y 1SP

SAGE Publications Inc.
2455 Teller Road
Thousand Oaks, California 91320

SAGE Publications India Pvt Ltd
B 1/I 1 Mohan Cooperative Industrial Area
Mathura Road
New Delhi 110 044

SAGE Publications Asia-Pacific Pte Ltd
3 Church Street
#10-04 Samsung Hub
Singapore 049483

Editor: Mila Steele
Editorial assistant: James Piper
Production editor: Imogen Roome
Copyeditor: Jane Fricker
Proofreader: Katie Forsythe
Marketing manager: Michael Ainsley
Cover design: Jen Crisp
Typeset by: C&M Digitals (P) Ltd, Chennai, India
Printed in India at Replika Press Pvt Ltd

© Chris Rojek, 2013

First published 2013

Library of Congress Control Number: 2012955760

British Library Cataloguing in Publication data

A catalogue record for this book is available from
the British Library

ISBN 978-0-85702-517-3
ISBN 978-0-85702-518-0 (pbk)

A revolutionary age is an age of action; ours is the age
of advertisement and publicity.

Soren Kierkegaard

One can trust anyone who babbles the jargon; people wear it in their
buttonholes. ... Simply to be there becomes the merit of the thing.

Theodor Adorno

Narcissism and the direct satisfaction of impulses are major obstacles
to the emergence of any collectivity worthy of the name.

Serge Moscovici

It is not clear to me how advanced large-scale societies can
fulfil the requirements of expressivism, other than by holding
Nuremberg rallies.

Ernest Gellner

and living'.[1] Ordinary men and women are urged to learn how admired members of the powerful and influential draw on strong, cleansing emotions and apply them to higher business and humanitarian causes. In a world in which people are often triply estranged from government, the state and big business, global events are cheerful testaments to people power. The Forum celebrated the best practice of celebrity trend setters in humanitarian and business enterprise and conjured a spirit of presumed intimacy between strangers. For a moment we are *team-world*, and there is no obstacle of nature, faith, church, economy or polity that we cannot overcome.

The desire to do good is magically combined with the satisfaction of feeling good. Events contribute to a positive self-image. They possess therapeutic value. Their scale and importance has ascended in direct proportion to the expansion of social and cultural injunctions to get more in touch with our feelings and to emote frankly and without shame. Ernest Gellner (1994) once speculated that as human societies develop more efficient and dependable infrastructures of security, the struggle for survival is replaced with a struggle for approval and acceptance. If he is right, global events are the biggest human-made objects of approval and acceptance ever devised. The Olympics, the FIFA World Cup, Live Aid, Live Earth, Live 8 and their cognates are catalysts for deep emotional arousal and exchange. They issue licence to break out of our daily bubble of existence and allow us to express our no-holds barred common humanity. It is as if global events supply ordinary men and women with the intimation that the 7 billion people on the planet constitute the fundamental human entity, beyond the walls of nation, race, class and religion.

Yet events are neither spontaneous nor free expressions of people power. They are closely organised, schooled in the methods of exercising persuasion over human cognition by market research, rigorously planned and monitored in detail. Events are publicised as expressions of 'people power', but event ownership and management do not rest with the people. To be sure the entire category of the event audience is problematic. The mixtures of stadium crowds and network publics constitute an *illusory community*, in which unity and commitment are largely apparitions.

Many commentators increasingly point to the control functions of events. Events are portrayed as radiant, symbolic representations of civil society coming together. In reality, they apply principles of hierarchical authority and keep citizens at arm's length from 'mega-project decision making' (Flyvbjerg et al., 2003: 5).[2] Citizens are not directly involved in planning, commercialisation and securitisation. In cyclical events like the Olympics and FIFA World Cup, the use of CCTV (closed circuit television) and UAVs (unmanned aerial vehicles) is a standard part of the security package. Global events are actually among the most controlled, regimented settings devised.

As Stephen Graham (2010, 2012) observes, the securitisation of the London Olympics (2012) involved the deployment of more troops than the war in Afghanistan. Anti-terrorism and crowd control measures involved the use of unmanned drones, surface-to-air missile systems, and a thousand armed US diplomatic and FBI agents policing an Olympic zone divided from the rest of the city by an 11-mile, £80 million 5000-volt electric fence. Investment in electronic surveillance included a new range of scanners, biometric ID cards, number plate and facial recognition CCTV systems, disease tracking surveillance and checkpoints.

Intensive risk assessment and adequate security and surveillance provision are now part of the global event planning process. It is subject to well-oiled lobbying interventions from the security and surveillance industry. Pressure from this quarter led to the investment of a $300 million 'super panopticon' CCTV and information system for the Athens Olympics (2004) (Samatas, 2007). Graham (2012) estimates that the cost of providing security for each athlete in the Athens Games was £90,000. For the London Olympics he puts the cost at £59,000 per competitor.

Investment on this scale puts a huge strain on metropolitan and national finances. The Athens Games are widely regarded to have created a culture of easy borrowing which was a major factor in the collapse of the Greek economy after the 2008 financial crash. In the bidding process, the estimated cost of the London Games was £2.37 billion. By the opening ceremony, this was held to have climbed to £24 billion (Graham, 2012).

All of this is done in the name of protecting 'the people'. Yet citizens are not a genuine party to the decision-making processes. Post-event, the security and surveillance provision is transferred to providing 'more effective' community and city-wide policing. A version of Naomi Klein's (2007) famous 'shock doctrine' is at play here. Namely risk assessment of event anti-terrorist and crowd control security requirements underwrites colossal investment in security and surveillance systems which contribute to the more intensive policing of domestic populations in the post-event scenario.

Event concepts frame the event for the media and the public. The formation and application of the event concept is pivotal. Generally, it is simple, eye-catching and designed to appeal to the emotions, not the mind. 'Feed The World' was the event concept that defined Live Aid. Simultaneously, it demarcated solidarity and defied criticism. It is still rolled out today to combat academic and media accusations that post-event fund distribution squandered the Live Aid money earmarked for relief.[3]

As the event planning stage unfolds and moves into event proper and post-event relations, the event concept is a convenient short cut to override jarring sentiments and conflicting meanings that individuals and groups bring to, and take from, the event process. The concept is the brand. In an age where self-advertising and impression management are automatically accepted as the key to gaining personal impact, branding is everything. Selling the cause to the public effectively means developing the right concept, in the right place and at the right time. Event concepts work best when individuals accept, without reflection, that universal issues and problems are on team-world radar and that they *must* act upon them *as one*.

Outwardly, events are ecumenical. Unconsciously, they exhibit many elements of religious evangelism and old style salvationism. For example, the event concept is presented as bringing the ordinary man and woman *into confidence*. The issue or problem is a *message* about which 'good' people should know. The Make Poverty History campaign, which the Live 8 (2005) event showcased, aimed to turn people of all nations into *disciples* in the march against hunger, disease and inequality.

Global events focus on problems of misery, want and collective improvement. But their internal hard drive, which gradually becomes more palpable as the event process unfolds, is to bring the message of *good news* to people. Needless to say, good news does not lie in the human wreckage that follows a natural or geopolitical disaster. Rather it is the image of the true and noble response of the people to get stuck in, sort things out and affirm a fellowship that is admirable and appealing. Although we habitually feel powerless and impotent in the face of the world's problems, events permit us to feel that we are *making a difference*. Our *conviction* and *energy* provides an infusion of hope to the wretched. When we see a gay rights float at the Sydney Mardi Gras or a costume parade featuring the *pessoas humilde* (humble people) at the Rio Carnival or the image of starving African infants broadcast on the video screen of a concert to relieve hunger, we become part of an irresistible wave of global unity.

All for One and One for All

The popularity of global events reveals important changes in the culture of charity and problem solving. It is not for nothing that Chris Hedges (2010: 200) observes:

> The belief that we can make things happen through positive thoughts, by visualizing, by wanting them, by tapping into our inner strength, or by understanding that we are truly exceptional, is peddled to us by all aspects of culture.

The most seductive mouthpieces that entreat us to make these acts of virtue are celebrities. To name but a few, George Clooney, Angelina Jolie, Cameron Diaz, Bono, Bob Geldof, Mia Farrow, Michael Stipe, Jay Z and Madonna are celebrity advocates and diplomats who preach on global issues and problems. In doing so, they impart a reviving, *can do* attitude to the public. Events are out of the ordinary experience, so it is no surprise that they use people who are culturally defined as *extraordinary* to inspire ordinary people to act. Celebrities have become an adjunct of the event brand. They humanise event goals and provide event management with sparkle. By assuming a noble, imploring attitude to help, they place themselves on the same footing with those whom they address.

Events are portrayed as virtuous responses to international emergencies or commemoration of long-standing injustice (such as gay repression or racial exclusion) and business and government are cast in the part of clumsy, inefficient operators. Audiences receive not only the gratification of being invited to help, they also have the self-confirmation of being 'in the know', i.e. being conversant with real world issues that ordinary people are unaware of, in which George, Angelina, Cameron and Bono confide with us. Additionally, there is the rhetoric of direct action which contrasts sharply with the image of muddling through that is associated with so much of what business and government do. Thus, events are presented as belonging to people with 'modern' attitudes. By implication, those who do not attend to, or participate in, events are 'pre-modern' or 'traditional'.

But what do events really accomplish? To begin with, we should allow that it would be foolish to dismiss the reality and force of goodwill. Corporate events, for example, provide the workforce with an opportunity to revive and reinforce *esprit de corps*. Business and humanitarian events are no different in this respect. Businesses have long recognised the value of corporate events to improve camaraderie among the workforce and build the brand. Events switch resources to displays of corporate pride and unity. The strong emphasis upon 'speaking frankly' during the business event awayday provides a showcase for management to exhibit a caring, listening attitude. The professional event literature is vocal in claiming social integration and organisational image enhancement as standard event outcomes (Bowdin et al., 2011; Getz and Wicks, 1994).

Turning to humanitarian global events, there is no doubt that they bring people together and are fully capable of generating resources for the relief of misery and want. Events aspire to the condition of a people party. They provide the strong and winning image of people power. Nonetheless, questions are raised about both the longevity and concrete results of event people power. A number of studies suggest that event consciousness is finite (Collins, 2001; Elavsky, 2009). That is, popular interest in event causes fades away after the stage is dismantled and the perimeter fence and portable toilets are packed away.

Moreover, event consciousness is largely communicated through votive behaviour. It lies in the *pledge* to donate money to relieve suffering and the *promissory* grace-note to convert ludic energy into a moral crusade to change the very system that blights the world with hunger, injustice, carbon fuel emissions, nuclear power and so on. The question is, how far is votive behaviour removed from meaningful action? Do we change the world by attending a pop concert for famine relief or are we subconsciously participating in a gaudy enterprise whose consequences are incapable of rising above leaving the scaffold of power that protects the engines of inequality, injustice and irresponsible enterprise intact? Some research into event participation claims to expose the shallowness in the crowd and network public of the promissory grace-note to change the world. Instead it presents event participation more prosaically as a break from the routine of work, the monotony of unemployment and the activation of undiluted escapism (Tickle, 2011).

Might it not be that global events are more accurately viewed as part of the latest consumerist move towards what some observers in the USA have called 'self-gifting' (Carroll, 2011)? That is, the therapeutic practice of periodically and ostentatiously giving presents to yourself in order to provide self-gratification and serve notice to others of personal worth.[4] Dean MacCannell (2011: 24) speaks of the rise of a new world of consumer experience that is already among us, in which behaviour takes the form of 'staged authenticity', in which appearance is all. In these conditions, concludes MacCannell, 'raw ego' has replaced personality.

Certainly, given the scale of human resources required, the money and manpower raised by global single-issue events like Live Aid and Live Earth, or cyclical events like the FIFA World Cup and the Olympics, offer little more than pinpricks of relief. Further, while global events are estimable outpourings of personal compassion, they are in reality a distraction from the severe economic, political and social issues on the world agenda. What is required is a fundamental thorough-going revision of fiscal responsibilities to remove toxic debt burdens in the developing world and create secure fair trade frameworks (Easterly, 2007; Moyo, 2010; Sachs, 2010, 2011). Instead of fixating on incidents, emergencies and episodes, events should contribute to a popular understanding of the underlying structures of power and causal sequences that reproduce inequality, injustice and exclusion.

These criticisms suggest that it is dangerous to take events at face value. A more searching attitude to *who* defines events, *how* they are managed and *what* they achieve is required. These are substantive questions having to do with how power is generally distributed and operates. However, overwhelmingly, the professional event literature provides a *technocratic* view of events. It focuses on the nuts and bolts in the machine and when and where to oil the parts. The crucial issues of who owns the machine, who controls it and what is its purpose are confined to the backwaters.

Event capitalisation is not merely a matter of economics. It encompasses the cultural capital and psychological energy that events generate. For too long a blind eye has been turned to the questions of how this capital relates to social ordering and the politics of self-gratification. What needs to happen is greater transparency about event aims and outcomes to ensure that events are understood clearly and the resources that they generate used appropriately.

In order to do this the relationship between events and emotional governance must be addressed. Events are important links in the chain of communication power that influential social networks deploy to regulate global populations. While the roots of causes generally lie in the work of activists, the media and associated power networks take them over and use their message for their own ends (Castells, 2009: 331–2). In gratifying individuals that they make a difference to world affairs and boosting social consciousness about global incidents and emergencies, events provide succour to all who suffer from pangs of guilt about colonialism and world inequality. They replace the logic of political economy with the romance of charity. They offer a sense of transcendence and the comforting feeling of personally providing something that is missing in the world. There is a child-like purity in putting your shoulder behind the wheel that feeds the world, ends poverty, halts pollution or celebrates brotherhood. However, the publicity radiance that precedes and accompanies a global event has the effect of making us brain-blind.

The scale of economic, humanitarian and environmental problems facing the world is bigger than the competence of any single event or amalgamation of events to solve. When we come together at a company meeting as one entity, the conflicts of interest that divide us, and the differences in authority and power that separate us from one another, melt away on stage, but stubbornly persist after the wine and canapes at the post-event party are consumed. In any case, a pragmatic focus on the ends of the event concept is the wrong place to concentrate energies. This is hard to articulate candidly, because events are so securely positioned on the moral high ground in our culture; but to the extent that events deflect efforts from strategic issues of power and inequality which are not merely divisive, but antagonistic, they are a red herring.

This book is written in the conviction that events *do* provide something that is missing: pinning the tail to the donkey. They stir up a global media *mazurka* that unintentionally obscures the structural transformations that are necessary to make the world (or the corporation) a better place. They perpetuate a homespun philosophy that ordinary men and women have hearts of gold, who think of their neighbours first. They make us feel like heroes, just for one day. But who is driving the donkey and to what end?

Notes

1 Clooney was advertised as 'an actor, activist and co-founder' of the charity Not On Our Watch; Martha Stewart as one of 'the world's greatest entrepreneurs'; Muhammad Yunus as CEO of Grameen Bank and Nobel Peace Prize Winner; Russell Simmons – founder of Def Jam Records and Phat Farm clothing and author of *Do You! Twelve Laws to Access the Power in You to Achieve Happiness and Success* – as one of the 'most influential people in the past 25 years'; Michael Fertik as 'founder of reputation.com'; and Jeff Taylor, as 'founder of Monster.com and Eons.com'. Planned and managed by the Growth Faculty, an Australian education and public relations organisation, the event billed itself as being about 'unwrapping genius'. Reserved tickets were advertised at $A595; Premium Reserve at $A880; VIP Reserve at $A1100; and the VIP Cocktail Pack, providing seating at the VIP front section, access to VIP catering and networking and a ticket of entry to the VIP Cocktail Party in which all speakers, except George Clooney, 'will attend'.

2 Events are typically presented in terms of a partnership – between event organisers, audiences and network publics, between chief executives and the workforce. In reality, the professionalisation and commercialisation of global events has created a monopoly over security and cost control in the event management team.

3 The strong self-image of global events as providing worthwhile pedagogy, contributing to cultural literacy and fundraising goes hand in hand with an exceptionally defensive attitude to criticism. When BBC reports alleged that Live Aid money had been appropriated to buy munitions and arms for the war in Ethiopia, Bob Geldof responded with the furious indignation that we associate with an Old Testament prophet. As we shall see later, there is a good deal of evidence to show that Live Aid funds *were* used to purchase munitions and arms that prolonged the war in Ethiopia (pp. 127–35). But because this evidence conflicts with Live Aid rectitude it is denigrated and pulverised by event planners and managers.

4 Even votive behaviour (to make a financial pledge) carries strong positive associations in event participation.

1
WHAT IS EVENT MANAGEMENT?

Event management refers to the targeting and managing of designed public events geared to invest emotional energies and economic resources to selected goals. Events are a branch of the hospitality, leisure and tourism industries. The field they address concerns aggregate issues known in the trade as Meetings, Incentives, Conventions and Exhibitions (MICE). The foremost examples of global events are single-issue international charity-building and consciousness-raising events such as Live Aid (1985), Sport Aid (1986), the Nelson Mandela 70th Birthday Concert, aka 'Freedomfest' (1988), the Indian Ocean Tsunami Relief Concert (2005), Live 8 (2005), Live Earth (2007), the Haiti Relief Concert (2010); and global cyclical events like the FIFA World Cup, the Olympics, Oktoberfests, Burning Man City, annual international literature, film and drama festivals, trade expositions, Carnival, Mardi Gras and heritage festivals.

At the local and national levels, events are also commonplace in the form of neighbourhood festivals, corporate meetings involving the whole workforce, management awaydays, horticultural shows, literary, comedy and film festivals, livestock shows and flower festivals. Event management therefore covers a large territory encompassing the general production, design, publicity and management of events (Getz, 2012).

However, as will become apparent in the course of this study, the scale and variety of events render blanket propositions pointless. In this book the foremost emphasis is upon the analysis of global events. While some of the points made in relation to event planning, strategy and consciousness apply to non-global events, it would be wrong to infer that differences of scale, organisation and level of impact can be ignored. There is all the difference imaginable between organising a jumble sale to save the parish youth club and launching an international programme of attractions, with multinational sponsors, telecast live in support of emergency relief or global consciousness raising.

The focus upon global events in this book reflects the extraordinary profile that they have attained in tackling questions of want, promoting narratives of belonging and imprinting subjective psychology with a sense of shared purpose. They are a highly visible branch of what Ulrich Beck (1992) calls 'sub-politics', meaning the social interests and movements that are located outside the field of organised party politics and pressure group lobbying. For large numbers of the population the subsidiary importance implied in the term 'sub-politics' is redundant. Personal responses to humanitarian events, international sporting competitions and counter-cultural festivals, like the annual Burning Man event in Nevada, have emerged as one of the most revealing life-scales measuring personal character and integrity. They allow us to weigh both the validity of a cause and the worth of a person.

Indeed, there is a case that it is most useful to think of them as components of lifestyle architecture through which we now build competent, relevant, credible images of ourselves. Lifestyle architecture is critical in the question of holding a tenable self-image, and pivotal in portraying ourselves as competent, credible actors in social networks.[1] Not least, because to show support for a cause or identify unimpeachably with corporate or national values affords a short cut to recognition, acceptance and impact. Demonstrating support for an event 'says it all' about who you are and what you aspire to be.

At the social rather than psychological level, events are part of the urge to interrogate and utilise space and time to define occasions as special and worthy of commemoration. As such, they are frequently taken to be a sign of the health of the community and the vitality of ethics of responsibility. However, the expansion and size of some global events raise separate concerns about issues of social ordering, performative labour, task-centred regulation, manipulation and communication power. Events are powerful, short-hand mechanisms of social theming. They confer a readily comprehensible brand and glamour upon event management, organisation and participation.

Politicisation has emerged as a keynote theme in the contemporary analysis of events. In other words, event consolidation and the responses to events have become important proof of personal worth and social membership. Global events, which are also known as mega-events (Roche, 2000, 2002), involve the building of sports stadiums, hotels, blasting highways and constructing slip roads that often require the eviction of inner-city populations and the destruction of areas of outstanding natural beauty. The FIFA World Cup in South Africa (2010), the Beijing Olympics (2008) and, as we shall see in more detail in Chapter 5, the Vancouver Winter Olympics (2010), produced widespread evictions and protest.

Some events celebrate lifestyles and beliefs that have been traditionally marginalised or stereotyped in negative ways. For example, the annual Gay and Lesbian Sydney Mardi Gras originated as a political protest in 1978. It was designed as the legitimate, transitory occupation of inner-city space to celebrate both the validity of nonconformist sexual values and to air the values of the counter-culture against the prejudice and narrowness of the heterosexual establishment (Forsyth, 2001). The event is telecast globally and draws a network public of 300,000. Less well reported is the continuing undercurrent of heterosexual resentment at the temporary annexation of urban space for the celebration of nonconformist sexual values. On closer inspection, events which are portrayed by the mainstream media as enhancing social integration often carry an undertow of social tension and spatial resistance (Mason and Lo, 2009: 97). There is circumstantial evidence to suggest that this undertow was a significant factor in the decision to drop the 'Gay and Lesbian' prefix and redefine the event as the Sydney Mardi Gras dedicated to the new event slogan of 'the freedom to be' (Munro, 2011).

As we shall see in more detail in Chapter 9 when we consider the question of event appropriation, the Carnival in Rio de Janeiro, which has grown into one of the world's foremost hallmark events, has generated controversy from activists who claim that it has been cut adrift from its roots. The Brazilian tourist industry and government present the Carnival as the distillation of national identity and a positive image of Brazilian miscegenation. However, the lower income levels of the black population, whose traditions are associated with inventing the samba form of dance and exhibition upon which the Rio Carnival is based, now find themselves priced out of full participation (Sheriff, 1999).

Because drama, theatre and melodrama are integral to the event form, events illustrate in unusually graphic ways how the display of fellowship inadvertently produces conflict and how messages of global unity are exposed as media gloss. In modern cultural settings where a person's connection with others is often fragile and provisional, events exhibit unity and solidarity. By validating the self, the ideology of emotionalism that is central in event planning and management conjures up a form of emulsified spirituality that makes us feel personally affirmed and relevant. By being recognised as a small but necessary cog in a wheel at the company general meeting or donating $50 to feed Africa during a concert relief telethon, we publicly exhibit social credibility and self-worth.

The therapeutic aspect of event participation is a fundamental reason for the vast expansion in event visibility over the last three decades. Events provide a forum for public recognition and personal confirmation. People nail their colours to the mast, not merely by supporting a good cause, but being *seen* to do so. Increasingly, this visual dimension requires a record in the form of an image captured on a mobile phone, SLR camera, iPad, lap-top or video recorder. Psychologically speaking, global events allow the individual to briefly enter into the romance of charity while submitting, in the rest of life, to the dominant, implacable logic required by acquisitive, divisive political economy.

In these opening pages another aspect of event culture must be remarked upon, not least because it appears to have gone unnoticed in the professional event management literature.[2] Events provide a compelling material analogue for the peer-to-peer, open-sourcing and advance of creative commons that has become such an exciting and prominent feature of the digital economy. The event is the material embodiment of new forms of cooperative labour, social recognition and social networking that are now commonplace on the internet (Baym and Burnett, 2009; Turner, 2009: 82–3). Like the net, events seem to represent *people power*. This carries unmistakable anti-corporatist, anti-government and anti-consumerist overtones. Cooperative labour, volunteering, social recognition and social networking through the digital economy are popularly represented as a 'break' from traditional modes of production and associated systems of politics. Similarly, events are often portrayed as part of the new politics, unlocking the power of the people in the digital age.

The Importance of Performative Labour

The concept of performative labour is especially important in understanding event management and event consciousness. It is widely used in studies of the workplace, especially those relating to the hospitality and tourist industries (Crang, 1994; Edensor, 2001; Hochschild, 1983). Nonetheless, while these studies go a long way to clarifying the concept, they omit to do justice to its importance by confining it to the shallow orbit of the work setting. For example, Alan Bryman (2004: 103) defines performative labour as 'the rendering of work by managements and employees alike as akin to a theatrical performance in which the workplace is construed as similar to a stage'. In a book of many insights, he applies the concept specifically to the Disney theme park industry where Disney personnel use surprisingly tightly formulated and well-honed 'people skills' (rather than old-fashioned empathy, hospitality and spontaneity) to regulate crowd behaviour. As Bryman (2004) and other commentators make abundantly clear, the concept of performative labour has become pivotal in the sociology of Western employment market economies because of the growth of the service sector. Blyton and Jenkins (2007) calculate that seven out of ten workers in the advanced economies of the West are now employed in service work. This work is intimately connected with performative labour since it is based on communication, knowledge, information and broader 'people skills'.

However, central to the meaning of performative labour is the idea that communication, knowledge and information are integral to all forms of human interaction. In the digital economy, where data relating to personal life enhancement and modes of people skills are ubiquitous through television, the internet and the media, access to performative labour resources is continuously available. These resources are vital, not only in landing and keeping a job, but in developing effective relations with your partner, your parents, your children, your next door neighbour and so on. The internet, the iPad and mobile phone are now foundries of performative labour training which are of equivalent importance to schooling and the workplace.

In this study I want to expand the concept of performative labour from the workplace setting to apply it to *a central means of status differentiation and social impact in popular culture*.[3] In doing so, I draw to some extent on the work of Judith Butler (1990, 1993), who deploys the concept of performativity in explaining how social identities and practices are moulded and disciplined. Butler's work chiefly addresses the relationship between performativity and gendered power differences. Concretely, it focuses upon how female embodiment and character are coerced to assume specific values privileged by patriarchy. While Butler's work is a useful resource, the emphasis she places upon the relationship between performance and gender is too restrictive. I submit that performative labour is now so generalised in society that it is essential for understanding *all* forms of social interaction. For a multiplicity of reasons, personal life has become increasingly preoccupied with standing out from the crowd and making social impact.[4] We not only desire to believe that we are different, we need to register social impact as a mark of personal validation. Important questions of the meaning of personal authenticity and trust follow from this, but, for reasons of space, for the most part, they will be treated as separate from the core considerations in this book (but see Bauman, 2000; Sennett, 2003).

This way of thinking about the growing importance of social impact has been found useful in a number of fields that have nothing to do with event management. To take a dramatic example, the sociologist Mark Juergensmeyer (2003) has argued that the foundational element in terrorism is what he calls 'performance violence'. A conscious part of planning and executing a terrorist incident is the use of extreme violence to register maximum impact upon social consciousness. Personal validation does not lie first and foremost in the violent act, rather it resides in the incident being recognised as 'mind numbing', 'mesmerising' political theatre *for an audience*. The network public in question is of course connected to each other and to the incident through the global communication network. The camera has become fundamental in weighing up the social worth of an action. Just as extensive TV coverage 'validates' a suicide bomber, a kiss at a concert for emergency relief has more personal meaning *if it is filmed.*

In part, my interest in expanding the concept of performative labour goes back to the work on 'performative utterances' by the late J.L. Austin. For Austin (1962) when words are articulated in appropriate contexts they have the power of enforcement. For example, when an employer makes an offer of employment in the workplace it has an effect. It changes your identity. You cease to become an applicant for the post. You become an employee and generally, you perform the role that you have obtained through the job selection process. In this sense talk *is* action.[5]

In the present study the term performative labour will be applied to forms of behaviour designed to exhibit integrity, compassion, solidarity, competence, credibility, relevance and other types of status differentiation and social impact. As such, I depart from Austin in as much as I do not restrict the concept of performative utterances to speech acts. A much broader notion of *social linguistics* informs what I understand by performative labour. To be sure, this includes speech, but it also encompasses dress, grooming, manners, attitudes, values, politics, brinkmanship, flirting and other techniques of impression management.

Further, I maintain that performative utterances are primarily motivated by the object of building and managing confidence and achieving social impact in interpersonal relationships. No relationship between brokering confidence and being honest is assumed. Performative utterances are designed to be noticed and build trust. They are not necessarily related to virtue or sincerity. The purpose of these various techniques is to acquire recognition as a person of 'the right sort', 'good character', 'appealing', 'sexy' or 'sound'.

Because social impact depends so much upon being in the know and looking right, according to the mores of the peer groups to which one is attached, performative labour is now a perpetual, seven days a week undertaking. The articulation of choices about matters like diet, transportation, clothing, posture, car ownership, attitudes to sexism, racism, gainful employment, terrorism, animal rights, climate change, etc., are designed and exchanged as *utterances* that express wants of personal impact. Performative labour is the visual and linguistic means through which people convey what they take to be, or wish to be seen as, the mark of their inner personalities.

That theatre is inherent in performative labour has long been recognised by sociologists. Although the concept predated the work of Erving Goffman, his (1961, 1963) extensive writings on dramaturgy and the presentation of the self make transparent use of the concepts of performance, gaining advantage and making social impact. From Goffman we acquire the idea that the self is not bounded by subjectivity. Rather it is enmeshed with complex and multi-layered codes and symbolic networks of affirmation, solidarity and differentiation. These codes are much extended and additionally nuanced in the digital age where personal scripts, forms of grooming and impact strategies owe as much to *para-social* relations developed through television and web as primary relations (Horton and Wohl, 1956).[6] Even participation abounds in rich ethnographic material that exhibits scripts for emoting in public, acknowledging solidarity and engineering performance to achieve personal impact.

Essential to my use of the concept of performative labour then is the notion of theatre. That is, I do not hold that it is necessary for people to believe in the values and attitudes that they articulate. Rather I see the articulation of these matters as what might be called cultural chips exchanged in the roulette wheel of social encounters with the end in mind of making a notable and, usually, positive impression. Social impact is the name of the game (Rojek, 2010, 2012).

The same rule of thumb applies to event culture. On one level, the disinterest, social inclusiveness and concern for suffering and corporate solidarity expressed in events are genuine responses to issues and emergencies. I don't wish to be understood as proposing that events do not enhance social consciousness or raise funds. Nor are they simply exercises in unrealistic pedagogy and wishful forms of cultural literacy, i.e. by hiding the real roots of power in society and distracting us from the necessary structural transformations required to produce meaningful contributions to problems of, for example, global inequality, injustice and environmental pollution. All the same, in addition, if we do not see them as performative utterances designed to display qualities of personal worth which have telegenic impacts we do not get the full picture of their effect in modern culture.

As popular culture has become more sceptical about the prospect of fundamentally transforming dominant political economy through collective resistance, the biomedical idiom has become more significant (Furedi, 2004: 173). We now use the body to resist. This involves tattooing, piercing and other forms of body styling, but it also encompasses using other speech acts to *display* resistance.

Global humanitarian events are group speech acts designed to dramatically highlight issues and problems. They have not, however, produced a form of transformative politics that is a genuine threat to capitalist hegemony. The old idea that the personal is political has been replaced by the more general, but vastly more superficial notion, that *representation is resistance.*

In network society it is impossible to underestimate the centrality of the media in agenda setting and conditioning the content and vernacular of performative labour. The pivotal importance of communication networks in the formation of identity and life politics means that, as consumers, we use para-social prototypes of display and representation drawn from television studios, film sets, concert halls and radio mikes at all levels of interpersonal communication.

Work by Manuel Castells (2009: 167–90) demonstrates the indisputable effect of network communication power in framing public agendas and encouraging preferred readings of news. It is, of course, still the case that we think for ourselves, but it is necessary to add that the media, dominated by transnational corporations, like the Murdoch family's News Corporation, Time Warner, Viacom, Bertelsmann and Disney, provide the electronic eye through which we cognitively register understanding, exchange information and reach conclusions.

However, it is not just a question of communication networks providing content. They also set the parameters of the form of language used to make sense of the world and the style of exchange that provides speech utterances with social impact. Television, film, pop music and social networking widen and refine the ideas of theatrical performance and stagecraft in every avenue of everyday life. The vital importance of communication networks in life politics and perpetuating para-social relations means that we borrow media-based forms of display and performance at all levels of interpersonal communication and redeploy them in our own speech utterances. The mimicry that follows a widely seen reality TV show in which catch-phrases and looks achieve instant circulation and general recognition provides evidence of the integral power of communication networks in contemporary social encounters. When the Scottish singer Susan Boyle appeared in *Britain's Got Talent* in 2009 she was an instant, overnight global sensation causing unprecedented levels of blogging. It was not just that people instantly knew her name, they became automatically adept in mimicking her look and manner so as to have impact over others about a happening event in the media sphere. In a word they *performed* her in social settings that were disconnected from her or reality TV in general.

More worryingly, as Castells (2009: 167–90) demonstrates, transnational communication networks condition general perceptions of politics, economics and culture. They colluded in the programmes of misinformation launched by the White House, Downing Street and elsewhere to persuade Allied forces to invade Iraq (2003). It would be wrong to cast the media as a monolithic force in proliferating subjective passivity. For the same channels of information that are used to misinform the public about the threat of, for example, armed Iraqi aggression under Saddam carried a backlash from those who accused Western governments of distortion and manipulation. Whether or not misinformation and exposure is balanced is a question for empirical investigation. However, at the analytic level the proposition that media communication power inscribes and perpetuates the cognitive maps which the public use to read reality is well established (Curran, 2010, 2011). Communication network power is therefore central to life politics. As such, it is fundamental to any enquiry into global event management.

Para-social Relations and Media Networks

My understanding of the concept of performative *labour* links it closely to communication technology and the social conventions that have grown up around this technology. Horton and Wohl's (1956) classic concept of para-social relations is relevant here. A para-social relation refers to relations of presumed intimacy and fellowship that network publics develop with media presenters. Horton and Wohl (1956) coined the concept at the dawn of the TV age. Today media communication power is much more sophisticated and penetrating (Castells, 2009; Curran, 2011). The concept therefore needs to be elaborated from the fronts of presumed identification and fellowship of the airwaves, to concrete mimicry of attitudes and opinions of personal validity to every area of life. By the term performative labour in connection with para-social relations then, I mean *the construction of a valid self-image through actions and practices as well as language, that are heavily, but not, of course, exclusively, modelled on the motifs, role models and preferences supplied by the media.*

It is a convention in the field to refer positively to the creative power and knowledgeability of social actors. This has grown up in reaction to cultural and social determinist approaches to human behaviour. While I have no wish to depart from the convention, I must stress the foundational importance today of the media in planting and nurturing the resources that are exploited and developed through performative labour outside media settings. The media are part of the *invisible government* of day-to-day relations.[7] They pump-prime audiences with a sense of urgency, an agenda of issues, values, norms, identity and a mode of cognition (Curran, 2010: 39). Their impact in this respect is all the more significant since the dominant motif of airwave transmission is speaking for the common man. But global media networks are not owned by the common man. Most are privately owned by influential individuals who have interconnected corporate interests. They can hardly be expected to suspend these interests when it comes to the management of multinational broadcast policy. The *communication power* of the media reflects the *network power* of the influential individuals that own and ultimately control them (Castells, 2009).

Para-social relations breed *para-social impacts*. By the latter term, I mean forms of activism that rely upon theatre, spectacle and other forms of representation for validation. Causes and dilemmas that emerge from the mouths of celebrity activists on TV certainly generate media interest and mobilise social energy. But they create an imitative form of activism that is based on glamour, impact and the appetite for personal recognition. Para-social impacts may have real consequences in alleviating hunger, poverty, injustice and other forms of distress. Notwithstanding this, they are also a means of interpersonal validation and self-gratification. Global events constantly slip between matters of sober international problem solving and the messier world of interpersonal politics of self-affirmation and self-aggrandisement.

In all of this the media are no innocent agent. They transmit issues of public interest, including news items and issues that may constitute the basis of events. However, the public is not directly involved in the selection, management and presentation of these issues. These questions are defined by the social interests that finance the media. For them, para-social impact is no less important in the ratings war than lobbying governments and corporations for multilateral fundraising or geopolitical intervention. The broadcast agenda shapes personal behaviour. This is why I opt to use the term 'invisible government' to describe the effects of the media.

In this study, I propose that the media, together with the public relations industry (the PR–media hub) are central in the social ordering of popular conduct.

Social ordering may be defined as the process of conditioning social behaviour through both formal processes (education, the law, policing) and informal processes (tacit understandings of rights and justice, the display of compassion and a 'can do' attitude). Performative labour is therefore the means through which particular types of social ordering are initiated and accomplished. This ordering is neither arbitrary nor random. If we begin to use catch-phrases from the TV adverts that punctuate programming we utilise a resource devised and implemented by the PR–media hub in order to generate economic value. The PR–media hub is most effective when it *naturalises* a particular kind of social order. When we come to believe that it is 'normal' or 'common sense' to have the freedom to bear arms or to pay for health care and education rather than receive them as rights of citizenship, to regard the catastrophe in New Orleans in the wake of Hurricane Katrina (2005) as an act of God, and to uncomplainingly pay mortgage and credit rates that are substantially in excess of inflation, the PR–media hub in alliance with business interests and government has achieved an optimum social reaction in social ordering for the interests of corporations and the state.

Now I do not wish to be understood as claiming that because the media are part of the process of invisible government they are wholly unaccountable to the public. There are instances in which the interests behind media power are forced into disclosure and public scrutiny. The phone-tapping scandal that engulfed the *News of the World* in the UK in the summer of 2011, led to Rupert and James Murdoch of News Corp submitting themselves to uncomfortable parliamentary investigation. The decision to close the *News of the World* to calm public disquiet about the newspaper's involvement in illegal phone-tapping raised difficult questions about journalistic rigour. The role of News Corp in titillating and inflaming the public, rather than informing became a widespread matter of global debate.[8]

That said, the occasions in which the invisible interests that own and control the media are required to account in public for the use of media power are relatively sparse. The most compelling reason for this is the vast concentration of power in the world's leading media corporations.

To remain for a moment with the example of News Corp, the most recent GAO Report (2010) shows that the Murdoch-owned company operates 782 foreign subsidiaries, of which 152 are based in tax havens such as the British Virgin Isles, the Cayman Islands and Luxembourg. Not surprisingly, most commentators concur that the independent policing of News Corp assets globally is challenging, with all of the journalistic regulation and fiscal control problems that this implies. Multinational corporations typically develop what I refer to as a *bespoke aggregation* model of accumulation. By this I mean businesses and brands that have the external appearance of autonomy and independence but which are in reality interlocked and operate in mutually reinforcing ways to build and augment brand capital. This equips media multinationals with immense global resources to coordinate publicity and accumulation strategies.

For example, News Corp dropped the BBC from its Star TV satellite in Asia to appease the ruling elite in China, and it uses Fox TV News, which it owns and controls, to create a public climate that is sympathetic to deregulation, since this accords with its business interests. The framing of public opinion largely occurs through socioeconomic interests that are invisible to public scrutiny. This has consequences not only for the character of performative labour that prevails in a geopolitical territory, but also the types of representation and resistance that can be mounted against them.

As we shall see, performative labour is seldom disinterested and its articulation always reflects social institutions. In other words, performative labour involves a perceived dividend in terms of generating some form of impact and recognition. In Marxism, the metric in which this recognition is expressed is usually economic value. This study does not discount the importance of this measure. Nonetheless, it treats performative labour primarily as a means of status differentiation which is integral to maintain a general cultural sense of 'normality', i.e. social order.

At this point in the discussion these somewhat *minimalist* definitions will have to suffice. Make no mistake, the concepts of performative labour and social ordering are crucial for the arguments outlined in this book. Neither is as simple or straightforward as it looks at first sight, not least because each must be contrasted with older ideas of the public sphere and transformative politics (Habermas, 1989). For this reason we will be obliged to come back to consider them at greater length in relation to a specific comparison with Habermas's argument at a later stage in the discussion.

Notes

1 In a social world which is so responsive to visual culture, the metaphor of architecture to describe lifestyle is appropriate and just. Design and representation are important features of resistance. Lifestyle architecture immediately provides us with a sign of to whom we belong and from whom we depart in social values.
2 With origins in hospitality management, leisure studies, tourism studies and business studies, the professional event management literature has not developed a strong critical profile. The present book is an attempt to rectify this state of affairs. The aim is not to be critical, but *constructively* critical. I take a receptivity to criticism as a sign of the maturity of a discipline or field of academic study.
3 Status differentiation refers to honorific distinctions that derive from either specific forms of social practice or occupying particular social roles. Chief executives who insist on corporate awaydays as sessions that allow management and workers to have a frank exchange of views are regarded as progressive. Similarly, celebrities like Sir Bob Geldof or Bono who engage in advocacy or diplomacy gain social respect.
4 See MacCannell (2011: 22–7).
5 Needless to say there is many a slip between cup and lip. Talking about an action or actions is a precondition of positive outcomes, but nothing is guaranteed. In general, approaches to action that separate discourse from the material level are methodologically flawed.
6 Para-social relationships refer to the imaginary relationships that a network public has with performers in the media. Horton and Wohl's (1956) concept is hugely important and has been underutilised in the fields of event management and celebrity studies.
7 The term 'invisible government' was coined by Edward Bernays (1928). He used it as an anodyne description of what public relations specialists do to present policies and strategies in the best light. In the present study I use the term in a more critical way to refer to the state–corporate amalgamation of power that oversees resource distribution, social investment and the manipulation of social reactions.
8 The News Corp scandal exposed dirty tricks in journalism. It resulted in the closure of the *News of the World* and compensation payments to public figures on grounds of invasion of public privacy. However, it would be naive to imagine that phone-tapping is banished from the journalistic repertoire. The nature of the social reaction to the issue is dictated by the ends of journalism. Thus, phone-tapping celebrities to find sensitive details of their private lives is deplored. But phone-tapping which exposes financial irregularities or crime is applauded.

2
WHAT ARE THE MAIN TYPES OF EVENT?

I want to be clear that this book is not to be understood as a critical sally against all types of event management, *sui generis*. My critical focus is upon high profile, global events involving pressure groups, corporations and the state. I hold that there is much of interest, and a good deal that is new, in the role of this level of organisation in the social ordering of contemporary life. Not to beat about the bush, it has emerged as part of the heavy artillery of governance in the battle for the public mind, and it deploys the full range of public relations expertise and media communication network power to pursue this end.

Right at the start, the distinction already made (pp. 1–3) between single-issue and cyclical events must be substantiated and the planned consequences of these events elaborated. Single-issue events focus on one topic, such as famine relief, aid for the victims of the earthquake in Haiti (2010), disaster relief for the victims of the *tsunami* in Japan (2011), etc. Cyclical events are part of the annual, periodic calendar, for example, the FIFA World Cup, the Olympics, the Sydney Gay and Lesbian Mardi Gras, the Carnival in Rio, the Munich Oktoberfest, the Venice Carnival, the Glastonbury festival, the Burning Man City festival and so on.

Among the social and economic outcomes claimed for events are establishing a sense of camaraderie, promoting euphoria, generating economic resources for worthy causes, relieving suffering, building brands, growing the client base, educating dealer networks, attracting tourists, producing sponsorship income and nurturing wealth creation (Allen, 2000; Rutherford and Goldblatt, 2003; Tassiopoulis, 2000; Yeoman et al., 2004).

As I have already noted, chiefly in this book I address global, humanitarian and environmental protest rather than local or corporate events. I do so because my object is to address the unique role that events play today in the social ordering of popular psychology, international networks of communication (including social networking) and global initiatives of control and resistance. I see global events as part of a mainly neoliberal initiative to use ludic energy in the task of global problem solving and adding therapeutic value to popular relations.[1] I maintain that they are couched in the rhetoric of new types of prototypical global citizenship in which ordinary people are urged to *perform* an 'heroic' role involving 'fun' activities in the name of helping, essentially abstract, others. For most of the audience in rich nations, the invisibility of the starving, the victims of famine, genocide and inequality is only modified by para-social information through media broadcasts and media-based celebrity activism. Recognition through para-social relationships is a requirement of the communication networks that stage global events and the PR–media hub that manages them.

Since these considerations are uppermost in my concerns, I will not deal at length with the question of event origins. That discussion would require another book. Yet even in the present enterprise, a compass-bearing on the question of origins is not out of order because it sets the scene for what follows. While I want to convey the full extent of the role of events in social ordering, I also wish to understand events as a response to a specific species need in humans.

The Necessity of Transcendence

I hold events to be, at bottom, attempts in the business of social transcendence. They are contemporary solutions to responding to the species need for a sense of a bigger something in life. At this point I wish to apply the term *transcendence* fairly loosely to refer to the urge to go beyond narrow, private concerns and the rigmarole of habitual, regimented existence. Supplementarily, I maintain that the need for public transcendence above individual worries and the monotony of life is a species universal. That is to say, I maintain that every human society has devised events to provide individuals and groups with intimations of transcendence.

In this sense, strictly speaking, there is nothing really new about the use of events in the task of social ordering. John Keane (2005) is right to redeploy the old term *theatrum mundi* to refer to the tendency of global communication power to present events as sensations that overcome cultural, religious, national and racial divisions to unite 'everyman'. The media portray global events as a world stage in which questions of personal and social worth are publicised, weighed in the balance and judged. Doubtless, this cannot properly be described as an invention of the media. However, only advanced industrial societies, organised around networks of mass communication power, have produced global events which claim to present the facts 'impartially' to a whole world that is watching, judging and acting. Just as only now, through the media, does a metric for calibrating, or at least making educated quantitative guesses, about the social impact of events exist. This involves partnerships between international pressure groups, corporations, communication networks and states which are new.

To return to the question of origins, organised religion might be said to be one of the first human responses to the species need for tran-scendence. The foundation of religion is the acknowledgement of a finite gap between the Creator and the creatures of creation. The desire for union is mirrored in various ceremonies and rituals of elevation (Kolakowski, 1982: 98–151). This produces auxiliary celebrations and festivals designed to signify a dramatic departure or outright escape attempt from the boundaries of regular social order.

Religious festivals and worship ceremonies have been sociologically explained in terms of the remaking of collective life.[2] However, their primary characteristic is the deliberate, flagrant *discontinuity* from mundane, routine existence. They do not so much remake everyday life as dramatically produce a break in monotony to yield an intimation of a bigger reality and a higher purpose. At the psychological level, this contributes to a personal sense of meaning and the representation of kinship. The qualities aroused in games, carnival and festival do not generally lead people to forsake the day job. Spiritual matters have their place, but their public expression is carefully controlled. Although there are historical exceptions, the real world of material striving abides and is typically fiercely defended by the authorities (Ladurie, 2003).

Politics, culture and society learned from religion. The application of drama, sport, music and oratory to activate the crowd and generate funds was commonplace in Ancient society and carried over into the Middle Ages, the Renaissance and beyond (Bakhtin, 1968; Callois, 1961; Stallybrass and White, 1968). The people of Ancient and Medieval times had their games, festivals and carnivals which were designed to impart a popular sense of transcendence. For example, Strauss's (2009: 21) account of the years that the rebel slave leader Spartacus spent as a gladiator, demonstrates powerfully that gladiatorial combat in the Roman games clearly supplied audiences with a sense – to use his word – of the *sublime*.

Events also have a long history in non-pagan religion. The first Jubilee in Christianity was organised by Pope Bonifacius VIII in 1300. It was a response to the increasing desire among European Christians to make a pilgrimage to holy sites in search of religious transcendent experience (Pipan and Porsander, 1999: 2).

Today, we would class these ceremonies and rituals as the forerunners of events. To be sure, the organisation and practice of contemporary events has mutated appreciably from their original religious incarnation. Nonetheless, comparisons are irresistible.

Like religious ceremonies and rituals, events are based in the chan-nelled diversion of collective emotions towards some sort of intimation of a bigger reality and higher purpose. Both employ devices of drama and melodrama to symbolise a break from ordinary experience. Both address the gift of grace, although in the event form, grace is understood wholly in secular terms. Both pinpoint a sacramental function to giving. And in both, a dimension of commerce is cultivated in conjunction with the bless-ings of transcendence.

Transcendence is naturally associated with giving and selflessness. However, it is as well to note that sharing, hospitality and charity are seldom exactly disinterested acts. 'There are no free gifts', writes Mary Douglas (1990: ix) in her Foreword to Marcel Mauss's classic work *The Gift*, 'gift cycles engage persons in permanent commitments that articulate the dominant institutions'. We will come back to examine this point, especially in relation to the issue of what these dominant institutions might be, at greater length later.

Transcendence or Escapism?

The accent placed here upon transcendence in event management con-trasts with the convention in the professional event literature which is to twin events with escapism as a means of establishing and reinforcing group identity. Thus, Haahti and Komppula (2006: 103) discuss the role of event design, publicity and management in producing themes or 'staged experiences' that conjure up a sense of unity, solidarity and shared meaning. Among the technical means of accomplishing this affective response are scenery, lighting, sound systems, props, cos-tumes and stage direction. Examples include the opening ceremonies of the Olympics, or the FIFA World Cup, global concerts for emergency relief and cyclical community parades and celebrations like the Rio Carnival, the New Orleans Mardi Gras and the *Dia de los Meurtos* (Day of the Dead) festival in Mexico.

Similarly, Mason and Lo (2009: 117) argue that a large part of the audi-ences drawn to the Sydney Gay and Lesbian Mardi Gras are not moti-vated by the celebration of nonconformist sexual values but the chance to participate in what they call 'the visual culture of transgression'. The display of nudity and frivolity are separated from the real political origins of protest against the dominance of heterosexual normative order. The audience has been drawn to Mardi Gras in search of a new sensation rather than the elaboration of a genuinely oppositional culture. Event planners seem to share this view. Arguably, it is one of the main reasons why they decided to drop the prefix 'Gay and Lesbian' from the Sydney Mardi Gras in 2011 (Munro, 2011).

The emphasis upon events as a gateway of escape leans on the work of Pine and Gillmore (1999) on the so-called 'experience economy'. The latter concept refers to a transition in value in consumer culture from material commodities to social experiences. As consumer culture matures, allocation of expenditure to events and settings increases. What is behind this is a search for novelty, diversion, networking and fleeing from routine.[3] These motivations are grouped together in the professional event literature as proposing mechanisms of escapism as the cause of events (Li and Petrick, 2006).

Intuitively, there is a good deal to support the view that a prominent factor in the organisation and participation of events is a search for escape. Events provide an attractive alternative to the drudgery of unemployment, the pressures of careerism or the sheer monotony of the 9–5 treadmill.

However, escapism does not explain the intoxication of getting carried away or losing yourself which are frequently expressed responses to event attendance. For want of a better term, when events work optimally they have a demonstrable *spiritual* quality (Gilmore, 2010). They provide people with a sense of a bigger reality. Events are often alluded to by organisers and some participants as life-changing. For this reason, I prefer to maintain that the search for transcendence has priority over escapism. The latter is not enough to explain the qualities of intense emotionalism and unrestrained exhibitionism that frequently accompany events as a social form.

It follows that I do not see events as primarily personal or private responses, but as social reactions that answer to power, discipline, resistance, performance and the species desire for elevation. Celebration and the search for transcendence beyond personal cares are integral parts of being human. The social dimension needs to be emphasised because, to repeat the key point, the anthropology of events demonstrates that they are invariably situated in social settings that require display and emotionalism to act as catalysts to boost the event concept or theme. In other words, there is a strong display element embedded in the organisation and practice of global events.

It goes without saying that the motivation behind display is not constant. Rather it varies with historical and social conditions. It is not enough for people to give, they must also be *seen* to give. The *performance/witness* elements have become axial in modern event psychology. Photography and filming are not simply means of commemorating events, they are also tools of personal validation which provide an independent record of involvement, self-worth and cultural importance. Global events must not therefore be seen simply as a means of solving external problems. They are also a catalyst of self-gratification and social acknowledgement. Their increasing incidence and visibility is not just the consequence of better news and information flows achieved by communication power. They are part of a wider social reaction in search of personal therapy in response to the dislocated, fractured and provisional nature of social relationships in most social settings (Furedi, 2004).

It is, I think, revealing that this dimension of event organisation is barely addressed in the professional event literature. As we shall see in more detail later, in focusing on the operational, technical aspects of event design, publicity and management, event professionals unwittingly obscure the relationship of events to deeper, wider questions of history, power, personal gratification, control and resistance (pp. 71–9).

For example, these are not covered by Goldblatt's (2008) influential model of the five Ws to create an event concept. Namely: *Why* is the event being held? *Who* will be the stakeholders? *When* will the event be held? *Where* will it be staged? *What* is the event product? This is a purely technocratic approach to event management which ignores questions of history, comparative experience and power that are essential if the event is to be successful. They raise meaningful questions of context and motivation, such as, *How* did stakeholders get into a position of having power? *What* is their agenda? *What* principles of social inclusion and exclusion do they apply? *How* are they connected to wider power interests both within society and at the global level? *What* are the meanings that audiences bring to the event and how do they compare with the goals of stakeholders? Unless these questions are asked, one only gets half the picture.

I would go further: a general weakness of professional event management literature is the remarkable underdevelopment of a critical perspective. In particular, questions of event meaning and theming tend to begin and end with the needs and wants of event sponsors, managers and ancillary staff. In my view, the critical questions of the meaning that consumers and participants bring to, and take from, events, and broader questions of how this relates to connected topics of power, validation, control and resistance, have not been adequately explored. Instead, the overwhelming focus in event management is upon the technical considerations of event concept formation, staging, sponsorship, security, health and safety, ticketing and media networks.

Naturally, I do not wish to be understood as proposing that these questions are irrelevant. Rather, what I am saying is that they also require a perspective which treats issues of history, difference (social inclusion and exclusion) and power as central. Further, this perspective is mostly absent in the professional event literature.

The dominant position in the professional literature creates an unhelpful convention of casting events in a perpetually positive light. That is, events are portrayed as grassroots solutions that the state and corporations are unable to achieve. This conveniently ignores the role that events play in social ordering and the nature of performative labour that characterises event experience. One of the goals of this book is to stand this convention upon its head in order to attempt a more complete, and hopefully, richer approach to the cultural significance of events today.

Event Metrics

Anyone who writes about events faces an immediate technical problem, to which I have already alluded. The term encompasses a vast range of phenomena. Everything from managing and promoting hotel attractions, budgeting for consumables and accommodation facilities to organising a global one-day concert featuring the world's top popular music acts or athletes telecast live. Obviously, events do not come in the same shapes and sizes. Ken Roberts (2004: 108–20) distinguishes between minor, major and mega-events. Although he neglects to give precise definitions, *minor* events are local (neighbourhood festivals, street or garden open days); *major* ones are national (national sports fixtures, music concerts); and *mega*-events are global (the Olympics, Live Aid and Live Earth).

An important sub-category of major events are *hallmark* events. They are usually recurring events designed to enhance the brand of cities as tourist destinations and multiply investment in attractions. Leading examples include the Edinburgh International Festival, the Berlin International Film Festival, the Munich Oktoberfest, Burning Man City and the Rio Carnival.

Despite complying in a rough and ready way with intuition, shape and size are not the best metrics to categorise events. For they ignore the deep social, psychological and cultural forces that precipitate the global phenomenon. The PR–media hub presents events as occasions for the demonstration of group empathy and the expression of altruistic sentiment. However, events also clearly exploit and romanticise three social psychological characteristics:

- *Catharsis*, that is the articulation of powerful private and public emotions in group settings. Events bestir altruism, empathy and the release of emotions. Openness to the marginalised, a powerful sense of mutual vulnerability and strong messages of social recognition and social inclusion are common.
- *Emotionalism*, that is a sense of righteousness, identification with the pain of others, the desire to help, criticism of those who either refuse to help or help in objectionable ways, the desire to do good, the wish to be publicly recognised as a team player or member of a social

group are strong incentives. Emotionalism supports direct action and uncluttered tactical responses to responding to misery and want.

- *Exhibitionism*, that is kinetic and symbolic behaviour designed to communicate powerful sentiments of unity and transcendence. Exhibitionism is often characterised by the spirit of occupying the moral high ground and folk camaraderie.

When these three characteristics are *in situ* individuals and groups experience a transcendent sense of emotional, and even spiritual, uplift which reframes the elements that compose everyday life and reduces it momentarily to subsidiary importance. Ordinary life is bracketed out in favour of higher concerns having to do with imagined, common responsibilities, *esprit de corps*, humanitarian undertakings, saving the planet, putting the interests of the organisation before those of the individual and the like. The salvationist mentality of events connects naturally to strong discharges of energy directed at personal validation.

Frank Furedi (2004: 37–9) argues that Western society has supported the development of ubiquitous therapeutic culture in which judgement about private emotions is the fulcrum of deliberating personal worth and the validity of public acts. For him, emotional determinism has replaced economic determinism in private and popular accounts of causality and motivation. In therapeutic culture the acknowledgement of private emotional pain through public exhibitionism is required for self-validation. It is not enough to feel. One must exhort others to recognise what one feels and comply with it. The act of emotional disclosure delineates lines of social inclusion and exclusion. By communicating private emotions and checking that they are recognised one regains a sense of kinship. In addition, communication offers a means of managing the responses of others. If you do not demonstrate that you feel what I feel, you provide an incentive for me to cajole your emotions and persuade you of the correctness of my inner feelings. The exhortation to join me in my private emotions is ultimately conformist since it involves you stepping into line with me.

Although they would strenuously seek to deny it, even in the midst of criticising established forms of power, celebrities like George Clooney, Bob Geldof, Bono, Angelina Jolie, Cameron Diaz and Madonna are engaging in a type of emotional manipulation that requires you to follow obediently, rather than think for yourself. What you follow is the self-evident validity of the celebrity case based on the rationed data that the mechanics of celebrity activism set before you.

From a critical standpoint, global event management may be defined as the professional organisation and government of scarce resources to optimally harness catharsis, emotionalism and exhibitionism to mobilise a sense of social transcendence in furtherance of client goals.

The technical accessories of this include the planning and application of sound principles of economic management and effective public relations and mass communication to achieve high impact factors. Impact metrics embrace media coverage (primarily features, interviews and news bulletins), donations data and pre- and post-event quantitative and qualitative research evaluation (surveys, questionnaires, structured interviews and focus groups).

In terms of event experience, the close correlation between global events, catharsis, emotionalism and exhibitionism readily persuades us that social reactions are heartfelt and spontaneous. The media language of events is sugar-coated with phrases like 'the generosity of the crowd', a 'fairytale response' and 'the heart-warming expression' of sincerity. Authenticity is the *lingua franca* in which event motivation and participation is articulated. Events are portrayed as cutting through pretence and obfuscation to mobilise the consciousness and action of 'the world'. A sense of overwhelming common purpose is orchestrated and shared.

In fact, global events are regimented with well-nigh military precision and professionally managed in order to convey the appearance of spontaneity and the presence of solidarity (Graham, 2010, 2012). Event planners set the stage for goals and technical considerations designed to enhance fundraising, build group identity, enhance the event concept and manage the event programme. They operate in combination with the PR–media hub which applies technologies of public relations and communication to strive for maximum global impact. Shared goals always presuppose a client who commissions the event, an event executive, usually a celebrity figurehead, and backroom and frontline staff who conduct financial, publicity, health and safety and security operations.

Designing activity programmes is a complex process. It requires selecting a leadership team, setting a budget, determining activities, constructing an event concept, devising an effective marketing campaign, building connections with the press, selecting the right public space and liaising with police and health officials to ensure crowd safety (Farrell and Lundegren, 1991). None of this is spontaneous. All of it requires chains of command, accountability and a budget. Much of it assumes the importance of theatrical staging and role play.

The proliferation of event management diplomas and degrees in recent years is a measure of the importance of events in income generation and influencing social consciousness. The number of events textbooks has mushroomed, and publishers, especially Wiley and Elsevier, have launched dedicated event management book lists. Likewise, several journals are devoted to the field: *Event Management* (formerly *Festival Management and Event Tourism*), *Journal of Convention and Event Tourism*,

World Journal of Managing Events and the online journal, *International Journal of Event Management Research*. Professional associations have also contributed to accumulating a body of specialised knowledge and dedicated practice, usually in the form of practitioner-oriented material aimed at single-type events (Getz, 2005: 535–6). Professionalisation has led to the codification of a body of transferable knowledge pertaining to budget setting, public relations, media communication, emotional management (people skills) and other operational issues.

The event management literature is, indeed, diverse and profuse. However, it is fair to say that, throughout, a congratulatory idiom prevails. Events are projected as drawing on the positive energy of the people to elicit a spirit of transcendence and the appearance of relevant problem-solving initiatives. The popular solutions of event management are often contrasted pointedly with the alleged inefficiency of big government and, likewise, the so-called shameful acquisitiveness and capitalisation requirements of multinationals. Events are characterised as holding a superior moral quality since they are portrayed as leaping straight 'from the heart' and offering direct, emotional uplift and spiritual cohesion. This often draws upon the reservoir of a 'can do', 'no nonsense' attitude. Events are referred to as the direct expressions of the opinion and will of ordinary men and women.[4]

On closer inspection, what emerges most unequivocally is the unsubstantiated, imagined nature of these hypotheses. For example, while it is commonplace for event managers to twin events with catharsis, there is little interest in exploring what kind of emotions are aroused or the personal meanings attributed to them. The emotions and questions of meaning that audiences bring to events are secondary to the event agenda which is ultimately determined by the clients who commission the event in partnership with the event executive. In the majority of cases, event planners court the crowd, but privilege the interests of clients. During the event, these interests are deemed to be optimally served if the audience is managed efficiently and reacts positively and generously to the event concept and programme.

Hiller (2000: 193) has gone further, alleging that global mega-events perpetuate a bogus idea of civic participation. They are based in 'top down planning' in which the event concept, on-site services and completion dates are monopolised by elites (Hayes and Horne, 2011: 750). As we shall see presently, it is a huge and unwarrantable leap from these considerations to propose that the interests of clients and the crowd are *synonymous*. Yet this claim is so frequently made in the global event management literature that it has almost become a presupposition of the field.

Although global event management professionals dwell upon their technical expertise and ethical probity, many of the claims made on behalf of the exercise turn out, on closer inspection, to be unsupported. Global event planning often cuts corners and avoids the burden of proof by invoking a short-hand model of the world as a unitary agent responding to urgent, impossible to deny, *emergencies*. Most commonly this takes the form of framing an economic, social, political or environmental problem as demanding the attention of the whole world. The idea of *the world* (or any other social organisation) as an agent which *thinks* and *acts* is deeply problematic. It presupposes a degree of unity and direction that cultural and economic differences between the people of the world fail to deliver. Likewise, depicting the world as a series of incidents, episodes and emergencies punctuated by short interludes of calm, that require the bold actions of determined risk-takers, obscures the degree to which human problems reflect mesmerising inertia on structural questions of power, inequality and injustice. Yet both are staples of global event management vocabulary.

The Elusive 3 Billion

Consider, the banner of the website for Live 8 (www.live8live.com) which avows, without qualification or evidence, 'an estimated 3 BILLION PEOPLE WATCHED LIVE 8, the greatest show on Earth. They came together with one message – make poverty history'.

The question is how does anyone know the real number of people that watched the Live 8 telecasts? No-one took a head count. The 3 billion figure, that was almost 50% of the world's population at the time, derives from the educated guesses of the TV syndication market. An educated guess is not a *bona fide* fact. Further, it represents a style of thinking that too easily conflates glamour and sensation with virtue and utility. Television companies have a vested interest in making a best possible case projection of estimated viewing figures since to do so enhances their appeal to advertisers and sponsors. Elements of grandstanding are at play here, for who in their right mind would wish to query a mandate supported by 3 billion people?

In communication networks the headline (dubious) quantitative data shade into a qualitative equivalent. The 3 billion who supposedly witness the event are presumed to have an identical response to what they see. Thus, to refer back to the Live 8 website: 'they' (the 3 billion) 'came together with one message: to make poverty history'. This statement is more part of the advertising executive's wanna-be world than tenable social science.

The truth is that people do not witness global events in an orderly, uniform fashion. Rather, they bring a variety of multifarious, multivalent and often contradictory meanings to events. Among the common motivations in event participation are the search for transcendence, escapism, star-spotting, peer reinforcement and public display. These *may* be connected with the economic, political and social goals contained in the event concept. But it cannot be assumed that this is the case. The capacity of humans to read meanings into events exceeds the disciplinary powers of event planners and managers to impose one preferred reading.

Even if we allow that many people – even the majority – watched the Live 8 concert with the hope of making poverty history, we need to make careful qualifications about the type of meaning involved. It is one thing to applaud Bono or Al Gore for speaking persuasively about global inequality and pollution. It is quite another to be fully conversant with the details of the social, economic, political and cultural issues raised by headline demands articulated by event figureheads, to say nothing of their consequences.

Few may have dissented from the Live 8 message in 2005. But how many made lasting lifestyle changes in consumption, charity donations and social consciousness to support the humanitarian goals behind the event? Ending poverty and fighting pollution inevitably have significant fiscal and consumerist ramifications. Higher taxes and the curtailment of consumer options by, for example, enhanced taxes on travel are unpopular because they interfere with personal freedom. Events may elicit high levels of emotional involvement from audiences, but they may also be in the nature of short-term responses that do not have enduring value. The blame for this does not necessarily lie at the door of event recipients. Events are geared to achieve a high emotional charge. For this reason, they often skate over the fine print of the stateless solutions that they support. Event publicity operates through banner headlines not balance sheets. Producing intense bursts of emotional commitment are close to the heart of event planning. 'Give us your money', shouted Bob Geldof during the Live Aid event (1985). But there is an uncomfortable issue here relating to the content of events that only a fool would not face.

Ludic and Moral Energy

Mixing the play form with the attainment of political and economic goals yields high levels of emotional discharge. Event footage often clearly shows audiences being carried outside themselves, shedding inhibitions, emoting unity and displaying righteous indignation. But viewers, no less than event mangers, often confuse the passion of the audience for the programme of event entertainment with firm social, political undertakings and enduring cultural commitments. The emotional energy that is multiplied in the audience through responding positively to stage-acts in the event programme is mixed up in unhelpful ways with superficial support for the 'serious' objectives of humanitarianism that are behind the event. It is not at all clear that the energy raised by watching U2 or Pink Floyd (briefly reunited at Live 8) is the same as the energy generated by relieving the hungry in Africa or writing off third world debt repayments. The former belongs to ludic energy, whereas alleviating hunger and writing off debt refer to forms of moral energy. Ludic energy is hedonistic. It values play and pleasure as ends in themselves. It is often based upon motor activity (dancing, running, shouting, singing, etc.) and emotional expressions which produce a spilling over, rather than an accumulation of energy. In contrast, moral energy is disciplined and constructive. It follows the goal of improving personal character or changing society for the better. It is predicated in the notion of an evolution of knowledge and skills. This, in turn, embraces the value of preparation, discipline and training as appropriate uses of energy. It is debatable whether ludic and moral energy are truly compatible.

While empirical research into the motivation of audiences to attend events is not extensive, the available findings do not add weight to the argument that events generate enduring moral commitments, with all of the attendant personal economic sacrifices and restructuring of time-budgets that this implies. For example Tickle (2011) quotes research by Bengry-Howell, which at the time of writing is unpublished, suggesting that the presiding motivation in event attendance is to experience a break from the monotony of labour or unemployment. This is generally tangled up with a semi-articulate wish to experience some form of social transcendence. On the face of it, neither the motivation of using the event to break with monotony nor as a catalyst for transcendence has much to do with developing a solid undertaking to solve the problems of the group or the world.

That entertainment has the potential to have political effects is not at issue (Curran, 2010: 58). Theatre, film, television and popular music have the capacity to contribute positively to debates about inequality, justice, empowerment and manipulation. However, this is different from a considered, layered engagement with these issues. Healthy democracy benefits from the portrayal through entertainment of complex geopolitical questions. However, entertainment tends to dramatise and polarise issues. There are inherent limits in what ludic energy can accomplish and dangers in using it as the yardstick of active involvement. Ludic energy can stop a crowd dead in its tracks, but is has difficulties in rising above what George Clooney has aptly termed 'an MTV level' of understanding.

Viewed thus, event management often seems akin to sorcery. Events are presented by the media as 'magically' solving problems that are beyond the ken or competence of governments or corporations to fix. People power, concentrated in celebrity figureheads, can solve global dilemmas just as wizards and magicians in some tribal societies can make rain out of drought.

In reality, the magical properties of events owes much to mixing play forms with problem resolution. Audiences are carried along with the emotion that a state of magical transcendence has been achieved – one capable of sorting out hunger, injustice and pollution. Post-event analysis of the effects of fund distribution is usually concentrated on the accounts sheets and board meetings of event organisations and their clients. Audiences are only requested to consider them if some sort of scandal is attached to how the money is distributed. As we shall see later, this was what happened to the planners and managers behind Live Aid funds. Now, global humanitarian events aspire to achieve what might be called a *chain reaction* between ludic and moral energy. The momentary excitement and sense of transcendence that the audience feels in seeing superstars is superficially transmitted to considerations of global problem resolution. However, it is questionable whether this chain reaction actually works in anything other than at the levels of publicity and wish fulfilment. If this was not the case, the outlook for positively managing hunger, injustice, pollution and other global issues would be on a much firmer footing than it is now. In a word, trying to combine ludic and moral energy in event forms is not mixing like with like.

As I have already noted, events are like religious ceremonies and festivals in possessing many prominent qualities of drama and melodrama. They are explicitly presented as offering contrasting experience with the humdrum. They use dramatic and melodramatic devices to offer transcendence, both in the sense of inspiring individuals and groups to reach out to recognise common humanity and in inferring that event participation projects people onto a higher spiritual ground. This contributes to the connotation of magic that frequently accompanies them.

Notwithstanding this, one should be wary of concluding that events change the world. Might it be that events allow passions to commute to this or that end, so reviving people's spirits which are jaded by routine and grey government, but leaving all of the fundamentals behind inequality, injustice and subordination intact? Further, might it be that what global events really produce is *compassion consciousness*, not trenchant, embedded economic and political solutions? Empowerment, social inclusion and distributive justice require coordinated, disciplined multilateral strategies and challenging fiscal disciplines.

When global event planners have attempted to bring this off by persuading leaders to put their money where their mouth is, as happened, for example, with the Make Poverty History/Live 8 (2005) campaign, the results have been mixed. On the whole they have not lived up to publicity communiques and pledges (Easterly, 2000; Moyo, 2010; Sachs, 2010, 2011).

Prima facie, events inspire people to noble objectives and boost publicity about social problems. By these means they certainly supply us with intimations of freedom, liberation and joy (Calhoun, 2001). Therapeutically, this compensates Western populations for general feelings of powerlessness and helplessness about the scale of most global problems, notably hunger, needless disease and pollution.

However, as Collins (2001) notes, peak emotional mobilisation is time-restricted. The over-production of publicity can precipitate compassion fatigue. As we shall see in more detail in Chapter 9, some commentators allege that this blighted the Make Poverty History campaign and Live 8 event (2005) (Ecclestone, 2011; Nash, 2008). Leaving the question of compassion fatigue aside, the stark fact is that the humanitarian objectives behind events require dedicated lobbying and repeat fundraising. They do not lend themselves to 'one-off' solutions. At best, global events provide sticking plasters. The wounds that they cover require a more profound and expensive course of dedicated surgery.

Typically, global events are presented as social and economic actions made by the rich for the benefit of the poor. The uncomfortable truth is that rich countries need events. Psychologically, events glamorise the redemptive power of the man or woman in the street. They make citizens believe that they count in solving the world's problems. This is an important source of self-validation and personal gratification (Moyo, 2010).

Nor is it exactly specious. Ordinary men and women do count. By generating compassion, events certainly mobilise resources that go some way towards alleviating distress. But they do not constitute a popular front of global resistance or transformation. Set against the scale of problems of hunger, needless disease, pollution and torture, the resources that they generate are a drop in the ocean.

To the extent that they divert moral energy from the questions of institutional organisational change necessary to achieve genuine empowerment, distributive justice and social inclusion, events compound underlying structural problems. The publicity they generate affords the illusion that power of the people is reforming the world. In fact, global reform requires agitation, the mobilisation of moral energy and concerted collective action to seize control from financial, governmental and informational capital. There is another problem.

Today this form of politics is widely regarded as discredited and exhausted. The ideas of eliminating private banks and creating a national bank to lend for the good of society rather than the interests of shareholders; seizing popular control of broadcasting multinationals like Fox (owned by News Corp) and CNN (owned by Turner Broadcasting) and using them to educate and entertain people rather than drill them with a news agenda dictated by private interests; or providing workers with direct participation in the decisions of boardrooms and government departments, are commonly dismissed as cranky or crackpot. Since the 1980s the successful mantra of the New Right has been 'there is no alternative'.

But is it really cranky to agitate and mobilise for genuine empowerment, inclusion and distributive justice by transforming ownership and control of the central business, governmental and financial institutions in society? What is crackpot about wanting an alternative to cyclical recession, bankers' mega-bonuses, unemployment, homelessness, environmental destruction, a culture of corporate-funded phone hacking and war mongering? If we discount alternatives on the grounds that they are unrealistic, are we not reinforcing the power of particular kinds of social ordering, over which ordinary people have been sidelined as mere isolated voters?

Ordinary people support events because they assume that direct action is positive. Getting off your backside and campaigning for event objectives by attending event programmes and even proselytising event causes is self-confirming. But it disguises the contradictory logic involved in the rich helping the poor. The same people that beat the drum for writing off international debt in the developing world, increasing vaccines for basic, treatable illnesses and dismantling the global culture that tolerates 2.7 billion people living on less than $2 a day, complain if their taxes go up or if funds are cut in other areas of public investment to pay for aid (World Bank, 2007). The leading political parties in the rich countries do not regard fiscal upgrading as politically expedient. Mostly, they take the view that it is unlikely that a manifesto to dramatically increase popular taxation would gain sufficient electoral support to become enforceable. Events therefore cater to the popular need to display activism. To take nothing away from her courage and determination, the number of Rachel Corrie's that they produce are statistically insignificant.[5]

In the long run, there is a big gap between appearance and reality in global event management. Audiences are drawn to events as effective people power in practice. In general, the moral energy that events generate is time-limited. Yet the public seem to have a yearning for the performative utterance of 'team-world' and a readiness to view governments and corporations as inefficient agents of problem resolution.

One can go further. Nowadays, ordinary men and women relate to public life as staging a serial procession of cyclical and single-issue *staged events*. Events have become an essential part of the repertoire of global social ordering. By this term I mean the presentation of events by media and public relations experts, designed to maximise social impact through the application of theatrical and cinematic devices that stress the value of emergency management and the moral obligations of the rich over the poor. Event publicity in the area of global humanitarianism symbolises overwhelming, positive messages: we are all in it together, everyone counts, we care. Further, it imposes upon everyone the head-line responsibility of direct action. Those who pass the buck are implic-itly designated as morally inferior. This endows the humanitarian global event with colossal moral privilege. Is there a real choice between dig-ging deep into your pockets or being shunned for having a heart of stone? The emotionalism and exhibitionism that surround events is not in question. What is debatable is how time-limited their consequences might be and their role in providing the populations in the rich world with temporary validation of their responsibilities with respect to the poor.

On balance, despite doing some manifest good, events reaffirm global layers of social ordering that operate to keep the system of entrenched, organised inequality *in situ* (Easterly, 2007; Moyo, 2010; Sachs, 2010, 2011). The *organisational* dimension must be stressed because so much of the professional literature on global event management emphasises the unpredictability of emergencies and the spontaneity of solutions. The use of ludic forms to generate publicity and raise consciousness is portrayed as automatic and irrepressible, but it actually involves rigorous planning and market research. Generally, global humanitarian event planners are backroom boys, although typically they rely upon a celebrity to humanise event management campaigns. Celebrity figureheads provide short cuts to carrying the claim that global events are momentous. In the case of Live Aid (1985) there is no doubt that the PR–media hub turned Bob Geldof into a figurehead for the elusive one in two of the world's population. As we shall see in greater detail later, the role of celebrities in articulating sustainable event targets and persuading the public to divest themselves of time, money and other resources is pivotal. But they are not the ring-masters.

Together with the corporate, state and voluntary sector clients that commission events, the event executive is part of a covert or semi-transparent band of interests pursuing discrete, planned targets of global emotional management. They are supported by the necessary accessories of media and PR experts who define and implement affirm-ative agendas of personal goal setting, practice and action. An explicit objective is to use free time to *engineer the consent* of populations for a variety of public goals (Bernays, 1928, 1947; Lippmann, 1922). As such, they now play an indispensable part in global *moral regulation*. Social ordering involves constructing a frame of experience that is cognitively and emotionally recognised as *shared* and pursuant to the business of looking after one another. Moral regulation has a more pointed meaning. It refers to the social construction of shared frames of meaning in order to fulfil dominant social and economic interests. Global event management is portrayed as a decent, socially responsible reaction, confirming community in the digital age and tackling world problems.

If this is allowed, what has the wish to help the poor and victims of disasters through the organisation of global events got to do with moral regulation? After all, helping is about standing up and being counted, getting things done and making a difference, often in defiance of authority. In contrast, moral regulation is about discipline, manipulation and control. On this basis, to venture that events enhance the purposes of moral regulation in accordance with the interests of invisible government, rather than express the free will of the people, may readily be dismissed as poppycock. Given the strong strain of emotionalism in event consciousness this is understandable. As the following chapter will endeavour to show, it is also wrong.

Notes

1   Ludic energy refers to leisure-related energy.
2   The *locus classicus* in the sociological tradition is Emile Durkheim's work on religion. Durkheim regarded organised play forms in urban-industrial society as possessing the capacity to generate the popular sense of unity and transcendence that was formerly associated with magic and organised religion. His sociology prefigures the idea of events. He saw public holidays and festivals, organised by the state, as occasions for 'collective remaking'.
3   Sociological discussions of modernity have stressed the inherent tension between social and economic forces directed to imposing order and those directed at change. These abstract forces translate into personality structure and human behaviour. Georg Simmel's sociology distinguishes between the blasé personality (punchdrunk by change that it becomes desensitised and routinised) and the neurasthenic personality (trapped by a foreboding sense of pulverising order and fearful of change). These psychosocial personality constructs are still useful in understanding behaviour today.
4   As with so much in event word of mouth, there is no empirical evidence to support the assertions that events are the direct expression of public opinion. How many people really supported the Concert for Hurricane Relief (2005), Live 8 (2007), Live Earth (2007), for example? The answer is we do not know. Enlisting an electorate to support your position without giving them the courtesy of voting would be decried anywhere else. Why does it pass as par for the course in the event field?
5   Rachel Corrie (1979–2003) was a 23-year-old American member of the International Solidarity Movement (ISM). She died acting as a human shield in front of an IDF Caterpillar D9 bulldozer, driven by an Israeli soldier scheduled to demolish a Palestinian home.

3

WHY IS 'MORAL REGULATION' RELEVANT?

To understand why, we need to go a bit further into what the term moral regulation means. Further, since global event management presupposes public relations and multinational communication networks it is also necessary to address the question of communication power and the related matter of events as vehicles of intercontinental consent engineering. We will go through these issues quite formally before returning to demonstrate their relevance to event management.

Corrigan and Sayer (1985: 4) define *moral regulation* as:

> a project of normalizing, rendering natural, taken for granted, in a word 'obvious', what are in fact ontological and epistemological premises of a particular and historical form of social order.

Organised religion and central state agencies have long employed schooling, the law and official ceremonies to 'give unitary and unifying expression to what are in fact multifaceted and differential historical experiences of groups within society, denying their particularity' (Corrigan and Sayer, 1985: 4).

In doing so an *illusory community* is created. Its interests are not articulated spontaneously. Corrigan and Sayer (1985) focus on the state because they hold that historically, the state has developed and exercised monopolistic or quasi-monopolistic powers over schooling, policing and licensing. In pursuing these objectives the state typically acts in the interests of the most powerful strata, especially the owners and managers of business corporations and the media.

Today it is by no means self-evident that the state alone provides this historic role. Indeed, in the digital age, it is not enough for religion or the state to school and stimulate public moral reactions. The PR–media hub, which is international in tendency, if not in nature, agitates for compassion on a global scale by adroitly positioning news of real events on the social horizon and employing dramatic and melodramatic devices to imprint them onto social consciousness. The media operate as a *theatrum mundi* taking us into confidence about agendas, players and plots in world affairs (Keane, 2005).[1] We have a sense of presumed intimacy, buoyed by the tit-bits fed to us by production controllers and the winning face of professional media presenters. This amounts to the manipulation of popular emotions to enhance social receptivity to formal, institutional definitions of reality and policy formation (Castells, 2009). The interests it serves have affiliated objectives, although whether the term 'class' is fit to describe them is disputable. Invisible government consists of international capital operating through multiple pathways in corporations, national states and the media. International capital is multinational, mobile and controls an agglomeration of institutions through which its interests are expressed.

For example, the French international media conglomerate Vivendi has its headquarters in Paris but owns Havas (the advertising giant in France), the Universal Music Group (based in Southern California), Maroc Television (based in Rabat, Morocco), GVT, a Brazilian telecommunications company (headquartered in Curitiba, Brazil) and has a controlling interest in the games company Activision Blizzard (based in Southern California).

The Sony Corporation, based in Tokyo, has subsidiaries in music, computer entertainment, electronics, magnetic device technology, mobile phones, creative software, television and games in over 30 countries, including the USA, UK, Australia, Brazil, Hong Kong, Mexico, Switzerland, Germany, the Netherlands, Turkey, Thailand, Vietnam, Argentina, Puerto Rico and New Zealand.

The organisational flow charts of these corporations are not untypical of leading multinationals. Although authority is ultimately located in central headquarters, power is distributed along multiple chains linking many different nodes in many different countries. Product lines are multiple rather than singular. Moreover, acquisition and development assume a plethora of mutual feedback loops between the various businesses.[2] For example, film production will be planned to add to the bottom line in music (film soundtracks), mobile phones (ring tones) and advertising.

Product diversity and internationalisation complicates policing and blurs lines of accountability. Multinationals lobby political interests throughout the world with a view to influencing public image and consumer responses. In this sense, moral regulation may be said to have slipped beyond the ropes of the nation-state. In the digital financial economy nation-states are local and bilateral whereas corporations are global and multilateral. Individual nation-states have limited capacities to monitor and police the activities of corporations like Vivendi and Sony. The strategy and enforcement of patterns of consumer choice are determined by corporate leaders and planning teams that are, at the composite level, invisible and only semi-accountable to the public. These agents do not confine themselves to selling products, they also operate to create new wants and new responsibilities in consumers.

What does it mean to 'morally regulate' populations? The question of moral government in advanced urban-industrial societies is tricky for three reasons. Firstly, unlike traditional, hunter and gatherer or agrarian societies, people are not integrated by powerful, monocultural magical or religious systems of belief. Morals that bind and unify do not stem from the mouth of a leader or pages of scripture. The moral relativism of populations means that agents of government cannot invoke the word of God or magical properties of design as spurs to obedience. Of course, monocultural systems persist, since one of the things that urban-industrial societies pride themselves on is moral relativism and tolerance of belief systems. In New York, Berlin, London and Sydney, therefore, we are still exposed to political parties who hold that it is the moral duty of all to work, or Islamic fundamentalists who insist upon inflexible respect for the word of the Prophet. However, in advanced urban-industrial societies monocultural belief systems do not exactly flourish. Attempts to impose them over-aggressively upon a population are met with resistance on many fronts.

Secondly, while physical force is concentrated in the hands of elected government, the boundaries within which it legitimately operates may be revised according to circumstance. For example, the use of the 3000 troops to clear up Rio's Rocinha *favela* in November 2011, in preparation for the 'cleansing' for the 2014 FIFA World Cup and 2016 Olympic city, were widely resented by residents as improper and heavy handed. The efforts of governments to use physical force to present a unifying moral front in cyclical or single-issue global events can open up a can of worms about issues of economic redistributive justice, marginalisation and social inclusion. Effective moral regulation therefore depends heavily upon engineering consent. This brings me to my third point.

To propose that advanced urban-industrial societies are tolerant to greater levels of moral relativism than traditional, hunter and gatherer or agrarian societies, is another way of stating the cardinal importance that they place upon what Ernest Gellner (1997) called 'the ethic of cognition'. That is, the respect for the liberty of assembly and freedom of speech. Contrary to the image of these societies as tolerant and open, they are, in fact, resolute and staunch in the defence of 'the pubic sphere' and, at least, the ideal of 'the open society'. This position is a threat to any system of belief and practice that goes by the name of being 'monocultural'. By the 'public sphere' is meant the right of free speech, which extends to the media, political parties and citizens (Habermas, 1989); and by the term 'open society' is meant the realm of guaranteed liberties that enable conservative and contrarian arguments to be expressed in the name of liberty (Popper, 1968). The ethic of cognition operates with a powerful notion of cultural literacy, but it is one that is presupposed to be multi-layered, flexible and morally diverse.

These three issues present moral regulation with formidable challenges. It is no longer a matter of merely policing people or schooling the population, it is a question of winning the battle for the popular mind in 'free' time activity. By engineering popular consent for externally defined ludic courses of action, usually based pre-eminently in pre-emptive emotive arguments, social interests divert popular attention from the hidden mechanics of invisible government that support and develop the whole system of organised inequality and injustice. Commercial media networks now operate ordinarily as channels of public persuasion, translating private considerations into urgent public interests and *causes célèbres*.

While global event planning presents itself as not playing the corporate game, the global nature of its activities and its reliance on the transmission capacity of the media mean that it is enmeshed in power relationships that inevitably compromise its reformist credentials. Event concepts are presented as the alternative to routine. Humanitarian events are depicted as offering solutions that governments and big business are unable to achieve. Corporate events are presented as occasions for the refreshment of energies, brainstorming and the flourishing of initiatives. The dominant motif is freedom of expression. This connects up with an idiom of participation that is openly libertarian and non-judgemental. Events are settings in which you are free to emote, share your problems with others and let your hair down for a good cause. Events certainly provide opportunities for reflecting critically on social and economic problems. They also provide a culture of disinhibition where subjective disclosure and the display of personal pain are cultivated. Events are associated with stepping out of stifling work roles and emoting deep feelings frankly.

Further, because this is also very often a matter of mobilising ludic energy, the play forms that mark the event muddy the waters about the level of personal commitment to the moral questions defined by the event concept. It is as if the stirring up of ludic energy encourages personal efforts to spill over into the exuberance of mere play activities. The relationship between the play form of cyclical and single-issue events and the moral designs that they are planned to fulfil is complex. I will take it up in more detail later. At this juncture in the discussion, I simply wish to suggest that there are tensions between ludic and moral energy. Having a party to achieve moral objectives means that ludic energy may be expressed in types of self-gratification that frustrate moral design by providing the show of resolute action while merely tinkering with remedies rather than rigorously enforcing them.

Leaving aside matters of moral relativism, cultural literacy and the ethic of cognition, in the question of the relationship between events and moral regulation it is profitable to examine the matter of moral regulation from another angle. This refers to the commercial and security aspects of event management. Popular expressions of events portray them as the embodiment of people power. One is pulled up short, then, by observing that the search for belonging, freedom and transcendence through events takes place in some of the most tightly controlled environments in contemporary society. General controls over crowd flow, sponsorship restrictions upon what the crowd is permitted to carry to the venue (alcohol, cameras, recording equipment), dress codes, the range of tolerated contrarian values, the policing powers of show stewards, the use of biometric surveillance and CCTV, UAV patrols, municipal health and safety requirements and the ticketing conditions impose a heavy tariff upon personal liberty and fundamentally regulate collective behaviour. The reality is that, even where events make a virtue of low levels of organisation such as the Burning Man City festival, the crowd is vetted (searched for offensive weapons, alcohol) and monitored for behaviour that conflicts with event protocol. Global event settings may be portrayed as 'free'. In reality, they involve the barracking of populations and directed ludic behaviour (Graham, 2010, 2012).

While the rejection of routine and discarding the straitjacket of standardised roles are cogent motivations, personal feelings and behaviour are subject to strong moral regulation. Outwardly, event practice is required to reinforce the event concept. Dissidence is not tolerated. In this sense events are hardly the celebration of personal freedom but, more properly, the politics of public affirmation of the event concept. People are not chiefly encouraged to develop themselves through their experiences and achievements. Rather they are prevailed upon to conform to the event concept by accommodating to the presiding politics of giving. Through these, and other means, the engineering of popular consent is pursued.

By 'giving' I do not just mean financial contributions or pledges. I mean displaying the emotions to an externally defined cause whether it be providing food for the starving or committing to the company five-year plan. The narrative of giving organised around the event concept frames how people are expected to respond.

Identification with the concept validates the self. Public validation provides individuals with a sense of personal recognition and self-worth. By displaying that you are a supporter of the Make Poverty History campaign or the Global Day of Action (Against Climate Change) (2007) you communicate that you are not only committed to helping others but that you answer to deep needs for acceptance and personal recognition. Emotional giving then is not simply a form of charity. It is also a type of personal therapy, since by lending support you represent active involvement.

Now, linking events to therapy does not mean that the stateless solutions to economic, political and social problems that they proffer are bogus. Events provide public settings for critically reflecting on dehumanising conditions and relieving organisational bottlenecks. They make a real contribution to fundraising and expanding the horizon of social consciousness about questions like global poverty, disease, torture, injustice and pollution. It goes without saying that in general, as we shall see, the solutions which they proffer do not live up to the publicity that accompanies them. The distraction that glamorous events produce from questions of political reform and fiscally prudent approaches to global and organisational problems is one of the main sources of criticism directed against event management (Easterly, 2007; Moyo, 2010; Sachs, 2010, 2011). The 'can do' spirit of event 'people power' also distracts from the therapeutic function that events perform for participants.

The suggestion that events are popular because they afford a degree of personal therapy is likely to be resisted by most event professionals. The dominant self-image of the profession is that events provide practical, rational solutions for fundraising and social integration that the free market and the state are unable to accomplish (Arcodia and Reid, 2004; Bowdin et al., 2011; Getz and Wicks, 1994). Yet the main currency through which people are required to give is not money, but the emotions. Through performative labour, by contrasting personal awareness with a supposed state of general indifference, individuals are persuaded to feel more alive and in touch with themselves. Event management does not simply make the event concept the focus of attention, it places the individual at the centre of problem solving. Who among us would not feel good about themselves if they act to 'save' Africa or confirm the corporation's commitment to provide service to customers and the community? That there is a gaping disproportion between the personal act of giving and the scale of the social, economic and political problems that global event concepts are designed to address is beside the point. Personal giving, and being seen to give, is at the fulcrum of the event process and the immediate, self-justifying principle of personal involvement.

The strong culture of conformity in the event process is not noticed because event managers promote events as the antidote to the dehumanisation and sterility of everyday life. Yet in fleeing standardised routine individuals are required to submit to a new order of emotional disclosure. Events exhort us to emote. Sharing emotions in public boosts the worth and publicity of the event concept. By association, the worth of the individual who displays emotion is validated. Conversely, by implication, the worth of the individual who refrains from displaying emotion is devalued. Either way the social impact of the event is enhanced.

There is nothing new in the application of celebration to achieve transcendence. The state has long exploited and developed sporting events, ceremonial processions and international trade fairs to build pride and loyalty (Roche, 2000, 2002). The event management partnerships between lobbyists, social movements, corporations and state departments to raise funds and publicise causes are a continuation of well-established precedents. What is new are two things.

Firstly, they are being forged and applied in the midst of growing awareness of globalisation and the limits of state power. Events offer stateless solutions to public worries and the illusion of global coalescence to shared goals. They provide individuals with the veneer of active citizenship and employees with the gloss of unity. We have a sense of making a difference by attending a concert for the fight against poverty or by speaking from the floor at a company meeting. In doing so we reassure ourselves with the thought that we are opposing the vulture logic of unrestricted capitalism. Yet we do not recognise that by privileging the romance of charity over the logic of political economy we reinforce the *status quo*.

Secondly, events have unprecedented force over social consciousness because they make full use of global media networks. It is impossible to imagine global events such as Live Aid (1985), Live 8 (2005) or Live Earth (2005) without the electronic eye of television telecasting images, gathering reactions and publicising concepts. While the media are hierarchical in objectives and organisation, they give the appearance of being informal and participatory. This is enhanced by the presentational styles of interviewers, analysts and talk show comperes. A state of presumed intimacy is orchestrated which nonetheless has real effects upon how people define and rank issues and responses to world affairs. Because global events are often associated with euphoria – at last, *something* is being done to provide genuine help for those in need and *finally*, the organisational gremlins that have been swept under the carpet are being *brought out into the open* – there is an uncritical acceptance that people are *all in it together* and that the media are *the honest, faithful servant* of popular will.

Yet event concepts are not expressions of popular will. Nor, *contra* Bernays (1923, 1928), are the media some kind of faithful drayhorse hauling the sentiments of the crowd to leaders and chugging them back, clop-by-clop, once again. Events, and the media representations of events, are conditioned by the mores of invisible government. What is meant by this term 'invisible government'?

The 'tone' of events and the public presentation of 'outcomes' comply not only with the judgement of event planners, but also with the requirements of unappointed financial sponsors who, in effect, act as cultural mediators, pushing public sentiment in this or that direction, mostly in service of the beck and call of the interests who employ them. While it is easy enough to identify most financial sponsors, since they declare and often advertise themselves, the question of cultural stewardship is rather more murky. Who are these people that set the 'tone' of events? How are they recruited? What systems operate to monitor their activities?

We are referring to the 'great and the good'. That is, persons of influence in government, the media and multinational corporations. They are not recruited from the same background, nor, in the digital age, is it necessary for them to have face-to-face contact. It is enough that they have similar interests in sponsoring particular forms of performative labour and piloting specific types of social ordering. The purpose of this labour and ordering is to maintain and advance the interests of the strata that have influential advantage in the conduct of world affairs.

To posit the existence of invisible government is not to smuggle in a version of conspiracy theory. Persons of influence in government, the media and multinational corporations do not need to aspire to take over the world because they already occupy privileged settings in managing world affairs, through work and ownership. There is no need to posit class dominance. If persons of influence have more power in achieving *hegemony*, it is nonetheless the case that inherent in the concept are the ideas of resistance and opposition. Notwithstanding this, the spheres of interest and access to instrumental and ideological power available to persons of influence enable them to exert significant, interlocking influence upon general cognition, belief and practice. The link with media networks is crucial in organising consent and social ordering.

Invisible Government Communication Power

Manuel Castells (2009) argues that *communication power* reflects the *social networks* that own and control the media. He provides several grounded examples of the phenomenon. For example, he notes that the prelude to the Allied invasion of Iraq (2003) constituted what might be justifiably termed an *information war* in which selective, and what turned out to be, incorrect readings of Iraqi military capacity were applied to soften up public opinion to be receptive to physical invasion (Castells, 2009: 165–88). Before Saddam Hussein's forces in Iraq could be conquered, it was necessary to conquer the hearts and minds of populations in the Allied countries so as to provide the varnish of domestic sanction for armed conflict. This was accomplished by the Bush and Blair administrations' deliberately entangling the 9/11 outrage with Iraq's foreign policy objectives. Many American service personnel and their Allies went to their deaths in the war against Iraq falsely believing that Saddam Hussein was either directly involved in, or complicit with al-Qaeda, in the 9/11 attack on the World Trade Towers.

For Castells (2009), communication power is now the normal opening move by means of which powerful global interests seek to impose their will over popular cognition. They do not merely reflect reality, they use various cues, scripts, transmission times, blends between soft and hard news and other devices to elicit preferred social reactions. In order to consolidate the point Castells (2009: 216–38, 254–64, 303–39) provides other detailed empirical examples: namely the election campaign method in the USA used to gain Barack Obama power in 2008; the conservative targeting of the political record of the socialist regimes led by Felipe Gonzalez in Spain; and the environmental movement in the West.[3]

Media Functions in Democratic Society

The emphasis on the role that media communication power plays in shaping social consciousness goes to the heart of the relationship between invisible government, entertainment and democracy. Pluralist and neoliberal accounts maintain that the media provide three key functions in democratic society: to inform, to provide an open arena of debate and to protect public interest. The theory of communicative power undermines each precept. It submits that the media:

- Frame issues around boundaries of validity, which limits the scope of information.
- Operate in accordance with the private interests of ownership and control rather than producing a level playing field of open debate.
- Protect private interests of ownership and control in ways that conflict with the public interest.

This falsifies pluralist and neoliberal approaches. For example, these accounts are fond of presenting action in terms of rational choice models (Chambers and Costain, 2000; Fishkin, 2009). That is, since the functions of the media in society are presented as operating in a perfect market of knowledge and information ordinary citizens possess the means to weigh up data and reach rational conclusions.

The theory of communicative power rides roughshod over rational choice models by holding that the market of information and knowledge is rigged. Further, it insists that the privately owned and controlled media operate in accordance with the invisible or semi-transparent interests that support and manage them.

On this reckoning, the media do not offer an electronic eye on the world. Rather, they provide tunnel vision on topics and issues that are determined by media managers who are enmeshed with the interests of private corporations and/or the state. This involves not only the content of what communication power transmits but also the information diet between hard and soft news. This diet contributes to the popular sense of what is important in the world and the weight of personal responsibility. Privileging soft news in media schedules produces a public that is less well informed and more plastic than in schedules where the privilege is reversed (in favour of hard news).

For example, Curran et al.'s (2009) comparative study of media coverage concludes that American TV news reports privilege soft news over hard news and feature half the international news topics and issues of Danish and Finnish TV news. Moreover, unlike Danish and Finnish broadcasters, American TV news situates programmes at the periphery, rather than the core of prime time transmission slots. Curran et al. conclude that the American public has an information deficit with respect to international news and issues and topics of public interest, compared with their Scandinavian counterparts. This information deficit suits the interests of the persons of influence who have access to the greatest effective power in running the USA.

The theory of communication power, then, refutes normative accounts of media and democracy engendered in the pluralist and neoliberal traditions. In contrast, it submits that the media are chained to the interests of oligarchy. These forces require values, debate and even basic processes of cognition to be hot-wired to their own interests. The orthodox role of the media in modern democracy is to inform, to provide an arena of debate and to represent public interest, but only if, in the long run, the media dance to the tune of the invisible oligarchy that has hegemonic advantage in reproducing the global social order.

The Symbol, the Leader and the Technology of Network Communication

Although Castells makes no reference to the history of public relations his discussion is remarkably reminiscent of the basic principle of effective public relations laid down by the so-called 'father' of public relations, Edward Bernays (1923, 1928), almost a century ago. Bernays submitted that there are three cornerstones to effective public relations: the *symbol,* the *leader* and the technology of *communication*.

The public relations symbol may be defined as a short cut to consent (in the event literature we would call this the 'event concept'). When used successfully it enables the group to automatically view the world and its problems in a positive light. As such, it is an indispensable tool for leaders in politics, business and the arts. At one and the same time the symbol is a means of galvanising opinion and manipulating responses to achieve predetermined ends. To quote Bernays (1923: 4):

> The very need of reaching large numbers of people at one time and in the shortest possible time tends toward the utilization of symbols which stand in the minds of the public for the abstract idea the technician wishes to convey.

Symbols have the technical capacity to match complex goals to scarce resources in impressive, compelling fashion. This raises a separate set of questions concerning who sets the goals, how resources are managed and why we accept the goals that are given to us. Bernays was notoriously vague about all of these topics (Ewen, 1998). Suffice to say that public relations regards symbols as indispensable in regulating majority opinion. Presuppositions here are matters of how symbols are formulated and communicated. This brings us to what Bernays considers to be the second crucial element in effective public relations: the leader.

The leader provides the group mind with focus and direction. Bernays was influenced by an earlier generation interested in the psychology of the crowd – writers like Gustave Le Bon and Wilfred Trotter.[4] 'A crowd is a servile flock', wrote Le Bon (1896: 72), 'that is incapable of ever doing without a master.' It may be objected that this is somewhat severe. For it implies that the majority are incapable of knowing their own minds. They require a leader to help make sense of the world and their place in it. To be sure, this is indeed the nub of Le Bon's view. However, in fairness to him, the judgement is made as much in response to the challenges of industrial society as to what he perceives to be innate flaws in the human psyche. That is, he submits that the division of labour is necessary for the health and prosperity of society. However, it corrals men and women into specialised activities and patterns of behaviour that blind them to ideas that fall outside their own speciality. Where the economic requirements of life oblige people to be specialised and divided, leaders supply the group mind with a sense of progressive collective responsibility and purpose.

Taking up these ideas, Bernays (1928) proposes that the leader is the servant of the people. Again, he concentrates upon the technocratic aspects of leadership and mostly leaves aside ticklish questions of political manipulation. Thus, he invites us to regard the leader as the voice of the people. As he (1928: 109) puts it:

> The voice of the people expresses the mind of the people, and that mind is made up for it by the group leaders in whom it believes and by those persons who understand the manipulation of public opinion.

These 'persons' are, of course, public relations experts. They determine the popular will through mass opinion research. In doing so they have complete recourse to the instruments provided by social research to acquire objective knowledge of the group mind: namely, structured interviews, questionnaires, focus groups, sampling, statistical surveys, content analysis, structured interviews, semi-structured interviews and unstructured interviews. By these means, the condition of the mind of the people is held to be *scientifically* revealed. These data are translated into symbols, policies and strategies that are, in turn, articulated by leaders. It is in this sense that leaders can be said to be the organ that expresses the voice of the people.

The third element required for effective public relations is the media. Newspapers, television, radio and websites are transmission belts communicating symbols, policies and strategies from the leader to the people and vice versa. Naturally, no self-respecting public relations expert would claim that the media is the mirror of society. To refer to Lippmann (1922: 279):

> Every newspaper when it reaches the reader is the result of a whole series of selections as to what items shall be printed, in what positions they shall be printed, how much space each shall occupy, what emphasis each shall have.

The same holds for television news broadcasts and websites. Instead of speaking of the media as the reflection of public opinion it is more accurate to regard them as framing cognition by producing a context of debate and an agenda by normative rendition, ventilating values, recognising belonging and directing action.

Interestingly, in his discussion of communication power Castells (2009) also alludes to the role of the media in 'framing' issues and responses. Drawing on psychological research Castells (2009: 142) defines frames as 'neural networks of association that can be accessed from the language through metaphorical connections. Framing means activating specific neural networks.'

As a nephew of Sigmund Freud, Bernays would have no trouble in accepting that frames operate at both conscious and subconscious levels. For both Bernays and Castells, communication processes imprint a stamp upon the agenda and significance of news and opinions and conditions judgement of validity, fairness and the necessity of action in the public mind.

According to Bernays the challenge of public relations is to make the communication process reinforce and develop the interests of 'invisible government'. This term recurs throughout his work, but it is a shadowy concept which is never precisely defined.[5] Reading between the lines it refers to leading business, government, military and media interests. It is not clear if Bernays sees these interests as interlocking. He maintains that in healthy democracies, in the medium and long term, the interests of invisible government always coincide with the interests of the people. Although short-term deviations are possible, they are subject to correction by popular protest and the ethical responsibilities of the professional class that manages the communication process, namely PR and media specialists. The use of communication power to regulate majority opinion is therefore not regarded as unbridled. For Bernays, the PR–media professional code of ethics prevents the wool from being pulled over the eyes of the people.

Castells (2009) also submits that social interests strive to dominate the communication process in order to frame the responses of the majority to questions of validity, fairness and necessity. However, he is less sanguine about the protective cover provided by the PR–media professional code of ethics. To quote Castells (2009: 192):

> By activating networks of association between events and mental images via communication processes, power-making operates in multilayered dynamics in which the way we feel structures the way we think and ultimately the way we act.

While Castells would doubtless concur with Bernays that many aspects of these 'multilayered dynamics' are invisible, he does not maintain that in the medium or long term the interests of invisible government and the people coincide. For Castells communication networks are governed by the agenda setting, managerial and editorial decision-making power of the interests that own and control multimedia communication networks, their employers and clients. His collective term for these interests is *network power* (2009: 419). They define and manage the event agenda and set the scripts of performative labour surrounding event networking. Their ultimate purpose is moral regulation, i.e. to conduct popular forms of behaviour that reinforce the hegemony of the interests behind network power. Castells does not, however, regard these interests to be omnipotent.

Communication power allows feedback loops of resistance and opposition to challenge the preferred readings of 'the facts' produced by network power. These are situated at both a grassroots level and in the campaigning role of activists. Nor does Castells regard the social interests behind network power to be fully interlocking. Networks allow social interests to develop a common front of action over specific issues. But his model acknowledges autonomy, difference and divergence between socioeconomic interests.

Notwithstanding the recognition of diversity, division and resistance, he sees the use of communication power to regulate majority opinion as an unequal battle. The PR–media hub act in *accordance* with commercial and state interests dedicated to the tasks of social ordering and moral regulation to manage global power. They have professional skills and privileged access to the greatest resources of communication power in human history. Castells (2009: 420–1) makes no bones about holding that network power has medium- and long-term ends that are contrary to the interests of the majority. That is, maximising margins in the global financial market, increasing political capital in support of government-owned corporations and attracting, creating and maintaining an audience as the means to accumulate financial and cultural capital.

The concept of communication power has a particular inflection that distinguishes it from conventional models of power. The latter identify power as a transformative resource that realises the will of private interests. Thus, in Weber's (1978) sociology, the crucible of power is the state which defines laws and regiments policing over a territorially located body of citizens. For Castells (2009), digital society diminishes the salience of Weber's position. He builds this case on a fundamental distinction: 'power is relational, domination is institutional' (2009: 15). The latter assumes a territory over which an institution, normally the state, holds dominion. In contrast, the former is *deterritorialised* since it presupposes that power is a universal in human relationships. More than a splitting of hairs is involved here.

Moral Regulation and Globalisation

In the golden age of statecraft, roughly between the Treaty of Westphalia (1648) and the Vietnam War (1955–75), states were held to have sovereignty because of the power vested in them by the people (Linklater, 1998). This was open to serious dissent in the period of monarchy. For monarchy is a system of rule founded in the principle that the head of state embodies the will of the people and is bound by God to act for the popular good.

Viewed from a republican standpoint, a hereditary monarch who is the servant of God is an absurd proposition. The question is how is the monarch cognisant of the will of the people? The pat answer is that he or she is acquainted with this subject by the grace of God. But since the existence of God is not a matter of universal assent, this rhetorical device is of weak leverage in enforcing government. Indeed, it is positively enfeebled when the monarch is seen to transparently act against the interests of subjects.

The Treaty of Westphalia also acknowledges the principle of legal equality between states and respects the legal right of states to manage their own affairs without the intervention of other states. All of this presupposes clear, unambiguous lines of sovereignty between the head of state and appointed government over a legally defined body of people.

Castells (2009) writes from the conviction that this entire framework is rendered obsolete by the rise of communication power and the digital economy. To continue, modern states still assert territorial domination. Thus, there is a law of the land and the citizens of the land are required to obey it. However, the ascent of globalised, digital society has fundamentally changed the rules of the game. Modern communication power exceeds the technical capacity of any state or combination of states to deliver sovereignty over information. Since effective policing of digital communication is technically impossible it follows that the state assertion of sovereignty is untenable.

The post-Westphalian state is *permeable*. The head of state and appointed government are enmeshed in global networks of communication that are not necessarily corroborative. This is what Castells means when he employs the term *relational* to describe the specific quality of network power. In post-Westphalian states, communication power *permeates* national boundaries. This vastly complicates the questions of framing, social ordering and moral regulation.

Most pertinently, it makes total domination an elusive quality in contemporary statecraft since there is no monopoly over information or communication. Politics is still the art of persuasion. But the permeable character of post-Westphalian states requires many more resources to be allocated to public relations and communication because the field of operation is so much bigger. Framing public opinion is a complex, multi-layered task, involving both local and global levels. Recalling here the words of Corrigan and Sayer (1985) already cited: the purpose of framing is to 'normalise', 'take for granted' and render 'obvious', the 'ontological' and 'epistemological' premises of a 'particular', 'historical' *form* of 'social order'. When these preconditions are in place, normative rendition has been accomplished. An 'illusory community' is *in situ*. Framing operates most efficiently when historically specific conditions are understood to be natural and unalterable.

Global events have emerged as an important weapon in this process of framing. They proclaim themselves to be popular, stateless solutions to problems that neither elected government nor the corporation can handle. Despite raising publicity and funds for emergencies and moral concerns, they lack the continuous, systematic qualities of effective problem resolution. A considerable critical literature now exists in the field of development studies that argues that events provide distractions from effective solutions to the development gap. The distractions are popular because they salve the conscience of the advantaged with respect to third world hunger, poverty, disease and other issues connected with global inequality. Their contribution is primarily to act as a device of first world therapy not as a means of structural reform in the global economy (Easterly, 2007; Moyo, 2010; Sachs, 2010, 2011). As such they are not really new, but rather one of the latest instruments in the task of moral regulation.

Stateless Solutions and their Conundrums

Global event managers present events as *stateless solutions* to local, national and global problems. The *relational* issue is for the citizens in the economically advanced countries to do something that elected officials abstain from doing 'for the world'. As we shall see in more detail later, an expanded version of global citizenship is being intimated here (Nash, 2008). Publicity blitzes for the Olympics, Live Aid, Sport Aid and Live Earth concentrate upon inspiring ordinary people with an heroic, 'can do' attitude which is not confined to processes within national borders. Implicitly, the call for motivation is based upon the recognition of unwritten but nevertheless, compelling and decisive responsibilities of *global citizenship*.

None of this makes sense in the Westphalian context. Remember, here the dual cardinal principles are for states to have sovereign authority over a legally defined body of people and to refrain from meddling in the affairs of other sovereign states. In this framework the people look to the state to act on their behalf. It is upon this basis that the head of state and the appointed government claim the right of legitimate sovereignty.

It is as if the Olympics, Live Aid, Sport Aid and Live Earth logic wave a magic wand of global citizenship dissolving, or at least, much reducing, the salience of national sovereignty and national citizenship in the matter of responsible conduct. This is posited in an unexamined premise that the 'fact' of common humanity imposes an ethical duty upon all in the economically advanced countries to act *as one* to relieve hunger, poverty, illness, torture and repression in the developing countries and to minister to the suffering of the Earth itself.

This is indeed a magical state of affairs in which Left and Right forget their differences, bury their quarrels, ignore distinctions of ethnicity, culture and religion, eliminate considerations of self-worth and self-aggrandisement, to heed to Mother Earth and her ailing children. Global event planners condemn the ideology of competitive materialism and party politics. Instead they position themselves as speaking on behalf of, and standing shoulder to shoulder with, 'the world'.

But this naively presumes that their position is neutral, preordained and universally shared. This is not the case. One-world/team-world philosophies are always latently authoritarian. For cultures are not all the same and their differences are not limited to negligible disagreements. Nor are the rights and duties of humanity universally recognised. They are conditioned and moderated by religious traditions which express kinship and fellowship in different ways and by cultural divisions which are not uniform.

Further, because the forces that commission events and the event executive have no interest in acquiring formal, elected power, their responsibilities are circumscribed and disaggregated. This has extremely pertinent consequences upon the traction of their policies. Those who act for the world in the name of reversing environmental decay in Mother Earth have no logical or necessary connection with others who take it upon themselves (since they are not elected and non-accountable) to represent the world in making hunger, poverty and war, history. Global events, it might be said, are occasions in which the romantic Left and the romantic Right meet in common purpose for finite duration. But this does not mean that the differences between them are eliminated or that the show of unity necessarily persists.

Global citizenship is in fact, a chimera. It may be desired, yearned for and, in some rarefied circles, which deal with the declaration of universal human rights, confidently asserted. But it is not universally enforceable and it is not recognised in practice by all people of the world. The obligations to strangers recognised by Berber tribesmen in the Atlas Mountains are profoundly different from the equivalent among metropolitan populations in Western welfare states. To discount these differences as matters of no consequence and to ride roughshod over them in formulating global policies and programmes of resource distribution is culturally insensitive and perilous.

So while the logic of events like the Olympics, Live Aid, Sport Aid, the Rio Carnival, the Sydney Mardi Gras and Live Earth can justifiably be said to clarify some issues of fellowship, injustice, suffering and risk, they obfuscate others and encourage unrealistic expectations of deliverance from misery, division and want. They produce a disaggregated unrealistic approach to relief, since giving is predicated in the romance of charity rather than the logic of political economy. This may have value in alleviating suffering, but it is the lesser adjunct to aggregated approaches at national government, bilateral and multilateral levels. For global problems of hunger, illness, poverty and environmental decay are continuous. What they require is planned, year-on, decade after decade, fiscal and investment strategies aimed at reallocating surplus from the economically advanced Western nations to the emerging and developing world and creating a common fund to tackle fossil fuel pollution.

Yet humanitarian global events often overshadow the operations of the less glitzy parts of the humanitarian relief sector and encourage an unproductive 'one-stop' solution outlook among large sections of the global public. Pay no tax, hold more comedy telethons, sports fixtures and multinational rock concert telecasts are hazardous solutions in humanitarian effort. Yet in spite of disclaimers from event planners this is often the net result of what they do.

To take up and develop a point made earlier, the festive element in global events contributes to obfuscation by twining reform strategies with play. Comedy telethons in support of the poor, international sporting tournaments in the name of fellowship and multi-venue international rock performances on behalf of famine relief or environmental reform aim to achieve transcendence through laughter, games and music. However, it is not at all clear whether the sense of unity and spirituality achieved through these means are of the same kind as the humanitarian response to suffering (Katz, 1999). Festivity may produce empathy, but it is also associated with escapism and self-help. Laughter, games and music may help to save *the* world, but they also transport people from immediate cares in *their* worlds and elicit what is often the illusory balm of self-healing. There is a thin line between helping others and self-gratification. Global event management crosses it repeatedly and without apology. The climate of empathy and kinship that it strives to induce is also a mechanism for group approval and self-validation. Some individuals and groups are radicalised by global events. Beyond question, they are in the minority. Make no mistake, this is not to attribute insincerity to them. Rather, the point to grasp is that only for a very few cases is it a once and for all commitment that changes the fundamentals of life.

Moreover, catharsis, emotionalism and exhibitionism lend themselves to dramatic representations of many hues and patterns. The dramatic element in events is not confined to the stage presence of celebrities, audiences in the stadium and at home are cast in the role of heroes. They take on the responsibility of adopting global problems that the state and business allegedly, carelessly abjure.

If this is correct, global event management can be seen as part of the psychology of performative labour which induces citizens to express emotions for the purpose of self-validation. Turning up and paying for a concert to save the world, dancing for climate change, phoning in donations to a worthy telethon cause, exhibiting heartfelt public support for the corporation that employs you or the party of which you are a member, display a good heart and provide the gloss of active citizenship. No matter that the concert and the telethon generally deal with social problems that require levels of fiscal rectitude that viable governments and political parties in the West dismiss as electoral suicide. The *display* of giving is as motivational as the act of giving (Furedi, 2004). By providing an outlet for anger and joyful celebration of humanity, global events contribute to the moral regulation of populations. They divert them from the central questions of the embedded, structural relationships between inequality, injustice and political economy. These questions demand profound revisions in international capitalisation, multilateral trade agreements, the allocation of labour, knowledge and other distributive resources, which ultimately lead to the issue of the structural transformation of power and wealth between the rich and the poor. Global humanitarian events do some good by generating limited resources and partially raising social consciousness. However, to the extent that they fudge the question of structural transformation they exert a pettifogging effect upon humanitarian efforts.

Notes

1   The Baroque term *theatrum mundi* is particularly apposite to describe the media. Communication power both frames the world as a series of incidents and emergencies and employs theatrical devices in the presentation of news, interviews and so on. The space given to the structural forces behind incidents and emergencies is strictly rationed, presumably because it does not have the same box office appeal as portraying the world as a teeming mass of incidents and emergencies. By neglecting the question of structure, a distorted picture of media-fuelled social reality emerges and is perpetuated. Thus, we focus on the burning towers and the man behind the assassins, not the geopolitical and economic structures that hatched the terrorist plot.

2   The cleansing operation was widely seen as a hammer to break a nut. The dislocation of ordinary life in Rocinha gained headline columns in the world media that supported the determination of the Brazilian government to mount a good, clean World Cup and Olympics. However, the gain in rolling back organised crime was comparatively small.

3   The same techniques of misinformation were used by corporate communication power in the USA and UK to soften up the public to the Allied invasion of Iraq (2003).

4   Le Bon and Trotter were among the first social scientists in the industrial era to pose the question of the origins, tension-balance and dynamics of crowd psychology. They tapped into the issue of subconscious drives emanating from unconscious forces which, for Bernays, would have deeply suggestive parallels with the work of his uncle, Sigmund Freud, on the structure of the mind.

5   Despite this, I am drawn to the notion of 'invisible government'. For my money it captures perfectly the faceless chief civil servants, financiers, industrial entrepreneurs and captains of industry whose influence on the conduct of life is achieved by clandestine meetings and secret deals. One would think that the age of communication power would render invisible government transparent. Instead, the age of the media has produced new layers of insulation and secrecy between decision-makers and those to whom they are accountable. Like modern-day celebrities, decision-makers are surrounded by a salaried team of cultural intermediaries who provide a media-friendly spin on decisions based in naked acquisition.

4

HOW IS EVENT COGNITION FORMULATED?

It is a cliché to maintain that we live in the information age. That is, a social, economic and political context in which electronic data are a source of value in conditioning social and economic relationships (Bell, 1976; Castells, 1997; Touraine, 1974). What does it mean to posit that information is a source of value and what is the connection between this and event management? To answer these questions we will eventually have to make a distinction between the means and ends of information.

Before getting there we need to take a sideways step. We must briefly consider how economists have elaborated the proposition that the uneven distribution of information in society reflects power differences that invalidate the notion of perfect competition.[1] The classical view treats the free market as an arena of perfect competition. The logic of this view is that economic fluctuations simply reflect the operation of the market's 'invisible hand'. Namely, that free market's are self-correcting so that when a disequilibrium between supply and demand occurs, the market corrects the imbalance by allowing resources that produce over-supply to go to the wall. By liberating 'unproductive labour' an incentive is created to boost enterprise and initiative. In effect, unproductive resources are eventually redeployed to productive outcomes. This is fine in theory. But it has one insuperable practical difficulty: it does not correspond to real market behaviour. Information is not perfectly distributed because power is not equal. The unequal division of information allows agents to influence economic value and must therefore be itself understood as an economic value.

Consider the recent economic crash in the Western economies of 2008. Most economists now agree that a major causal factor was the development of collateralised debt instruments (CDIs). These boost the market in what is known as derivatives. A derivative is an information value that is derived from other assets. Should I bet that the market value of a stock next Monday will be 10% higher than today I am deriving a value from a current asset based upon my hunch (or information network) that the stock value will climb. If you bet that my estimate of the stock rise is wrong, and invest in the proposition that stock value will *fall* by 5%, you are allocating resources on the basis of *your* guess (or information network) about market trends. This is known as making a derivative from a derivative (Stiglitz, 2010: 169). A big factor in the crash of 2008 was not just that derivatives were being based on faulty information values. They were also incentivising some speculators to rig the market.

Collateralised debt instruments also include the controversial investment tool of hedge funds. The basic idea is very simple. Fund managers use the investment resources of high capital investors to spread risk and opportunities over multi-levered, short- and long-term derivative assets. In effect, investments are made along a paper trail of derivative values. Bets upon what stock prices might be in the future are the source of income in the present.

By 2008 the problem with many of the largest hedge funds was that the layers of derivative investment were so complex that they exceeded the capacity of hedge fund managers to manage them prudently (Sachs, 2011). Derivatives are not simply the means of communicating value, they can become subject to the all-consuming end of profit maximisation. What has this got to do with event planning and event cognition?

Event cognition refers to how a planned event is publicised and popularly perceived. As global events have expanded in scale and financial turnover, the business of producing a favourable outcome in event cognition is a pivotal objective in the event planning process. Derivative values here fall into two sets.

Tangible derivatives refer mostly to quantitative forecasts of the economic boost in corporate sponsorship, inward capital investment, employment rates, tourist traffic and long-term infrastructural upgrades such as slum clearance, cleansing of crime-ridden areas and the enhancement of transport routes and hotel space. Cyclical events, like the Olympics, the FIFA World Cup, the Rio Carnival, the Sydney Mardi Gras and the Notting Hill Carnival, involve complex econometric measurement, growth forecasts and opinion research. The results are far from foolproof, but evaluations of derivative effects are mainly based on so-called 'hard' data.

But global events are catalysts for emotional exhibitionism. So it is no surprise that the derivative market extends to the use of soft data, having to do with the 'halo effect' of hosting events that symbolise, *inter alia*, fellowship, compassion, urban renewal, pride, prestige and civic virtue. *Intangible derivatives* refer to largely qualitative forecasts of the cultural and social benefits in national and international prestige, the cultural and economic maturity of the metropolis or nation, quality of life, cosmopolitanism, expanding multicultural/multiethnic tolerance, civic duty and humanitarian investment. These all come under the category of *intangible derivatives*. Events such as the Sydney Mardi Gras and the Notting Hill Carnival are credited with improving racial and gay integration with other communities and building the international reputation of the nation.

Likewise, the Olympics is often presented as an inherently 'good' thing because the athletic excellence that it showcases is thought to carry over into improved rates of gym participation, exercise and diet enhancement in the ordinary population. Governments of developing nations also identify hosting as an international sign of global economic and political maturity and acceptance. This was evident in the event management run-up to the Olympics in Beijing (2008) and Brazil (2016) and Korea's involvement in co-hosting the FIFA World Cup with Japan (2002) (Horne and Manzenreiter, 2004). The events were used to announce that these nations had 'arrived' at the international high table.

Global events have emerged as important elements in statecraft. The PR–media complex presents them as expressions of people power, but they have a diplomatic and financial life of their own. Of course, this reflects representations of people power, because that is why it has traction with the media. However, it recognises no necessity to respect or conform to popular will. It is perfectly capable of using this 'support' to achieve separate political objectives. Indeed, it is mostly interested in *representations* of popular will since, if this is properly handled, it enhances the global reputation of government and the nation. Global events are used by governments as resources for brokering trade agreements, diplomacy and other aspects of foreign policy. By awarding the nation and the government prestige in the eyes of the world, global events contribute to more effective statecraft. The global media representation of event people power is also the ignition key that sparks a rise in economic value in the derivatives market.

Global events took off during the neoliberal revolution of the 1980s. The derivatives philosophy developed by them therefore bears the hallmarks of neoliberal thinking. To this extent, global events are the focal point of an event derivative market that extends to retail values, capital investment programmes, property income and social engineering. This applies to both local values of hotel space, retail units and entertainment venues as well as general metropolitan capital values that climb when investors perceive effective urban clean-up programmes and robust infrastructural upgrades. In a word, global events have the capacity to inflate derivative values in ancillary business sectors in hospitality, conventions, exhibitions and estate management. This has led to charges that global events are vehicles for venture capitalists to engage in 'spectacular accumulation' in order to attract potential investors and sell off assets at super-profits as part of a deliberate pre- and post-event strategy.

Short-term profiteering is justified, or at least excused, by the proposition that event legacy outcomes are beneficial and enduring. The issues here are complex. For example, while selling off social housing and replacing it with high cost housing after the event is commonplace and often deplored, if land prices were not thus inflated the available funding for social housing would be even less. So while property investors can make a killing out of events, there are also solid legacy benefits of improved accommodation and transport for poorer residents (Poynter and Macrury, 2009). Typical additional claims for economic and social dividends include a boost to jobs, improvements to health, enhancing metropolitan and national pride and, increasingly, contributing to a balanced ecology.

However, boosting the market in event-related derivatives carries many social costs (Kennelly and Watt, 2011). A global event does not simply add to social order, it disturbs existing social relations, frequently in very profound ways. Typical event risks are an increase in crime rates, urban congestion, retail price inflation of hotel space and food and, the risk of terrorism. A variety of critical studies have demonstrated that cleansing urban space to privilege event settings has resulted, *inter alia,* in exploitation, the displacement of settled communities and the suspension of civil liberties (Andrews, 2006; Gold and Gold, 2007; Kennelly and Watt, 2011; Silk, 2012).

Harvey (2004: 246) attempts to capture this by maintaining that the 'organised spectacle' serves the interrelated dual function of capital accumulation and social control by re-spatialising inequality.[2] There is some force in this line of argument. The intervention of more than 3000 troops to 'clean up' Rio's notorious Rocinha *favela* (2011) in preparation for the 2014 FIFA World Cup and 2016 Olympics is the latest in a long line of attempts by host authorities to make event settings palatable to corporate sponsors, TV broadcasting companies and global consumers.

Likewise, the Vancouver Winter Olympics (2010) involved the police in a 'clean up the streets' pre-event campaign that focused on youth and homeless people. The measures were attacked by grassroots opposition groups, like No Games 2010 and the Olympic Resistance Network, who maintained that, in addition, the Games displaced the poor from inner-city communities, infringed aboriginal rights and squandered public money on the over-budget Conference Centre (Hiller and Wanner, 2011: 887; Kennelly and Watt, 2011).

Similarly, the London Olympics (2012) used popular perceptions of risk to augment securitisation of urban space that amounted to a retrenchment in inner- and outer-city policing (Fussey et al., 2011). In this sense events may operate as convenient excuses to implement politically sensitive long-term plans of regulation. Additionally, critics of the Olympics in Athens (2004) allege that infrastructural developments to support the event produced irreparable ecological damage (Karamichas, 2005). Hence, perhaps, the sensitivity of post-Athens bids to produce Games that are carbon neutral and eco-friendly.

The response of event planners to criticisms of the disruptive effects of events has been to seek to assuage negative opinion in two ways. In the first place, they argue that tangible and intangible derivatives will produce enduring benefits in the long term, for the whole community. This argument does not merely relate to the economic multiplier effect of cyclical or single-issue events. It also encompasses the argument that events produce social improvement, cultural integration, urban revival, civic refreshment and the enhancement of metropolitan and national prestige.[3]

Secondly, event planners make extensive use of celebrity figureheads to humanise and popularise events.[4] By drawing in 'representative' superstars from film, television, pop music and sport, events apply an emulsive lick of glamour and star power to the event process. The goal is to maximise media attention and make the event a global *cause célèbre*. Emphasising the benefits of the event for the community and enlisting the support of sympathetic celebrities are the central weapons in the global event planners' charm offensive to win over public cognition. The dynamics can be usefully elaborated here by focusing upon three case studies.

The London Olympic (2012) bid will be explored to demonstrate how tangible and intangible derivatives were set before the awarding bodies, corporate sponsors and the public in order to achieve a positive outcome. After that, we will turn to the deployment of celebrities in event cognition with reference to the role of Bono in the Make Poverty History/Live 8 campaign and the role that the late Steve Jobs played over many years in fronting the Apple MacWorld Exposition.

The London Olympic (2012) Bid

The London Olympic event concept was based in a trio of interrelated populist strategic undertakings to expedite urban regeneration, engage with youth and enhance ecological sustainability. In policy terms this was reduced to five headline commitments that defined the bidding campaign: climate change, biodiversity, efficient waste disposal, social inclusion and healthy living. The choices of settings for the Olympic Park and capital investment targets were designed to merge these themes with the pre-existing Thames Gateway Project, an ambitious monumental programme of urban rejuvenation centring on some of the most deprived boroughs in London. The project is conceived as an 'eco-friendly' programme of urban regeneration designed to upgrade transport, housing and provide new shops, schools, hotels, business parks, health centres and leisure facilities. Event campaigners posit the event as exerting a multiplier effect in income generation, civic integration and capital investment. The Games were also sought after as a high profile pedagogic ecological contribution educating the public about low carbon living (Hayes and Horne, 2011: 753).

With respect to the details of the Olympic bid, the main targets for capital investment programmes were the five largely deindustrialised East London boroughs of Greenwich, Hackney, Newham, Tower Hamlets and Waltham Forest. Each has a postwar history of severe urban deprivation, industrial blight, environmental pollution and high concentrations of youth dwelling in low cost housing (Poynter and MacRury, 2009). Approximately one-third of children growing up in households here are officially classified as 'poor', and 40% of the residents in Hackney, Newham and Tower Hamlets have no formal qualifications. At the time of the Olympic bid, 290,000 of the 1.25 million residents were unemployed (Kennelly and Watt, 2011: 767). Giving hope to ethnically mixed youth was a major legacy pledge of the Olympic bidding campaign. Lord Coe, who fronted the bid, brought 30 children with him to Singapore in the final stages of the bidding competition to present the London case as a 'young people's Olympics'.

Analytically speaking, the sprinkling of youth with bids for global event investment might be termed the 'Julie Andrews effect' in event management[5] – that is a PR–media organised campaign that promotes and fetishises the sincerity of event planners and the purity of their objectives. What could be more worthy and pure than winning a multi-dollar event 'for the children'? It shows how much event planners have learned from theatrical conventions and melodramatic infusions of film, music and other branches of entertainment into popular culture. The supposed innocence and purity of youth is enlisted as a tool of event venture capitalism. Adroit use of images of youth can be hugely effective in making the moral worth of the event 'speak for itself'.

In addition, the London bid promised to make the Games 'low carbon' and 'climate neutral'. Since the Olympics in Sydney (2000) and Athens (2004), the green card has become a more significant bargaining chip in the cycle of the event bidding process. The construction of the Olympic Park was portrayed as a 'blueprint' for sustainable living. The London bid therefore portrayed the Olympics as a catalyst in a much more ambitious project of urban regeneration, environmental detoxification and healthy, sustainable living in London and the South East of England. The bid was supported by an intensive national publicity campaign. Once the decision was made in May 2003 to compete in the bidding process, billboards and posters supporting the bid were introduced in main retail areas and transport routes. The Mayor of London and national politicians in the fields of sport, culture and trade used conferences, symposia, public speeches and press briefings to build corporate support and consumer demand to host the Games. By May 2005, 1.2 million Londoners had signed up to the 'back the bid' campaign and 10,000 volunteered to be helpers (Newman, 2007: 255). The publicity campaign highlighted the benefits to trade and tourism. But at its heart was the message that the event was an opportunity to 'reinvent' the nation by embracing multiethnic, post-imperial, intergenerational realities. The Labour government portrayed the Olympics as an extension of the 'Cool Britannia' brand that signified the renaissance of the country after the nationalistic introspection of Conservative administrations of the 1980s and 1990s.[6]

The original bid estimated that the Games would cost £2.37 billion. Fussey et al. (2011) calculate that the costs more than doubled, to £9.3 billion. Graham (2012) argues that when infrastructural projects such as Crossrail are included, the cost of the Games may be as high as £24 billion. While much of this has gone into urban regeneration, environmental decontamination and sustainable living investment, there has also been considerable leakage into securitisation and commercialisation programmes.

Consider the question of securitisation. National and international perceptions of the risk factor to public order and safety produced by the Games were heavily influenced by the Muslim terrorist London bombings on 7 July 2005. These attacks occurred within 24 hours of the announcement in Singapore that the London Olympic bid had been successful. The timing of the bombings played into the hands of police authorities and risk consultants intent on boosting securitisation programmes (Fussey et al., 2011). Event planners provided for an estimated Games audience of 3.3 million. Security human resources investment included 15,000 police and 6500 private security contractors. The security focus was on the protection of critical infrastructures and the transnational counter-terrorist coordination of intelligence (Jennings, 2012). As the planning cycle unfolded, international security and surveillance corporations lobbied that risk management provision was inadequate. The same process had occurred in the Athens (2004) and Beijing (2008) Games (Graham, 2012). The clear aim was to increase pressure on the International Olympic Committee (IOC) and allied government bodies to increase the budget on security and surveillance spending.

Unquestionably, the Games are a premier global event. Because of this there is a significant international security dimension in resourcing them. But risk inflation is now so blatant that it cannot be ignored as an abuse of the Olympic planning process. For example, in November 2011 US lobbyists criticised security arrangements for the Games and announced preparations to send 1000 of its agents, including 500 from the FBI, to provide protection for US athletes and diplomats. Partly through US pressure, the London Organising Committee of the Olympic and Paralympic Games (LOCOG) responded by proposing that the event required 21,000 guards (over double the original estimate) (Hopkins and Norton-Taylor, 2011).

Risk inflation and securitisation issues have become more prominent since 9/11. For example, during the Athens Olympics (2004) the Greek government and IOC bowed to post-9/11 lobbying from the American security and surveillance complex. The latter is an alliance between the established security industry and high tech surveillance and data controls. The aim was to create a fortress city. The Athens Games were incident free. However, Samatas (2007: 235) submits that this owed more to constructive behind the scenes diplomacy between the Greek government and Muslim, Arab, Palestinian and Israeli representatives than the high cost electronic surveillance system demanded by the US security and compliance lobby.

In the run-up to the London Games, tackling youth crime in East London also quickly emerged as a major policy objective. Once again precedents had been provided by civil order campaigns for the Games in Beijing (2008), the FIFA World Cup in South Korea (2002) and, as I have already noted, the Winter Olympics in Vancouver (2010). In the London case, Kennelly and Watt (2011: 776–7) point to the intensification of police 'stop and search' powers in relation to young people and related 'clean up the streets' operations in preparation for 'the inspection of the world's media'. Far from giving hope to young people, these measures stereotype them as public order risks.

In addition, the objective of sustainability was damaged when the event authorities scored an embarrassing own goal by the enforced closure of the Manor Gardens allotment site in Hackney Wick in order to make way for the Olympic Park. The allotments were established at the start of the 20th century as a philanthropic measure to provide local working-class families with what we would now call, a green alternative to urban living. The compulsory closure of this long-established amenity which had been dedicated to the ideal of sustainable, healthy living violated the philosophy of a green Olympic Legacy Park (Hayes and Horne, 2011: 757). It left the IOC vulnerable to the charge of double standards and hypocrisy.

Global events open up fresh avenues for trade, diplomacy and integration. They are also disruptive, and provide governments and venture capital with new opportunities for moral regulation and economic exploitation. National pride in winning the Olympic bidding war translates into personal responsibility to honour and respect the Olympic ideal and the national brand. As such, they are highly prized assets in engineering event cognition. The adjunct of this is that the temporary curtailment of civil liberties and the acceptance of pro-Olympic fiscal requirements are the price to pay for the national and global prestige of holding the Games. The London Games were protected by the London Olympic Games Act (2006), which legitimised the use of force, including, in theory, private security companies, to clamp down on Occupy-style protests (Graham, 2012). The suppression of ethnic and multicultural tensions are collateral costs. Events may be organised around illusory communities, but what they demand of all in the host community is to put your best face forward for the benefit of the international media.

Event cognition involves automatic acknowledgement of the event as an unequivocal statement of national pride and personal submission to the event concept and the national ideal. Moral regulation is achieved not by rapping a ruler over the knuckles, fines or the threat of incarceration. It works by the altogether more nuanced and elusive dynamics of waving the flag and not letting the side down. The individual unwittingly becomes involved as an agent in structural decisions of government and capital. Supporting the event commits one to a certain approved course of conduct and adds to the bulwark of established, institutional power, at both national and global levels. Event planning cultivates event cognition as a matter of support. In reality, it is a matter of capitulating to 'top-down' goals defined by a government that is invisible to the public and translated into ethically acceptable commitments and modes of behaviour by the PR–media complex.

Mediated Persona and Event Cognition: The Cases of Bono and Steve Jobs

John Corner's (2000) work on 'mediated persona' provides some useful analytic tools and a helpful framework to elaborate how celebrities are deployed in the event charm offensive and associated programmes of engineering cognition. He develops his analysis in relation to the construction of political persona, but his ideas transfer readily to the politics of event cognition. Integral to his case, and following Bernays (1923, 1928), is the proposition that engineering consent requires a persuasive leader. In democracies, the leader must be trustworthy, sincere and appealing without overstepping the mark by hinting that an ogre or oligarch lurks within. Event leaders and figureheads must be 'men and women of the people', achieved celebrities who, despite their wealth and influence, are 'one of us'. In this way event cognition can be turned in the right direction, i.e. to comply with the goals of event planners and the interests behind them.

Because of the powerful link between legitimate achieved celebrity and popular acceptance, the event leader is encouraged to act naturalistically in order to demonstrate the lack of personal barriers of status and hierarchy in 'working together'.

However, the leadership style of naturalism in event management is plastic, since it relies upon the PR–media hub to use opinion research and stage techniques to mould leaders and figureheads that can inspire and persuade ordinary people. Figureheads, then, are mediated personas who use the arts of public speaking and affiliated elements in what I earlier referred to as the battery of 'speech acts' to win hearts and minds.

Global event planners are only too aware that the objectives of inspiration and technology are heavily dependent upon the technology and studio tricks of television. The aim is to achieve a brand of mediated persona that is instantly agreeable to audiences. Event leaders and figureheads must be accepted as persons of quality to generate esteem and popular support. Event cognition depends upon strong, positive codes of identification from ordinary men and women with the event concept.

Drawing on Machiavelli's classic statement of the relationship between flattery, assertion and power, Corner portrays the construction of a favourable mediated persona as being a matter of producing and sustaining the appearance of virtue. The latter term is understood here in Machiavelli's usage, as the exhibition of nobility, generosity, competence, vision, grace and personal worth. By using the PR–media hub to enlist celebrities to support events, event planners seek to engineer consent over a population conceived as subjects, 'open finally to direct coercion' (Corner, 2000: 388). The construction of mediated personas deploys various types of performative labour to get the result of suasion and is mediated through three interrelated codes of communication:

- *Iconic:* The positive display of posture and demeanour in order to gain automatic endorsement from the public. The use of superstars in photo opportunities, informal interviews and lobbying political and corporate leaders promotes association with a *popular cause*. Iconic codes need to be vigilant against interventions by opportunistic journalism to cast the celebrity figurehead in an unflattering light by pouncing upon an offguard comment or expression of the 'wrong sort' of visibility.
- *Vocal:* The creation of an informal, confidential atmosphere in *what* is said (the event concept) is influenced by *how* it is said. Treating the audience as 'fellow travellers' or people 'in the know' and using theatrical devices of dress and vocal delivery are designed to build support. By pandering to the psychology of wanting to be different, vocal codes orchestrate an ensemble of speech acts to engender consent.

- *Kinetic:* The construction of the mediated persona uses the stage, props and the camera to present the mediated self in action and inter-action. Speech acts are not presented by talking heads. Every effort of staged presence is made to dissolve any sense of 'them and us'. Back footage of the mediated persona in ordinary settings, talking to ordinary consumers or victims is used to enhance the audience's sense of fellowship and diminished hierarchy.

We can illustrate how these codes work in the business of event cognition by referring to two case studies: Bono's role as a 'celanthropy' advocate and the part played by Steve Jobs in re-engineering Apple's market position with brand loyalists between 1997 and 2011.

Bono: The 'Celanthropy' Advocate

Since the 1985 Live Aid concert, Bono has emerged as one of the world's leading celebrity advocates and diplomats (Cooper, 2008). His forthright support for debt relief, fair trade and famine relief is legendary.

In 2005 he was a leading spokesperson and publicist for the Make Poverty History campaign and Live 8 concert. He captured the tone of the campaign nicely in the promotional video released to support Make Poverty History:

> Hello. My name is Bono. But you can relax, I am not asking you for your money. ... World leaders are meeting in Scotland in July – the G8. They're gonna discuss debt cancellation, more and better aid. They're gonna discuss making trade rules fairer for everybody, so that these people (the impoverished) can earn their own way out of poverty. It's a real chance to do something ... for millions. What will our generation be remembered for? The internet? Yes. The war against terror? Yes. Wouldn't it be great if we were also remembered as being the ones that set about making poverty history?

Bono's manner seeks to draw the viewer into his confidence. Despite having a reputed personal fortune of £400 million, with all the access to power and social advantage that goes with it, he presents himself as just like one of us (Scott, 2006).

His style of mediated persona depends upon convincing network publics that we all share the same worries and fears. The video does not lecture or hector but aims to persuade the audience to make common cause with superstars against manifest global injustice. Iconic, vocal and kinetic codes do not venture beyond headline details. Live 8 is presented as a chance to change history, improve justice and cancel debt. The audience is urged that each individual can make a difference, if only they act.

The means for this is presented in pure and simple terms as people power. The fine details of income accumulation, debt cancellation and fair trade requirements and resource distribution do not figure in the video. The attention of the viewer is focused on 'the big picture', as if the economic and political details of intervention can safely be left to event planners and managers who can be relied upon to silently act in the name of the people.

The promotional video is a mass market publicity device. It conforms to all of the characteristics of a standardised commodity. Yet the social reaction to it is one of personal rebellion, identification with the marginalised, uniqueness and authenticity. Bono appears to speak directly to you, even though he does not know who you are and, very likely, will never meet you. There is no personal relationship, yet the manner and tone of communication is steeped in presumed intimacy. Bono's pitch for ethically accountable conduct is a para-social relationship. Yet the idiom of the video is reassuringly natural and familiar. This is not just a superstar talking to you, it is a friend with a conscience. Bono's legitimacy in this respect is reinforced by the actions of the PR–media hub who portrayed him (and Sir Bob Geldof) in the popular media as an expert on debt relief (Street, 2011: 282).

The implication of the video is that ordinary people have the power to make permanent change possible. Furthermore, right-thinking people are portrayed as wanting to change the balance of power between the West and the rest. Unlike Live Aid (1985), which relied heavily upon *shaming* viewers into action, Make Poverty History concentrated mostly upon the issues of *empowerment* and *redistributive justice*. Bono presents these as human rights issues independent of political party objectives or traditions. Event cognition management is portrayed exclusively as a matter of raising consciousness and giving. No reference to overturning the dominant order of power and replacing it with more inclusive government is made. The tone of the video and the Make Poverty History campaign is about living with capitalism and reforming it rather than seeking to transcend it.

Steve Jobs: Re-engineering Cognition of the Apple Brand

The case of the legendary keynote addresses by the late Steve Jobs, CEO of Apple at the MacWorld Expo and other special events provides a useful counterpoint to event cognition management styles. For some, to refer to him as an example of event cognition management might be amiss. On the whole, the MacWorld keynotes were delivered to a captive audience of Apple devotees. They carried with them intense positive feelings for

Apple and its products. Thus, Jobs's keynotes were not, strictly speaking, about engineering consent but preaching to the converted.

However, this ignores two things. In the first place the keynotes were much more than Apple love-ins. Jobs took it upon himself to build the Apple brand by announcing breakthrough innovations in the development of devices and software. The keynotes were relayed online, providing a vast global audience for the event. Jobs played the part of a technological and business impresario to the hilt. Each keynote hinged around the release of new Apple breakthrough products and services to Apple fans, employees, the media, board members, shareholders, third party developers and competitors. Many now remember MacWorld keynotes featuring Jobs as fanfares of technological and service revolution that would change the world. The association of the keynote with mould-breaking developments was carefully engineered and is a major factor in the impact of the event with the audience, the media and network publics. This brings me to my second point.

The idea that the Jobs keynotes were simply Apple love-ins ignores the immense challenges facing Jobs when he resumed leadership of the company and addressed the 1997 MacWorld Expo.[7] His return to Apple occurred in straitened trading circumstances. The financial press widely reported that Apple was on the brink of bankruptcy. This required piloting a major shift in cognition relating to Apple's place in the market and trading arrangements. Jobs's address noted that Apple's sales in 1995 were $11.1 billion; in 1996, $9.5 billion; and in 1997, $7 billion. Jobs affirmed that since being appointed as CEO he had discovered that Apple was 'performing wonderfully' on many of 'the wrong things'. The remedy was presented as changing the board of directors, focusing on the core competencies of the business and forging new business partnerships. Jobs also mentioned product development, but refrained from specifying items, since presumably they were not in the corporate pantry, and, more importantly, he had to announce a business partnership to the audience of diehard Apple loyalists that he knew would be regarded as tantamount to sleeping with the enemy. This refers to a series of product development, software partnership deals and a $150 million non-voting share investment from the old enemy: Microsoft.

Jobs handled this highly unpopular announcement by insisting that the deal with Microsoft was a prerequisite for the company's survival. He noted Apple's capitulation to Microsoft's request to carry Internet Explorer as the default browser on Apple machines, but softened the blow and appealed to the renegade, autonomous side of the Apple audience, by observing that machines would be shipped with alternative internet browsers and that 'creative consumers' could simply change the default setting.

For sure, the 1997 speech was preaching to the converted. But many of them violently disapproved of Apple's survival plan and saw the deal with Microsoft as a betrayal. Jobs dealt with this head-on by insisting that the age when it was necessary for Microsoft to lose so that Apple can win was over. Instead of reviving the old competitive language, he chose to use a more inclusive analogy. He submitted that Apple and Microsoft were part of the same 'eco-system'. Thus, the new trading arrangements were not presented as the victory of one giant corporation over another, but as an intelligent, adaptive response to new environmental conditions. The headline message to critics of the Microsoft deal was simple: Adapt or Die.

The 1997 keynote provided a presentational template that Gallo (2010) and others argue remained a steadfast in Jobs's keynotes. Before coming to this we must refer to an additional example of Jobs's keynote successes. Aficionados regard the 2007 keynote announcing the iPhone to be the pinnacle keynote address made by Jobs. As he put it:

> Every once in a while a revolutionary product comes along that changes everything. And Apple has been – well, first of all one's very fortunate if you get to work on just one of these in your career – Apple's been very fortunate. It's been able to introduce a few of these into the world. In 1984 we introduced the Macintosh. It didn't just change Apple, it changed the whole computer industry. In 2001 we introduced the first iPod. And, it didn't just change the way we all listen to music, it changed the entire music industry. Well, today, we're introducing three revolutionary products in this place. The first one, is a wide-screen iPod with touch controls. The second, is a revolutionary mobile phone. And the third, is a breakthrough internet communications device.
>
> So, three things: a widescreen iPod with touch controls; a revolutionary mobile phone; and a breakthrough internet communications device. An iPod, a phone and an internet communicator ... an iPod, a phone ... are you getting it? These are not three separate devices. This is one device. And we are calling it, iPhone. Today, Apple is going to reinvent the phone. (Steve Jobs, 1997 keynote address, YouTube).

Jobs's use of iconic, vocal and kinetic codes was adroit and successful. In 2011, the year of his death, the Forbes Rich List estimated that his personal worth was $8.3 billion. Yet his trademark dress code consisted of a black mock turtleneck, blue jeans with no belt and grey sneakers. By any reckoning, certainly by the standards of the average billionaire, this was an extremely humble wardrobe. It was an iconic code that stressed accessibility, informality and contact with the end user.

The same was true of the vocal code that he deployed. His tricky 1997 address used popular colloquial phrases like 'serve the people' and 'do a good job'. The controversial announcement to collaborate with Microsoft was sweetened by observing that the two companies live in the same 'eco-system' and that the era of competitive mutual destruction was 'over'. All of this was addressed to the 'creative spirits' that are verbally positioned as the core of the Apple user market. His use of the collective pronoun and present tense in the 2007 keynote announcing the iPhone, engages the audience by persuading them that they are directly involved in the design of the device (Sharma and Grant, 2011: 18).

In an overview of the Jobs Apple keynotes, Gallo (2010) submits that they typically take the form of an audiovisual story consisting of nine elements: (1) headline, (2) messianic passion statements, (3) key messages, (4) metaphors and analogies, (5) demonstrations, (6) partners, (7) customer evidence and third party endorsements, (8) video clips and (9) flip charts, props and show and tell. Buzzwords and jargon are kept to a minimum. The core message is clear, concise and consistent, permitting no room for wavering or dispute.

For example, the 2007 keynote does not just announce a new product (the iPhone), it speaks to the transformation of an entire genre: the 'reinvention' of the phone. This becomes the headline of the keynote, or if you will, the event concept. Just as in 2001, in launching the iPod, Jobs stated that the device enables you to 'have 1000 songs in your pocket'. In both cases there is a strong positive association between the product and a better future. By pitching the product in terms of how many songs you have in your pocket rather than informing the audience that the iPod as a 5 gigabyte drive, the analogy offers instant consumer identification.

In addition, the Jobs vocal code also observes what Gallo (2010) calls 'a 10 minute rule'. That is, presentations were structured to convey all information within 10 minutes. Jobs's use of the phrase 'And one more thing', at the end of his presentations both wrap up the good news that the keynote is usually designed to impart and provide a cliffhanger suggesting impending breakthroughs just around the corner.

Turning to the kinetic code, one of the most effective elements in the keynotes was the practice of not just announcing the product or showing a series of charts demonstrating how it can enhance the life of the end user. A crucial, high profile accessory was Jobs's stage manner on demonstrating how the device worked by holding it in his hands and going through the functions. By enthusiastically showing the audience the lifestyle gains of the original iPod, Air computer, iPad and iPhone, Jobs shaped human cognition of the devices and set the lines for market anticipation. The kinetic code worked by allowing audiences to imagine that they would share the thrill that Jobs conveyed in owning a device which was 'insanely thin', 'neat', 'cool' and carried 'more power'.

For this to work in dramaturgical terms, Jobs demanded absolute secrecy about product development. Under him, Apple pursued a 'relentless' policy of litigation against leaks and rumours. For example, in 2007 the company closed down the 'Think Secret' website – devoted to making announcements about forthcoming Apple products – for releasing details about the Mac Mini desktop computer in 2005. Jobs ruthlessly held tight to a 'loose lips sink ships' principle. Employees were informed that any leakages to the media would result in instant dismissal and consequent legal action (Sharma and Grant, 2011: 11). This also applied to core trading arrangements. For example, when he briefed his inner team about the Microsoft deal before the 1997 Mac Expo he demanded strict confidence about the information and is alleged to have threatened, 'If it does [leave the room] I'll fire you. So look around and see if you can trust the other people. If not, leave now' (Deutschman, 2000: 246).

One fabled piece of kinetic gamesmanship occurred during the 2002 Worldwide Developers keynote in San Jose, California. Upon resuming control of Apple, Jobs was insistent that the Mac operating system (OS9), which was over a decade old, constituted a major impediment to Apple's trading position. The issue turned on the resistance of third party software developers to accommodate to Apple's policy of continually upgrading the system. The decline of compatibility with software applications was regarded to weaken consumer confidence in Apple.

In 2000, Jobs announced a complete overhaul of the OS9 system in favour of a 'next generation' replacement, 'Mac OS X'. In the 2002 keynote Jobs staged a highly effective mock funeral of the old OS9 system. Sharma and Grant (2011: 15) describe this theatrical device as exerting 'outstanding rhetorical effect'. Among the kinetic features and outcomes that they note are:

1 *Stage-lighting:* Brilliant white lighting from the ceiling conveying the impression of celestial contact with back screen backdrop, three storeys high, of a church interior, flanked by blue curtains.
2 *Smoke machines:* Decorating the stage with low level mist.
3 *Casket:* A casket that rises from the stage from a trap door, inside of which Mac OS9 packaging is prominently displayed.
4 *Music:* The accompaniment of Bach's 'Tocatta and Fugue' as the musical backdrop.
5 *Renegade CEO dress:* Jobs attired in his standard renegade CEO outfit of black mock turtleneck, faded Levi's jeans and sneakers.

This was reinforced by Jobs's vocal code which melodramatically heightened the software innovation by portraying it as part of the cycle of life and death. In standing beside the coffin, he adopted the manner of a liturgical minister officiating at a funeral:

> Mac OS9 was a friend to us all. He worked tirelessly on our behalf, always hosting our applications. Never refusing a command. Always at our beck and call, except occasionally when he forgot who he was and needed to be restored. Mac OS9 came into this world in October 1998, for a suggested retail price of $99. And was perhaps the best internet OS of his generation. Hundreds of retailers held special midnight madnesses to celebrate his birth. He was mentor to many younger technologies, including Sherlock, Keychain and Auto-Updating. He helped make them into what they are today. He was a humble guy too. Though he was fully optimized to take advantage of the G4's incredible performance, he never once flaunted his power with a Start Menu. We are here today to mourn the passing of Mac OS9. He is now in that great Bit Bucket in the sky, no doubt looking down upon us with that same smile he displayed every time he booted. Mac OS9 is survived by his next generation Mac OS X and thousands of Applications, most of them legitimate. Please join me in a moment of silence as we remember our old friend Mac OS9.

The liturgy was consummated by placing a red rose inside the casket and closing the lid.

Conclusion

Event cognition is a crucial element in effective event management. It can no more be done away with than the magician can do without the wand in his tool-box. It produces an ethos of acceptance which both legitimates the event concept and generates an appetite for event engagement. By correctly massaging event cognition criticism is minimised and resistance is automatically translated into incorrect behaviour. Bono and Jobs do not work the crowd, in the manner of an old fashioned fairground barker. Rather, they contrive to convey intimacy between strangers around a transcendent cause. That is, respectively, the elimination of poverty, and the beauty and technical superiority of the Apple brand.

The bid for the London Olympics (2012) deployed cognate devices – 'the young people's Games', 'carbon neutrality', 'urban regeneration' – to create a similar, spellbinding spiral of complicity with the event concept. Organisationally speaking, the end game is to psychologically convince consumers that if they are not part of the solution (supporting the London bid), they are part of the problem. As with the event concept, event cognition operates in bold, simple headline statements. The aim is not to represent complexity, but to reduce it. The public are not given options, they are deprived of them, and the event plan is to bring light to darkness. All cognition is staked around the event concept.

In commenting upon the Steve Jobs keynotes, Gallo (2010: 190–1) coins the notion of 'the bucket method'. That is, a five-stage model of presenting events to achieve cognitive affirmation. The bucket method consists of (1) determining a list of questions that define the event concept; (2) drawing up categories or buckets of issues; (3) deciding on the best response to each issue; (4) selecting a keyword for each bucket to trigger a required response; and (5) using the keywords to reinforce the event concept when a question is asked. This is the logic that event managers apply in massaging event cognition.

It might be objected that this is a circular logic, since it suggests no way out of domination. One need not go along with the idea that resistance is pre-empted.

Criticism of monolithic messages and appeals to social inclusion are not banished. On the contrary, something more interesting and infinitely seductive is going on here. Event managers see event cognition as a contribution to *resistance*. By presenting stateless solutions to global or corporate issues they regard themselves as opposing obstinate orthodoxy and breaking the mould. Using people power to attack poverty or realise that corporate rivals in digital technology are part of the same 'eco-system' is thinking outside the box. Event managers present event cognition as liberation from social conformity and the programmed workplace. Stateless solutions are about short circuiting hierarchy, offering direct action as the alternative to the politics of glacial change, getting in touch with our true selves and making a difference.

However, the closer one looks the more apparent it is that there is barely a scintilla of genuine utopianism about them. Global events apply the same rhetoric of dissidence and non-conformity that the advertising industry uses to defend and advance corporate sales. Apple encourages you to 'think different', Pepsi encourages youthful rebellion, Benetton makes a virtue of controversy to defy convention and Nike conflates its product range with a search for spiritual enlightenment. Live Aid exhorts you to 'feed the world' and Live 8 urges you to 'Make Poverty History'.

Global events operate in the currency of the gestural economy by which, and through which, politics now typically works. By the term 'gestural economy', I mean the logic of performance in public life that turns representation into resistance. The digital economy boosts the importance of visual culture as a signal of social status and resource distribution. Gesturing to 'feed Africa' or 'save the world' provides the social imprint of personal relevance and conscience. This is concomitant with self-gratification and positive social recognition. But it is not a serious contribution to social and economic transformation.

Social and economic transcendence of global problems of hunger, inequality, pollution and injustice requires three preconditions. First, collective *agitation* in which the resources of individuals are pooled around a coherent *cause célèbre*. Second, collective *mobilisation* that enables pooled resources to be meaningfully organised and directed. Third, a persuasive outline of a collective *alternative*, in which the causes of hunger, injustice, inequality, pollution and injustice are tackled and managed.

Global events meet only the first precondition. The agitation of media channels to capture a global incident or emergency manifestly influences pre-event cognition in network publics. It places the event concept on the social horizon for a finite period and, by this means, is capable of raising funds to provide temporary relief.

However, going beyond global conditions that produce incidents and emergencies requires disciplined organisation and the articulation of a compelling alternative. This raises wider and more challenging questions of correcting power imbalances, eliminating state subventions that pervert the fair distribution of economic resources, making social inclusion real and empowering the powerless. At the very least, this demands the complete overhaul of current fiscal priorities in the direction of seriously increasing corporate and personal taxation. Strategically speaking, this is politically unacceptable. Established party leaders judge that a policy of significant personal and corporate tax hikes is electoral suicide. Nor it is at all clear that the electorate in the Western advanced economic democracies would tolerate significant new restraints on disposable income.

Event planners are correct in regarding the structural conditions of the day being unable to support the combination of agitation, mobilisation and transformation required to transcend gestural economy. But there is a cost in doing so. In the course of time, human cognition will turn away from event management.

Because event planners will gradually be recognised to provide the wrong answer (temporary relief) to the right question: social and economic justice.

Notes

1   The economic theory of perfect competition is so at odds with observation and common sense that one must conclude that its origins were metaphysical and its persistence has been ideological. A self-correcting market guided by an invisible hand has unmistakable parallels with a belief in a divine creator and the notion that disequilibrium is temporary and reflects an abnormal state of affairs conveniently erases the question of social and economic divisions and the role that invisible government plays in normalising inequality.

2   Gentrification does not eliminate poverty. Rather it takes over latent values of inner-city sites and makes them manifest values by investment. The dispossessed are simply moved out to less visible parts within city boundaries.

3   Again it is necessary observe that concepts of integration, revival and prestige are multidimensional. The attempt to cast them in one light reveals the tendentious nature of much event planning and post-evaluation exercises. These exercises are pre-eminently concerned with impression management with, in turn, the objective of engineering consent.

4   Sir Bob Geldof, Bono, Angelina Jolie, Madonna, Sting and Annie Lennox have become so connected in the public mind with humanitarian events that there is real reason to doubt if their presence is not actually now subject to the law of diminishing returns. Within the field of celebrity studies, the term 'celebrity vamping' refers to a condition in which a celebrity engages in too much endorsement of products so that public trust in the celebrity diminishes.

5   The Julie Andrews effect refers to Andrews' role in *Mary Poppins* (1964) as a sort of agent of perfection, delivering sound leadership and kindness to her young charge of children. Sound leadership and perceived kindness is the holy grail of organisation studies.

6   It is interesting that the theme of Britain coming to terms with its colonial past was a detectable, nuanced theme of the Olympic bid. The Olympics were not really pitched as a national apology for the less salubrious aspects of the history of Empire. Yet the motif of national purification was also a detectable part of the process.

7   The company was on the brink of bankruptcy at this moment. Jobs piloted the astonishing feat of transforming the fortunes of the company. In 2011 Apple briefly took the leading US company spot from Exxon oil with a gross worth of $348 billion and an estimated $76 billion in reserves.

5

HOW ARE GLOBAL EVENTS ORGANISED?

Global events begin with clients or stakeholders noting either a disruption of social order through a natural or social catastrophe or the calendar triggering a publicity campaign for a hallmark or cyclical event. Clients and stakeholders initiate the process. They fall into four categories: corporations/multinationals, departments of government, non-government organisations (NGOs) and private individuals. They work in partnership, but the links between them are loose.

For example, cyclical events such as the Olympics or the FIFA World Cup involve bidding processes where local and national governments operate as hosts for the tournament and engage sponsorship with national corporations, multinationals and private individuals. Celebrity sponsorship through endorsement or participation in the opening and closing ceremonies is a particularly important way of humanising the event for global audiences and gaining additional publicity. Publicity is generally lavish, involving VIP attendance, controlled crowds and, of course, media coverage.

Celebrities have become increasingly important as patrons or entertainers for events. In some case, their involvement is even more fundamental. Disaster response global events like Live Aid (1985) and the Haiti Relief Concert (2010) were initiated by agitation from, respectively, Bob Geldof and George Clooney. Since Live Aid (1985) many celebrity superstars have adopted the humanitarian role of global 'big citizens' (Cooper, 2008). That is, self-appointed figureheads for the *global conscience* addressing international issues of poverty, hunger, torture, environmental decay, human rights and disaster relief. A number of global charity taskforces have been set up in the process, such as Band Aid (1984) (Bob Geldof and Midge Ure), the Elton John AIDS Foundation (1992) (Elton John), the Jolie-Pitt Foundation (2006) (Angelina Jolie and Brad Pitt) and Raising Malawi (2006) (Madonna and Michael Berg).

George Clooney is co-founder of Not On Our Watch (with Don Cheadle, Matt Damon, Brad Pitt, David Pressman and Jerry Weintraub), a charity committed to putting an end to mass atrocities around the world and generating humanitarian assistance and protection for the vulnerable, marginalised and displaced. Clooney organised the Haiti Relief Concert (2010), a celebrity-based response for the victims of the Haitian earthquake.

These initiatives are part of the growing importance of *celanthropy* in the conduct of global affairs. That is, the social force which casts celebrities as activists, advocates, organisers, fundraisers and donators onto the humanitarian world stage (Bishop and Green, 2008; Rojek, 2012).

The passage between a client or stakeholder demanding the formation of an event strategy and producing impact upon social units that translate into responses is usually handled by a public relations office. Leading international public relations corporations like Ketchum, Taylor-Herring, Edelman, IPREX, Pinnacle Worldwide, Grayling, Hoffman and Hoffman and Ogilvy liaise with the client and media outlets to plan, implement and follow up event management strategies. Their event portfolio typically covers designing forums, internal workshops, product launches, roundtable discussions, sales conferences, user focus groups, annual general meetings and social, humanitarian and sports events. The event services that they offer are customised to suit the needs of the client and the requirements of the audience base. Typical core services include: event strategy and planning; logistics; global or regional coordination; media targeting; content creation; social capital strategy; on the day support; producing event memorabilia; and post-event evaluation.

Event Strategy and Planning

This involves discussions with the client about the event's concept, size and structure of the event, location/venue, timing, key attractions, setting operations, consumables and market potential. It is now standard practice for PR companies to develop feasibility studies to test budgetary requirements, labour needs, sponsorship opportunities, media links, resource schedules and environmental impact.

Strategy and planning also encompass developing a vision, determining sponsorship, constructing a mission statement, a headline event concept and producing realistic goals and objectives. Visions, mission statements, goals and objectives are usually driven by the demands of clients and stakeholders. They cover issues relating to economic return on investment, media impact, attendance, network support from the police and health organisations and waste disposal arrangements.

A key component of planning is devising event teams and ensuring that the lines of command are fit for purpose. Typically, event team structures consist of six or seven key administrators, including: an event director, a head of finance, a head of marketing and media coordination, a head of sales and sponsorship, a head of service delivery and a head of content. Depending upon the size of the event, dedicated support staff will be recruited to implement strategy.

An increasingly important aspect of strategy is developing stakeholder partnerships. Because of the economic, social and ecological effects of global events, partnerships need to be constructed along many fronts to minimise conflict and mitigate risk. Different models have emerged. Thus, Reid and Arcodia (2002) contend that the central partnership is between *primary stakeholders* (employees, volunteers, sponsors, suppliers, spectators, participants and attendees) and their need to liaise and force contracts with *secondary stakeholders* (host community, government, essential services, tourist organisations and corporations). In contrast, Getz et al. (2007) offer a more nuanced stakeholder model which distinguishes between *facilitators* (service and resource providers), *regulators* (government agencies), *co-producers* (other participating organisations and groups), *allies and collaborators* (professional associations and tourism agencies) and those impacted (audience and host community).

A crucial task is to create or update the event concept. This is vital for event branding. It requires event managers to clarify the event brief, which requires detailed discussions with stakeholders. Once clarity has been achieved, the next step is to relate the event concept to the target audience. Corollaries of this are determining the right timing and the right setting. A prerequisite in global events market research is to test the power of the event concept. By testing the concept against market reactions the crystallisation of the concept for the target audience can be accomplished. Ideally, event concepts should be unambiguous and memorable so that they can spearhead advertising and marketing campaigns.

Logistics

This refers to the technical, operational nuts and bolts issues relevant to making events efficient and successful. They include accommodation, transport, cash flow arrangements, advertising, on-site facilities, artist support, ticketing, insurance, security, crowd control, event consumables, waste disposal, VIP and media requirements, emergency procedures, event opening and closure ceremonies.

Because events are presented as post-government/post-federal solutions to social issues, sponsorship is central in logistics planning. As global events have grown bigger with broadcasting rights income and syndication rights, the cost of sponsorship has rocketed.

Estimated sponsorship for the 1980 Los Angeles Olympics was $200 million. By comparison sponsorship fees for the 1996 Atlanta Olympics was around $1 billion. Sponsorship is presented as building corporate brands, refining the brand image, networking, launching new products and motivating the workforce.

A pivotal issue in global event management today is locating and employing celebrities to humanise the mission statement, vision, goals and objectives by providing attraction and glamour. The involvement of celebrities as figureheads for events is an extension of what Bishop and Green (2008: 8–9) refer to as *celanthropy*. Celebrities build the event brand.

The industry standard for logistics is twofold: to make events run like clockwork and to remain invisible to the public. Logistics fail when an event ceases to work on its own terms. When the omission of backroom personnel cannot be maintained for whatever reason, the event stops being experienced as naturalistic. Its calculated, assembled nature stands revealed. Exposure of this type is costly for event managers and clients.

One aspect of this is the growing attention assigned to risk mitigation in strategic planning. Events involve the concentration of large numbers of people in physical settings. Television networks may communicate transmission of events programmes internationally, creating a strategic agenda for effective data control and syndication fees. However, the question of concentration poses intrinsic challenges for optimal event management.

Events can go seriously wrong, putting life and limb at risk. For example, in 2010 in the German city of Duisburg 21 young people died and over 500 were injured at the Love Parade event. The deaths and injuries were caused by overcrowding in a tunnel between the train station and the festival site.

The tragedy is not isolated. In 1979, 11 people died of compressive asphyxia while attending a concert by The Who in Cincinnati, Ohio. In 1989, 96 people died at Hillsborough Stadium, Sheffield, during an FA semi-final match between Liverpool and Nottingham Forest. In 1999, 53 people died in a tunnel at the Minsk Beer Festival. In 2000, nine people died during Pearl Jam's set at Denmark's Roskilde Festival. In 2001, 127 people died of compressive asphyxia at the Accra Sports Stadium in Ghana. In the same year, 43 people died and over 150 were injured at the Ellis Park Stadium in Johannesburg, during a match between the Kaizer Chiefs and Orlando Pirates.

Tragedies of this sort have enlarged strategic interest in questions of venue design, crowd-flow issues, crowd information systems and crowd stewardship (Fruin, 1987). Management failure in crowd safety control is now a core area of strategic planning.

Global or Regional Coordination

Coordination of attractions, support staff, consumables, media coverage and security is the prerequisite for successful global event management. Live 8 (2005) was a massive operation of global and regional coordination, involving concerts in 10 venues (UK, Hyde Park, London and Eden Project, Cornwall; France, Palace of Versailles, Paris; Germany, Siegessaule, Berlin; Italy, Circus Maximus, Rome; USA, Museum of Art, Philadelphia; Canada, Park Palace, Barrie; Japan, Makihari Messe, Tokyo; South Africa, Mary Fitzgerald Square, Johannesburg; Russian Federation, Red Square, Moscow). The event involved 150 bands and 1250 musicians. People were asked to donate money and pressure governments to increase aid. The broadcasts involved 182 televised networks and 2000 radio networks.

Analogously, the Live Earth concert, promoted by Al Gore in 2007, involved over 150 musical acts on seven continents The concert was broadcast live over 24 hours through television and radio and streamed through the internet. Live Earth attracted 2 billion viewers (Cottle, 2008: 136).

Mega-events require giant, multi-layered networks of publicists, advocates, managers and support staff interacting over multiple time-spaces dealing with a plethora of people, objects and technologies. The aim is to create fluid or 'liquid' operational structures that deliver events without disclosing dangling roots or awkward cables (Bauman, 2000). The organisational aim is to coordinate smooth audience responses purely and fully connected with vision, mission statement, goals and objectives. Inevitably, this involves manipulation of people, objects and technologies by clients, stakeholders and event managers.

Media Targeting

Public relations companies work closely with the media to communicate event strategy and manage public responses. The father of public relations, Edward Bernays, understood that the first task of successful public relations is to develop campaign messages that will attract and persuade the public. Focus groups, interviews and questionnaires are key instruments of data collection. However, the second task is developing an effective media network to transmit organisational goals to the public. Bernays holds that media targeting involves the use of dramatic and melodramatic devices to create news items that capture popular instincts. To quote him:

> In order to appeal to the instincts and fundamental emotions of the public ... the public relations counsel must create news around his ideas. ... He must isolate ideas and develop them into events so that they can be more

readily understood and so they may claim attention as news. (Bernays, 1923: 71)

This involves publicists developing links, interviews and roundtable discussions with representatives of the press, radio and television. The BBC alone was estimated to provide 16 hours of coverage for Live Earth (2007) publicity, for example (Cottle, 2008: 136).

Exploiting and developing social network sites like Facebook, Twitter and Flickr are becoming more central in media targeting. By setting up web-based competitions, encouraging the exchange of photographs and promoting blogging sites, event profiles can be substantially raised at relatively low cost.

Content Creation and Social Capital Strategy

Events require messages and symbols. This involves intensive brand design work to create an appropriate symbol and aggressive marketing to communicate vision and mission statement to the public. According to Bernays (1923), the centrepiece of effective content creation in public relations is content creation. This is a 'bottom-up' rather than 'top-down' process. That is, data collection, through qualitative and quantitative methods of social research, provides the raw material for building content. This involves textual development in the forms of policies, campaign catch-phrases and slogan. Crucially in a culture dominated by visual communication, Bernays understood the importance of sifting through symbols and selecting key images to brand the campaign. The specialist development of symbols that instantly and positively convey complex campaign messages is the difference between success and failure in event strategy. As Bernays (1923: 4) puts it:

> The very need of reaching large numbers of people at one time and in the shortest possible time tends toward the utilization of symbols which stand in the minds of the public for the abstract idea the technician wishes to convey. ... Such a use of appeals must, it goes without saying, be studied by the expert.

Clients, stakeholders and event management have a vested interest in presenting events in a positive light. In addition to highlighting the aesthetic and cultural benefits of the attractions, it is now common to link capitalisation schemes to the long-term upgrade of housing, transport and recreation facilities in the host community. The Toronto Olympic bid (1996) sought to garner public support by undertaking to turn mega-event accommodation into affordable housing after the closure of the event.

The Cape Town Olympic bid (2004) went even further. It presented capital schemes as post-apartheid 'upliftment' ventures to revitalise communities, exploit and develop affirmative action initiatives and improve public transport. However, the strategy backfired when plans revealed standards of new housing that were below IOC guidelines. In addition, the planned uplift in the housing market was not sufficient to meet the domestic demand for housing. The result was to increase levels of disquiet among the host population about questions of access to housing and distributive justice (Hiller, 1998: 52–4).

In nearly all global events management today, issues of creative content are bound up with questions of social capital. It is therefore necessary to consider events in terms of a package. That is, around the core event radiate various issues relating to quality of life and environmental issues in the host community. Event strategy and day-to-day management must be cognizant of this package and produce a governing rationale which balances short- and long-term benefits to the community over potential costs. In particular, event jingoism which produces inflated, one-sided presentations of benefits is counter-productive. Effective PR integrates local and regional populations by offering compelling, insightful strategies executed with the appropriate 'local flavour' to win over hearts and minds.

On the Day Support

Event management on the day includes supervising the programme, extending hospitality to VIPs, liaising with the media, ensuring effective ticketing and security and monitoring the delivery of consumables. On the day support typically includes provision for crisis management issues such as bad weather, crowd disturbance and glitches in the event programme.

Event Memorabilia

The emotionalism of event consciousness is not only expressed in attendance and participation. It also requires a souvenir of the event. Event memorabilia has developed into a significant income stream. Merchandising the event is now a standard part of global event organisation and practice. Determining the range and price of memorabilia is part of event strategy. Events create a number of auxiliary markets in DVDs, soundtracks, clothing (including T shirts), programmes and mugs. Effective event management creates a comprehensive business plan in which the cross-subsidiary financial advantage of memorabilia sales is built into the financial balance sheet.

Post-event Evaluation

Post-event evaluation takes two forms. First, internal management evaluation designed to assess event outcomes against mission statement, vision, goals and objectives. Typical issues here are evaluation of finance, optimal resource use, coordinating arrangements, team performance and audience satisfaction.

Second, external evaluation of clients and/or stakeholders. Common topics are the financial balance sheet, media impact, size and satisfaction of audiences and sponsors and environmental impact (Williams and Bowdin, 2007). Local development guidelines usually make post-event evaluation a precondition of contract awards. It is generally accepted the global events have a multiplier effect on local and national economies. Of course, the ratio of surplus to cost is not guaranteed. The New Orleans World Fair (1984) is considered to have been a financial failure, although the value of long-term infrastructural effects is still regarded as equivocal in the literature (Dimanche, 1996). While the immediate impact of global events in job creation and inward investment may be considerable, in the long run capital expenditure may not be recouped. For example stadiums and highways built to host international sporting mega-events may be under-used by the host population and hotel vacancies and empty restaurant tables may be problems for the hospitality industry after tourists have gone home.

The Montreal Olympic Games (1976) are estimated to have been a financial failure for the city. The Games cost well in excess of $2 billion (CAN) in capital and interest costs. Nothing like this sum was recouped. Granted, pre-event (1974–6) growth was significant, with hotel chains and major Quebec construction firms gaining good business. However, after the mid-1970s the economy of Montreal went into recession which lasted for nearly two decades. Between 1975 and 1982 property prices collapsed, unemployment doubled and the hotel trade in the downtown area shrank to pre-Olympic turnover (Levine, 1999; Whitson and Horne, 2006).

In addition, analysts should exert care in reading the headline statistics on the multiplier effect of global events. The employment boost provided by events is one thing. But it must not be allowed to obscure data relating to the quality and stability of jobs. To return to the example of the Montreal Olympics, it is reported that the number of jobs in the local tourist economy actually declined between 1990 and 1995. Moreover, nine of the 25 worst low pay jobs in Canada were reported to be tourist industry jobs (Whitson and Horne, 2006).

For charitable foundations a deficit is embarrassing and may be disastrous. If the cost of running an event exceeds the income generated through donations and advertising questions are inevitably raised in the media about financial prudence and probity. This extends to post-event income distribution and value for money issues relating to project management. Live Aid, for example, was subject to withering media criticism by the BBC regarding the serious misallocation of funds. Specifically, the report claimed that charity funds were absconded by the Tigray Liberation Movement in Ethiopia to buy arms and munitions. Although the allegations were subsequently withdrawn after a highly public critique by Sir Bob Geldof, the reports undoubtedly harmed the public image of Live Aid and Band Aid for it left many members of the public believing that there is no smoke without fire.

The fund potential of global events means that issues of financial prudence and probity with respect to the allocation of charity money and project management is often a protracted business. This runs the additional risk of charity foundations opening themselves up to public criticism that money that was intended to provide relief is squandered in management fees and investigative support structures. Global event planners must be highly sensitive to the potential criticisms that derive from substantial income generation. These criticisms are not confined to the immediate response to fund disbursement and project investment. They are matters of the *longue durée*.

The main tools of quantitative event evaluation are econometric analysis and event experience scales. However, since events are multidimensional, doubts are sometimes raised about the validity of these methodologies as instruments to provide a comprehensive picture of event outcomes (Wood, 2009). Nevertheless, post-event evaluation procedures are now widely accepted as an industry standard. Moreover, since global event management often involves sensitive issues involving public accountability and impeccable financial probity in handling and distributing charity funds, there is a clear preference for independent evaluation.

In any case, the claims for event outputs made by clients and event management teams are not always calculable. As with the Live 8 banner headline which claimed an audience of 3 billion to which I have already alluded, they are at best estimates. As such, they are legitimate targets for critics who allege over-exaggeration and wishful thinking. Work on event legacy outcomes demonstrates that it is wise to adopt a medium- to long-term perspective in event evaluation. The term event legacy refers to the aggregate of planned and unplanned, positive and negative outcomes that outlast the event itself (Preuss, 2007: 211). It is distinct from the term 'impact' for the latter refers to immediate, short-term results. In contrast, event legacies are often more intangible and may take many years to reach fruition.

Researchers have distinguished several dimensions of legacy outcomes, including (1) economic legacy, (2) infrastructural legacy, (3) educational legacy, (4) urban legacy, (5) public life and cultural legacy and (6) symbols memory and history (Cashman, 2005; Chappelet, 2006).

Examining Event Management in Practice

So much for the blueprint of event management. The strength and combination of elements obviously varies in different cases and circumstances. But the considerations of the blueprint are common.

What of events in practice? How do the objectives of event blueprints play out? What are their achievements? What kind of unintended consequences follow from them? The next chapter uses three case studies of cyclical events to examine these questions. The first is a fairly short account of the core of Lewis PR in managing the 2010 FIBA World Championship. The second is a more detailed study of Edelman PR's management of the 2010 Winter Olympics in Vancouver. The third is the Burning Man City event in Nevada, which has become the world's event *cause célèbre* for anti-corporatist, anti-government, anti-counter-cultural, anti-consumerist values. The latter is particularly instructive. The main dialectic in event management is between inclusion, open participation, spontaneity and commercialisation, commodification, professionalisation and control. Burning Man City is part of the counter-culture. As such, it valorises inclusion, participation and spontaneity. Because of this, the record of resistance it has mounted against commercialisation, participation, commodification, professionalisation and control is of note.

6

WHAT DO CYCLICAL EVENTS DO?

It is useful to illustrate the principles behind event services in action by briefly considering three case studies. Needless to say, this should in no way be regarded as exhaustive. The purpose of the exercise is to provide indicative content of the practical application of event blueprints and event management dynamics.

In this chapter I have chosen to focus upon cyclical events. Chapter 9 will turn to the case study analysis of two single-issue events, the Concert for Hurricane Katrina Relief (2005) and Live Aid (1985).

Cyclical events are regenerative. They aim to celebrate and strengthen unity, solidarity and kinship by providing a global arena for tournaments of sporting prowess and artistic performance, layered identity and multi-lateral citizenship. A major objective is to strengthen integration between professionals and fans, governments and citizens. Events like the Olympics, the FIFA World Cup and Burning Man City are designed to highlight human cooperation, camaraderie, *esprit de corps* and common humanity. That they do not always achieve these goals goes without saying. That they are also seized by strong counter-cultural forces which trigger resistance and opposition is slowly becoming recognised as a major issue in the field (Gorringe and Rosie, 2008; Juris, 2008; Routledge, 2011). Within the event sector, concerns often focus on the over-professionalisation and commercialisation of events.

For example, the Sunset Junction Street Fair, a long-standing celebration of music, the arts and community in East Los Angeles was cancelled a few days before the start date in 2011. The official cause was that event organisers failed to provide the city's public works department with a cheque to cover expenses. The festival had evolved over three decades as a prestigious event in Los Angeles generating camaraderie and prestige among the gay and Latino communities in Silver Lake. It was launched as a genuine, home-grown event celebrating social inclusion and ethnic and multicultural diversity. However, after the festival introduced a ticket fee structure to support management costs and publicity and introduced chain-fencing and policing in response to city health and safety considerations public perception gradually changed.

Commercialisation proved to be unpopular with the local community who associated the origins of the festival with carefree spontaneity, festivity, transcendence and freedom. Two reporters who covered the cancellation, which was controversial in the Los Angeles metro area, Randy Lewis and Margaret Wappler (2011: D1), quote the remarks of a Silver Lake Neighbourhood Council member, Sarah Dale: 'The trouble started when they began charging a mandatory fee to get in. It sends the wrong message: "I celebrate diversity but there's a price-tag on it." It's diversity for those who can afford it.'

In addition, as the size of the event ballooned locals complained of over-crowded streets, litter and traffic congestion. Some businesses located outside the festival footprint said they lost money during the event because customers could not get to them. Cancellation therefore occurred in a climate of mixed event cognition. Event planners were unsuccessful in providing a strong, unequivocal event concept that clearly demonstrated that event benefits to the community outweighed costs.

The *travails* of the Sunset Junction event illustrate some of the common technical and administrative problems that emerge when cyclical events become established in the social calendar. Size leads to health and safety issues, questions of security management, the supply and disposal of consumables and provision of measures against trespass that require support funding and administration. All of this threatens to undermine freedom, festivity and spontaneity. Thus, events run the risk of being the victims of their own success. So the qualities that bring them to the attention of the community grow encumbered with bureaucratic controls, commercial imperatives and professional interference. The protection of the spirit of event spontaneity and the quality of transcendence produce special challenges for event planners and managers.

To come to the questions of the event blueprint and history of event dynamics in respect of three case studies: the FIBA World Championship, the Vancouver Winter Olympics and the Burning Man City festival.

Lewis PR and the FIBA World Championship Campaign

Lewis PR was appointed by the International Basketball Federation (FIBA) to manage the profile of the FIBA World Championship in Turkey (2010) The Lewis bid stressed that basketball is the world's second biggest sport and has unique potential to unify populations throughout FIBA's 213 member countries.

The main tasks undertaken by Lewis PR were advising strategy, leadership profiling, social media planning and managing 1800 journalists during the tournament. Central objectives and goals developed in conjunction with the FIBA Executive were: to raise the profile of FIBA and the World Championship in the global English language media; raise the reputation of the FIBA secretary general, Patrick Baumann, as a global leader in world sport; maximise sports coverage of the tournament in the USA and UK; achieve sponsorship backing; and engage new fans using social media channels such as Facebook and Twitter.

Event strategy was built around three planks. First, to harness basketball's global fan base and attract new fans by using social media to boost FIBA's profile. Second, to communicate the professionalism of organisers behind the sport by making secretary general Patrick Baumann available for selective interviews prior to, and during, the championship competition. Third, to boost the image of FIBA by proactive placement of news items and issue-based stories in international sports, lifestyle and national media outlets.

Post-event evaluation was intensive and presented the following results. The media hospitality event to announce the success of the Spanish Tourism Board sponsorship of the 2014 FIBA World Championship was attended by 50 key journalists and reached 30 media outlets.

The profile of FIBA and Patrick Baumann was raised by media coverage in advance of the championship in a plethora of press and broadcast outlets, including *The Economist*, BBC Sport, Bloomberg, TV Turkey, BBC Radio 4's *The Today Programme*, Press Association, *The Guardian*, Reuters, NBC Television, BBC World Service, CNBC, CNN International, *London Evening Standard*, Webcom Brasil, *La Vanguardia* (Spain), *Expansion* (Spain), *The New York Times*, *The Wall Street Journal* and AP (US).

Media coverage hits during the tournament included ESPN, AP, *The New York Times*, Fan-House (US), BBC World Service (live coverage), *The Daily Telegraph*, *Daily Mail*, *MVP Magazine* (UK), *El País* and AS (Spain), *L'Equipe* (France), *La Nación* (Argentina), *La Gazaetta Dello Sport* (Italy), *Primero Hora* (Puerto Rico), *Goal News* (Greece) and *Hurriyet Gazetsei* (Turkey).

Two 'on the ground' strategic roundtables involved more than 30 key media from around the world. Feature stories in tier one media outlets included BBC World Service, ESPN and *Sports Illustrated*.

One of the most interesting and novel features of the campaign was the extensive use of the web to publicise the event. The Facebook campaign before the tournament commenced to encourage fans to develop 'virtual jerseys' for their nations. This encouraged product identification between consumers and event providers (FIBA). Supplementally, FIBA organised a weekly competition on Twitter introducing web users to Turkey 2010 and encouraging high profile basketball players to tweet about the event.

During the event live commentary of the championship was posted on Facebook and Twitter. A Flickr account was created to store photographs taken during the event to enhance access to international media and bloggers.

Impact evaluation analysis indicated that 92,000 Facebook followers were added before the competition and a further 32,000 plus 62,000 'virtual jerseys' were created during the competition. Followers on Twitter increased by 8000. The Flickr account received 64,000 hits during the course of the championship and FIBA.com logged over 50 million visitors. FIBA officials estimated that 1 billion people in over 200 countries watched the contest. The FIBA website received over 30 million visitors. There were no press reports of significant anti-FIBA protests or crowd violence.

However, it is now routine for major cyclical events to draw protest. The potential for media coverage is irresistible for counter-culture movements. So events are often exploited as occasions for wider protests having to do with opposition to the state, anti-capitalist movements, the rejection of militarism, various pressure group issues and so on.

In addition, cyclical events such as the Olympics and the FIFA World Cup are centred on metropolitan centres. They require considerable capital investment in the construction of new stadium space and infrastructural support in the form of highways, athlete villages, hotel accommodation and so on. As we shall see, this often involves the enforced displacement of traditional communities. Pledges to replace dwelling space with low cost housing often gives way to the development of mixed or luxury condominium property. In this way national and municipal councils use global events to legitimate slum clearance policies or wholesale changes in the mix of housing that would be difficult or impossible to achieve without the halo of the event around them. While the FIBA 2010 tournament in Turkey was conflict free, the 2010 Winter Olympics in Vancouver were associated with a number of layers of resistance and opposition, to the consideration of which we now turn.

Edelman PR and the Vancouver Winter Olympics Campaign

Edelman PR were awarded the contract to cover all marketing, communications, public relations and social media outreach for Live City, Vancouver's two celebration sites for the 2010 Winter Olympic Games. It developed a comprehensive, integrated campaign involving interviews with the chief executive, John Furlong, and the media, sponsorship, interviews with dignitaries and celebrities, media targeting and exploiting and developing social media networks. The Hudson Bay Company, North America's oldest corporation dating back to 1670, was appointed as the official outfitter of the Games. In conjunction with Edelman and VANOC (the Vancouver Organising Committee) it set about providing a distinctive 'Canadiana' look to enhance the Vancouver Games as a national and global brand. Sponsors included Coca-Cola, Acer, General Electric, McDonald's, Omega, Panasonic, Samsung, VISA, Bell, RBC, Petro-Canada, Air Canada, Proctor & Gamble, BC Hydro, Canadian Pacific, Ricoh, Tech, 3M and Molson.

Edelman used Twitter, Facebook, mobile applications and developed a dedicated interactive website to promote the Games. Again, a noteworthy feature of the event was the increased use of the web as a prime networking and data exchange resource. Facebook was estimated to engage 29,000 fans locally and around the world. A national digital contest was implemented to drive consumer engagement. Celebrity torchbearers included Bob Costas, Arnold Schwarzenegger, Wayne Gretzky, Shania Twain, Matt Lauer, Michael Bublé and Justin Morneau.

Edelman signed a subsidiary contract with the Resort Municipality of Whistler to update and refresh the venue as the Host Mountain Resort of the 2010 Games. This involved the design of a new logo and world-mark, the development of an environmental graphic package for the Whistler Discovery Centre, reports and printed material.

The mission statement reflected a vision and specific goals and objectives tied to making the Games a green event. Before the Games, 70 Olympic and professional athletes produced a petition urging public support to back VANOC's stated aim of making the Games carbon neutral. The petition was developed in partnership with the David Suzuki Foundation, an influential Canadian environmental organisation. One hundred days before the commencement of the championship VANOC announced 25 partners to invest in the '2010 Carbon Partner Program'. Simultaneously 'Project Sky Blue' was introduced, a movement designed to inspire individuals committed to climate change to contribute 1 billion kilometres of carbon-reducing activities from their daily lives by the end of the closing ceremonies.

VANOC's legacy strategy embraced environmental and social and economic opportunities for the host region. It introduced a new sustainability model for large sports and event organisations and a sustainable sports event toolkit for mega sports events. It pioneered partnerships with local aboriginal people through schemes with the Four Host First Nations and encouraged participation programmes for socially disadvantaged groups. Inner-city businesses benefited from C$5.7 million in Games-related procurement opportunities. There were 528 Buysmart contracts issued to a value of C$277 million, ensuring that sustainability goals were considered in VANOC's procurement and licensing activities. The VANOC chief executive, John Furlong (2011), reported that corporate sponsorship for the Vancouver Olympics totalled $750 million (CAN) in cash, goods and services.

The Games provided multinationals with a classic product placement opportunity to enhance their brands by associating them with improving health, excitement, diversity and glamour. Proctor & Gamble showcased 17 of its health and beauty brands such as Cover Girl makeup, Pantene shampoo and even Pampers. The target group for promotions campaigns was young women. It is estimated that 76% of the US Olympic TV audience were women between the ages of 18 and 34. Lisa Baird, chief marketing officer for the US Olympic Committee commented that 'the Olympics are centred around storytelling. Women love it.' Proctor & Gamble has invested heavily in the sports market since the $57 billion acquisition of Gillette, with a long history of sports advertising, in 2005 (Burkitt, 2009).

However, Edelman PR was unable to ring-fence bad publicity deriving from the Games. On the eve of the opening ceremony the media ran reports of police investigations centred upon people who opposed Vancouver's decision to host the event. Christopher Shaw, a professor of ophthalmology at the University of British Columbia, authored a book that was highly critical of the Olympics and the decision of Vancouver to host them. Shaw was interviewed by plainclothes officers from the Integrated Security Unit, an Olympics operation led by the Royal Canadian Mounted Police, who wanted to discuss his book and review his negative views of the Olympics (Austen, 2010). In his book, using archival research, scrutiny of public documents and media reports, Shaw (2008) accuses the IOC of engaging in profiteering in conjunction with British Columbian real estate developers. He maintains that the IOC avoids taxation on its operations.

According to Shaw (2008), criticism of financial exploitation is stifled by the strong associations of peace, harmony and unity with the Olympics and the campaign manipulation strategies of the PR–media hub in promoting this message. Shaw (2008: 15–16) calls this 'the Olympic frame'. He contends that it damages civil liberties by identifying criticism as being against the spirit of Olympism and fellowship that is the manifestation of the Olympics as a brand. Elsewhere, Hoberman (1984: 6) submits that this ideology has massively overestimated the value of the Olympic Games as a means of 'cohesion' in the 'world community'.

Shaw's book examines legacy strategy in the 2010 Games. It submits that in common with other recent Olympic bid strategies, the Games are linked to a variety of positive urban development outcomes relating to economic growth, the provision of new facilities, additional housing and revitalised infrastructure. Shaw exposes the mythology of Olympic 'stakeholder' rhetoric by revealing how linkage between various business, government and NGO interests operates to the advantage of these backroom groups. In particular the commitment for new housing and infrastructural development in Vancouver shored up and boosted a market in private speculation in those ventures.

In the bid strategy for the Games the city's Inner City Inclusivity Commitment Statement (ICICS) made clear environmental and social sustainability undertakings to the city population. The ICICS contained 14 areas of concern and 37 concrete commitments to be implemented by the organising committee (later known as VANOC). To quote Eby (2007: 1):

> The ICICS commitments explicitly promised to ensure Vancouver's inner-city residents would have meaningful input into the processes surrounding the 2010 Olympiad, would experience no undue hardship including homelessness or displacement as a result of the Games, and would enjoy housing and other legacies that would contribute to their community as a result of the Games.

For the most part, these promises were not honoured. Programmes of gentrification and infrastructural support produced waves of evictions, the loss of affordable housing and the criminalisation of the homeless and low income people in the city's downtown Eastside area. In addition, the ecologically sensitive Eagleride Bluffs region was bulldozed to create space for a major Olympic highway to ski venues, riding roughshod over VANOC's green vision and mission statement which was endorsed and finessed with the help of Edelman PR.

Shaw (2008) condemns the environmental and social sustainability legacy of the Games. He contends that civil liberties are trampled by publicity campaigns that fixate upon providing the public with positive, 'feel good' imagery of the Games while drawing a veil over closed-door business/property deals and financial chicanery. For Shaw, the mega-event is a pretext for organising bumper-to-bumper lucrative business deals that, above all, benefit private investors. His conclusion parallels broader research on sporting mega-events which maintains that the positive publicity campaigns which are connected to them typically underestimate costs and overestimate benefits (Whitson and Horne, 2006). The economic multiplier effect of the World Cup and global sports events in general is challenged by many commentators (Coates and Humphreys, 1999; Eisenger, 2000; Owen, 2002; Teigland, 1999). Immediate economic gains are often offset by longer term costs as, for example, when stadiums become under-used and tourists who would otherwise visit the hosting country are put off by event traffic. Security budgets can be easily overstretched by crowd control problems or terrorist threats. Lee and Taylor (2005) estimated that the real tourist flow to Korea during the months of the 2010 World Cup was one-third short of predictions, and was much lower than tourist arrivals in the same month in previous years. Bills to pay for infrastructure (new stadiums, roads, accommodation space, etc.) are considerable and subject to the vagaries of inflation. Other researchers argue that sports mega-events benefit business by diverting public resources into private corporations (Baade and Matheson, 2002; Judd, 2003).

In fact, before, during and after the Vancouver Games anti-Olympic protest groups flourished in the city. Organised around a loose coalition called the Olympic Resistance Network (ORN), as well as several other independent individuals and groups, they aimed to challenge the official PR–media hub by highlighting the impact of the Games on indigenous groups, low income communities and the environment. Demonstrations during the Games were mostly peaceful, with few arrests. However, the focus of dissent expanded from anti-Olympic activist resistance and opposition to VANOC's legacy strategy to encompass a bid to 'block the arteries of capitalism' (Mackin, 2010). Strategic provision and policing considerations infringed civil liberties by permitting the rationed colonisation of public space by 'Olympic space'. Axiomatic to this recolonised space was the exclusion of dissent or deviance from the Olympian ideal (Hoberman, 1984; van Luijk, 2010).

A separate set of questions is raised by setting VANOC legacy undertakings for aboriginals against delivery. The Games took place on the ancestral lands of the Squamish, Lil'wat, Musqueam and Tselil-Waututh. In the absence of a treaty, the Province is legally required to consult and accommodate the First Nations when proposing projects on First Nation territory. The Squamish and the Lil'wat agreed to 122 acres of land allotments in and around Whistler in exchange for their cooperation in the 2010 Games. In addition, the Canadian government allocated financial compensation to the First Four Nations. VANOC pledged $8 million (CAN) for youth sport and recreation programmes.

According to Laura Robinson (2011), the money river never materialised. The $8 million (CAN) pledge was contingent upon $5 million (CAN) from corporate donations combined with the $3 million (CAN) earmarked for aboriginal youth by the government of British Columbia (BC). Corporate donations did not amount to planned projections. According to Robinson (2011), received corporate donations amounted to less than $300,000 (CAN).

Legacies Now, the NGO that currently manages funds, estimates that, of January 2011, only $1.3 million remained of the BC grant. One reason given for the deficit was a VANOC spend of $350,000 (CAN) on the aboriginal component of the opening ceremonies. The Aboriginal Youth Legacy Programme, which is devoted to education, culture and sustainability projects as well as sport and recreation, was allocated $282,000 (CAN). In addition the fund has assigned support finance to aboriginal athletes and communities since 2005.

For Robinson (2011), however, this is a trifling sum. Her research indicates that the IOC sold international broadcasting rights to the Vancouver

Games and the 2012 London Olympics for $4 billion (CAN). The host broadcaster for the 2010 Games, CTV, paid $90 million (CAN) for broadcasting rights. VANOC's financial accounts list a further $61.5 million (CAN) in ticket sales for the opening and closing ceremonies. In addition, Robinson (2011) alleges that a substantial portion of sponsorship funds were assigned to the OTP (Own The Podium) programme that was intended to showcase the achievements of Canadian athletes in the Games. OTP is an initiative of VANOC and the Canadian federal government. It has contributed $110 million (CAN) over five years to elite Canadian winter sports and athletes. After the Games, the federal government committed $22 million (CAN) for winter sports and $36 million (CAN) to summer sports annually.

Black Rock City LLC: Burning Man City

Burning Man is an annual counter-culture event held in the Black Rock Desert, Nevada. From modest origins on a beach in San Francisco with a handful of spectators in 1996, it has developed into a multi-million dollar enterprise drawing nearly 50,000 participants. The event planning organisation behind Burning Man is the Black Rock City LLC (Limited Liability Company). This organisation is responsible for all Burning Man's financial and legal obligations. It handles accounts, expenditures, sponsorship, guaranteeing indebtedness, litigation, the acquisition, management and disposition of assets, the negotiation of contracts, the management and licensing of trademarks and copyrights, human resource management and training and the selection and dismissal of employees, volunteers and contractors. In addition Black Rock City LLC is responsible for external relations with county, state and federal agencies, the media and strategic planning (www.burningman.com).

Turner (2009: 91) defines the spirit of the event nicely as 'a living model of commons-based peer production carried out for non-monetary purposes'. Exchange is based upon gifting rather than monetary transaction. Participants are welcomed on condition of providing their time, labour, imagination and other resources freely. The event's multi-million dollar budget is funded almost exclusively from ticket sales. This underwrites Black Rock City LLC expenses consisting of a small team of salaried managers, the provision of basic on-site infrastructure, as well as meeting the per person/land use fee required for leasing the site.

Additional funds are set aside to support the art installations that participants bring to the venue each year (Gilmore, 2010). These works are important pathways of social integration around the Burning Man concept because they involve pre- and post-event planning and messaging. Although the Burning Man event lasts a week, the cycle of activities that it supports is conceptualised as year-round activity. A web team numbering 2000 facilitates an open-source information and social network, posting stories, photographs and supporting a writers' forum. The Playa bulletin board handles listings to 'connect with Burners'. 'Decompression' events in the Bay area are held after the festival. These consist of art, performance, bonfires, dance, theme camps, lectures, circus acts, live music and DJs.

From the start, the Burning Man organisation sought to maximise decentralisation and the autonomy of citizens in a manner consistent with environmental sustainability, health and safety. However, as the scale of operations climbed from a minor to major event organisers faced increased pressures on administration and financial resourcing. In the course of this, the event concept expanded into the idea of establishing not only a series of themed art works but building, maintaining and tearing down an entire city around them.

Burning Man is, arguably, the world's biggest counter-cultural cyclical event. The event concept positions spontaneity and transcendence over officialdom, standing bureaucracies and rules of procedure. Burning Man sets itself up as a freedom festival. It sets great store in welcoming alternative culture, personal idiosyncrasy and peaceful innovation. While funds are used to pay essential staff in planning and operations functions, the organisation is resolutely not-for-profit. Any surplus above essential costs is reinvested to improve the quality of event experience.

Burning Man is therefore a notable case study of resistance against the materialist drift, over-bureaucratisation and intrusive professionalisation of cyclical events. It is committed to respecting the spirit of spontaneity and transcendence over the profit motive. Black Rock City LLC aims to achieve a type of event experience that is self-directed, self-forming and personally transformative. To these ends, event management seeks to curtail hierarchy, reward creativity and champion experimentation. This is captured nicely by the lynch-pin phrase in the central organising event philosophy which is to treat *creative chaos* as virtuous (Chen, 2009).

What is the history of the event? The original Burning Man was an 8-foot statue, conceived by artist and landscaper Larry Harvey, and ignited on Baker Beach, San Francisco. The burning is thought to have been part of a impromptu exorcism after a failed love affair. However, the event cycle of closure and renewal suggests deeper roots. Indeed, the Burning Man website reports that the first improvised wooden figure was built partly in honour of the summer solstice. Burning as a symbol of closure, destruction and revival goes back deep into pagan culture. The phoenix always arises from the ashes. In a modern context its use implies both primordial, magical properties and cosmopolitan separation from metropolitan order. The flight from the moneyed metropolis to build a desert city in which money, government, the media and corporate power are replaced by gifting, cooperation, open-source information and fellowship carries strong ritual overtones of erasure, cleansing and renewal. The burning of the wooden statue at the climax of the event patently consolidates this.

Gilmore (2010) argues that social behaviour at Burning Man is semi-religious in form. Participants bring a vast array of artistic and religious symbols and motifs ranging from porta-temples and labyrinths to angels, demons, gods, goddesses, priests and even corporate logos. However, although pagan and new age elements are to the fore, they are woven into a complex and arresting tapestry of bricolage with cultural, anti-corporatist and anti-consumerist symbols and motifs. The event aspires to be radically inclusive, respects free exchange and locks down any attempt by commercial interests to commodify Burning Man as a brand.

The Burning Man event is now also known as Burning Man City. This is because the event now draws thousands of people who, for one week, are encouraged to build and maintain the fourth biggest city in Nevada. The horseshoe-shaped, retro-futuristic tent city stands 12 blocks deep. It stretches about a mile and a half from end to end (Turner, 2009: 83). The tents are laid out around a grid of streets in which participants set up and run 'theme camps'. Event managers provide minimal basic services (camp placement, public information, refuse bins, porta-potties). Participants are advised to bring their own food and water supplies.

Each year the week-long festivities are themed around an event concept. Recent concepts include Rites of Passage, Metropolis, Evolution, the American Dream, the Green Man, Hope and Fear, Psyche and the Vault of Heaven. The focal point of the city is the Burning Man wooden sculpture which is illuminated with multicoloured neon and packed with fireworks that are ignited at the climax of the seven days of festivities.

Other cyclical events maintain a strong distinction between performers and spectators which is reinforced by event planning regulations and policing. Burning Man City seeks to erase this distinction. The City is conceptualised as an organic creative whole, in which all participants are citizens, each of whom is designated as an active participant in the event. A 'no spectators' policy is rigorously applied. Activities are organised around the annual event concepts and include art works, debates, lectures, exercise classes, games, theme camps, dancing and fireworks.

In the study of organisations, self-directed, self-forming order is often seen as the holy grail of event management. Burning Man City applies volunteering and the gift economy as the touchstone to achieving it. Although salaried staff and ticketing prices have escalated as the event has become bigger, the primary resource is still volunteers who devote their labour *gratis*. The only commodities for sale in the desert city are ice, tea and coffee. Catering and hospitality are conceived as a matter of self-help and community fellowship. No advertising is permitted. The city is raised, maintained and deconstructed by unpaid volunteers who are encouraged to treat the building and clean-up process as obligations of active citizenship. The mantra of city dismantlement is *leave no trace*. The ethic of environmental sustainability requires the organisers and participants to leave the setting for the event in pristine condition. Written codes of practice have not been entirely eradicated, since Burning Man City is now a mega-event, which requires a salaried staff to run the managing body, Black Rock City LCC, office space in downtown San Francisco, health and safety services, arrangements for waste disposal and insurance cover. In addition, the organisation is based around 10 principles, which are deliberately expressed in general formulations, and which operate as a sort of minimalist constitution. Briefly, the following principles are:

1 *Radical inclusion:* The event is open to all. Although a ticketing structure has emerged in order to cover running costs, no-one is debarred from applying to be a volunteer or participating.
2 *Gifting:* The event is run around a gift economy. No expectation of profit or equal return is made in gift giving. The gift is regarded as unconditional.
3 *Decommodification:* Commercial sponsorships, advertising and transactions are banished from the event. Participatory experience is the main currency of exchange, thus breaking down the old distinction between producers and consumers.
4 *Radical self-reliance:* The event requires each City citizen to utilise and express his or her inner resources.
5 *Radical self-expression:* The culture is non-directive and rejects punishment-centred styles of management.
6 *Communal effort:* The ethic of creative chaos is built upon foundations of spontaneous cooperation and non-directed collaboration. The City community decides what is best for City members.
7 *Civic responsibility:* Citizens are required to obey local, state and federal laws. The purpose of activities is guided by responsibility to public welfare and communicating civic responsibilities to all participants.
8 *Leaving no trace:* Burning Man City respects the sustainability of the environment. The space occupied by the City is cleared after the event and restored to a state of nature.
9 *Participation:* Citizens are called upon to act collectively to build, maintain and dismantle the City. There are no distinctions between leaders and followers. Every citizen is designated a creative worker.
10 *Immediacy:* Attendance and activities privilege experience over rational engagement. The barriers between mind and body that exist outside are suspended within City boundaries. (www.burningman.com)

Needless to say, a major event of this scale does not exist in a vacuum. Over the years Black Rock City LLC has evolved strategies to deal with the three main external agents that influence the context of event management operations: government departments, the media and business (Chen, 2009: 120–49). What makes Burning Man distinctive is that it is defiantly located outside the event mainstream. Consequently, the Black Rock City LLC has been determined to avoid conventional routes in handling external agents. For example, attempts by government departments, especially the Bureau of Land Management (BLM), to regulate the event in compliance with sanctioned recreational norms, provide adequate hazard insurance cover and impose onerous land fees were headed off by the mobilisation of volunteers, the establishment of taskforces and eventually departments (such as the 'Earth Guardians') and the evolution of a code of standards.

Similarly, when drug use, alcohol consumption, public sex and nudity threatened to precipitate a full-scale moral panic, with lurid stories of the event trailed in *Playboy* and attempts by MTV to place undercover agents to film site activities, the LLC professionalised ranks by establishing a Media Mecca department of press and public relations. Activities that might provoke a moral panic, such as the possession and use of loaded guns, were banned. Media Mecca restricted media access to the site and developed publicity around the banner headline values of the event, namely gifting, community, creativity, freedom and environmental sustainability.

As word of mouth and organised publicity about the event spread, Burning Man attracted the interest of advertisers, brand development agencies and other commercial investors. The use of Burning Man imagery, the name and venue for commercial exploitation violates the not-for-profit, community ethic of the event. The LLC appointed a legal team to target the unauthorised use of event images in commercial websites, print and film. Volunteers were also mobilised to monitor commercial infringement on the internet and television, in pop music or other branches of the entertainment industry. The Black Rock City LLC has a few of the features of orthodox corporate culture. For example, Larry Harvey is paid an executive director salary and is president of the Black Rock Arts Foundation. However, the hallmark of Black Rock City LLC dealings both within the organisation and with external agents, is solidarity with anti-corporatist and anti-consumerist sentiments.

That said, the introduction of new departments and the appointment of outside professional bodies to uphold the ethos and the interests of the event imply a level of *realpolitik* in Black Rock City LLC event management style that threatens the spontaneous, transcendent and creative qualities for which the event is popularly known. How can event management achieve spontaneity and the spirit of transcendence without leadership, a command structure, written documents, general rules and accountability?

The entire history of the event has been a see-saw between avoiding the straitjacket of over-organisation and the perils of under-organisation (Chen, 2009). In 1996 the event came close to disintegrating. Just before the event, a worker was accidentally killed in a crash between a motor-cycle and truck. This attracted censorious media coverage, which was exacerbated in the closing stages of the event, when an inebriated driver drove his car into tents and seriously injured several campers. These trag-edies were seized upon by hostile elements in government and the media as evidence that Burning Man had grown into a recreational demon that the event managers could not control. The philosophy of creative chaos was blamed for producing a management style of irresponsible under-organisation which risked the life and limb of participants.

Circumstantial evidence to support these arguments was indeed pro-vided by the strong growth trajectory of the Burning Man event. The first event in San Francisco involved 20 participants. By 1989, 300 participants attended, causing Park Police to object that the event was in violation of noise abatement and health and safety regulations. As a result, in 1990, the Burn location was switched to Black Rock City, Nevada; 800 partici-pants attended. In the course of establishing Burning Man in the desert, the event concept was modified from a festive, educational, localised, temporary event, into the vision of a fully functioning temporary city with pre- and post-city construction undertakings which involved event man-agers and volunteers in all-year-round activities. By 1993, participants had climbed to 1000; by 1988, 15,000; by 2003, 30,586; and by 2008, just under 50,000 (www.burningman.com.timeline).

The under-organisation charges made after the 1996 tragedies prompted adjustment in the event management strategy. Volunteer recruitment was tightened up. Medical and public communication ser-vices were upgraded. On-site driving was banished. The anarchic 'no leader, no rules' philosophy was amended by introducing a new empha-sis upon individual and community responsibility. These moves were resisted by some participants who contested the imperative to move towards greater centralisation and sought to reaffirm the event ethos of tolerance, decentralisation, freedom and support for personal idiosyn-crasy and self-realisation. However, police pressure on the BLM not to renew the Burning Man land use permit after the 1996 tragedies weak-ened the force of these arguments.

The 1997 event was transferred from BLM-managed land in Pershing County to private land in Washoe County. Relocation brought new chal-lenges to the event managers, most notably in negotiating with Washoe County officials and private land managers about questions of access, accountability and governance. However, the make-or-break nature of the relocation move strengthened the pro-administration Burning Man lobby (Chen, 2009: 32–4). In 1998 the event moved back to BLM-managed land. But the administrative structures developed in Washoe County were retained. The organisation aspires to a state of constant creative balance between control over infrastructure and creative expression.

What attracts participants to Burning Man? A variety of motivations come into play. Some people are drawn to what is generally acknowledged to be the premier cyclical counter-cultural event in North America. The event appeals to the anti-consumerist, anti-corporatist, anti-government, do-it-yourself sentiments in American society.

For others, the Man symbolises the tyranny of the workplace. So the festivities around the statue and the eventual burning symbolise temporary release from the 9–5 treadmill. There are utopian overtones here, in as much as the atmosphere of experimentation, gifting, cooperation, innovation and non-judgementalism is clearly trailed as some kind of post-industrial blueprint.

In furtherance of this point, academics have discovered that one interesting, and perhaps surprising, constituency of Burners is workers in computer-related industries (Kozinets, 2002; Turner, 2009). Google's founders, Larry Page and Serge Brin, Amazon's head, Jeff Bezos, John Gilmore, a co-founder of the Electronic Frontier Foundation, and Brian Behlendorf, a major open-source advocate, are long-standing Burners (Turner, 2009: 83). Google employees have attended company parties in Burning Man derived costumes and hosted internal websites devoted to the event (Cohen and Whelpley, 2007). It is worth going into the motivations of this group more deeply because the issue points to structural changes in the labour market and popular culture that may raise the chances of the Burning Man model being more widely adopted.

Several commentators have contended that the digital economy is eliciting new orientations to work and the renewal of old obligations to the community. Notably, with respect to the former, cooperative labour is becoming an adjunct of mere personal gain. As for the question of obligations, volunteerism and gifting are becoming more prominent aspects of social membership. Richard Florida (2002) contends that high tech, web-based workers have developed cultures of creativity that are defined in opposition to conventional corporate models. These cultures are apparent in dress code, work design, work attitudes and recreational choices. Originally, 'creative class' workers in digital technology took profit-driven corporations like IBM and Microsoft as the embodiment of the 'dark forces' to which they were opposed. Hence, for example, Wikipedia and Google have each developed 'services' rather than 'products' and pursue a philosophy of cooperative labour over hierarchy. Both companies follow a strong ethic of service to the community and peer-to-peer sharing. Thus, the entries in Wikipedia come from users, just as Google uses unpaid developers. For commentators like Florida (2002) and Baym and Burnett (2009) the creative opportunities offered by the web and digital economy in general have fossilised traditional concepts of producers and consumers.

It might be objected that the creative class and new bohemianism in the workplace arguments are exaggerated. The use of unpaid labour in ventures like Google and Wikipedia is not so very different from the exploitation of paid labour in conventional multinationals. For the effect of the labour distributed is to augment the stock value of the company that receives it by workers adding more value than they subtract through the labour process. While a philosophy of peer-to-peer creative commons obtains at the level of production, reward follows the orthodox capitalist model. For example, the Forbes Business 2011 billionaires list, estimates that the founders of Google, Serge Brin and Larry Forbes each have a personal fortune of $19.8 billion while Jeff Bezos is listed as being worth $18.1 billion (www.forbes.com\billionaires\list).

If the creative industries, like old style factories, are producing billionaires this does not, in itself, falsify the thesis that new labour market regimes constitute a structural transformation in attitudes to work and community membership. The open-sourcing, anti-corporatist, peer-to-peer networking and volunteering that characterise network modes of doing business find a compelling parallel in the Burning Man City project. Workers in the high tech digital information and communication industries are drawn to the event as a showcase for their art works and a gathering of fellow travellers against the corporate, consumerist, state-controlled mainstream. Some commentators suggest that Burning Man City even permits workers in the digital communication and information industries to try out prototypes that feed back into the workplace. As Fred Turner (2009: 91) puts it:

> [Burning Man] is not only a ritual space but a potential factory. As with multiplayer online role-playing games or open-source projects in various fields, Burning Man is becoming a site at which the traditional features of artistic bohemians – collaborative commons, visibility, subsidy, project labour and fused pursuit of self improvement, craft and reputation – help to structure the manufacture of new information goods.

However, if this is indeed the case it is a by-product of the festival and applies only to a minority of Burners. The majority come to the Burning Man cyclical events carrying utopian meanings that seek confirmation in the festival desert space. The realisation of these meanings is contingent upon a complicated interchange between over-organisation and under-organisation (Chen, 2009). The event seems to be constantly on the brink of falling apart. Yet the low levels of control and high levels of openness to diversity and experimentation are compatible with utopian affirmation and personal transformation. The spontaneity and spirit of transcendence of the event have not ossified into closed options and frozen routine.

Burning Man therefore offers a model of a mega-event which has successfully avoided the pitfalls of over-professionalisation, bureaucracy and commercialism. However, its accomplishments in these respects owe much to the meanings that Burners bring with them to Burning Man City. Because the event is located in a wider cycle of counter-cultural activities that fall under the umbrella of Burning Man, the disjointed, commuter mentality of event consciousness that afflicts other global events is not conspicuous. The levels of display and emotionalism for which Burning Man City provides a catalyst are *continuous* with the lifestyle values that Burners bring to the festival. In as much as this is the case, the event can look forward to retaining its vitality and sense of building and maintaining a society beyond the player.

Cyclical Events: Costs and Benefits

Burning Man benefits because the majority of Burners carry values, beliefs and lifestyle choices that conform to the spirit of spontaneity and transcendence organised around event counter-cultural values. The issues facing other cyclical events in which the meanings that participants bring to the event are not so solid and directed are more problematic. The FIBA and Vancouver Olympics campaigns both made extensive recourse to transcendental images of fellowship, unity and solidarity. On the whole the FIBA event successfully achieved these goals, but the Olympics faces similar cyclical problems to the FIFA World Cup in requiring massive infrastructural development that produces conspicuous costs as well as benefits for the host community. When event mechanics become transparent or falter, the desired state of festivity and transcendence is compromised because the cogs of organisational manipulation become visible. Unfulfilled obligations in social investment and the creation of a market of property racketeering can take some of the shine off the enterprise.

Similarly, building the infrastructure to support global events in urban settings has implications of enforced evictions, demolition and homelessness which may produce counter-productive event publicity. The replacement of poor housing stock with higher quality accommodation has the additional consequence of out-pricing poor residents from traditional inner-city neighbourhoods. For example, the 2008 Beijing Olympics involved the demolition and clearance of 171 urban villages with an estimated displacement of 370,500 permanent residents and migrants (Shin, 2009).

Another well-documented case is Blikkiesdorp in Cape Town. This so-called 'temporary relocation area' was designed to accommodate panhandlers and people made homeless by the redevelopment programme for the 2010 FIFA World Cup. Constructed in 2008, Blikkiesdorp is an 'emergency housing development' of 3000 one-room shacks built of wood and iron, currently housing 15,000 people. In some cases five or six people are crammed into a living space of 3 x 6 metres with inadequate ventilation or heating, no showers and no paving between the living cubicles. The settlement has become known as 'Tin Can Town' by residents and other locals. It invites unflattering comparisons with the townships created under apartheid (Siegel, 2010; Smith, 2010).

Such is the scale of some cyclical events like the Olympics that resistance now accompanies the pre-event run-up. The widespread rioting and looting in London and many other major British cities in the summer of 2011 achieved saturated global media coverage. The spark to the tinder box was the controversial police shooting of a black criminal suspect in North London which precipitated protests of unlawful killing by the black community. However, this was surrounded by a climate of resentment and opposition produced by the authoritarian deficit reduction policies enforced by the coalition government. While it would be going too far to claim that opposition to the Olympics was a leading factor behind the riots, the press certainly contrasted massive expenditure on new Olympic stadiums and infrastructure with severe cuts to grassroots facilities such as youth clubs and benefit support in the troubled areas.

Cyclical events generate inner investment through international sponsorship, merchandising, broadcast syndication rights and tourist flows. However, there is now a large critical literature that questions the profitability of global events (Coates and Humphreys, 1999; Eisenger, 2000; Owen, 2002). Certainly, the costs of cyclical events are enormous. Leaving aside infrastructure development costs, cyclical events now carry heavy costs of security. Event planners for the London Olympics (2012) estimated the participation of teams from 205 countries, at least 120 heads of state and 50,000 journalists. The activities stretched from May to September. Policing costs were concentrated not only in protecting official venues, but in hundreds of parallel events which attracted large crowds such as televised screenings in London parks. The planning team did not limit security provision to crowd control issues. The showcase nature of the Olympics made it a global media circus, and therefore a prime target for terrorist activity. The London Olympic planning team recognised four possible threats of terrorist bombing or assassination: plots by al-Qaeda or affiliated jihadist groups; a rogue Irish republican group seeking spectacular glory; a lone wolf assailant; and 'imported problems' – dissident groups who see the event as an opportunity to strike against the head or representative team of a hated government (*The Economist*, 15 October 2011).

Money attracts corruption. The sheer scale of the money generated by global events invites profiteering and a sense among the propertyless of being ignored. Fall-out from the riots in London in 2011 required multi-level strategies of management which encompass positive publicity benefits and modelling in inner-city investment, policing and public relations. Particularly sensitive issues here are infrastructural event capital projects and post-event social project management. Organisational dynamics extend beyond the event preparation and duration to the impact of social, economic, political and cultural consequences of events which may take years to register in social consciousness. The long-term nature of event dynamics contrasts with general social awareness of event impacts which is immediate, emotive and typically clusters around a fairly narrow range of reactions. Characteristically, social reactions are handicapped by short-term responses that concentrate upon the quality of the event programme and event publicity that occurs over the duration.

Nonetheless, cyclical events can serve as a useful chess piece in diplomacy and politics. Later, we shall examine some case studies of event appropriation. That is, the political and commercial seizure of folk events to achieve goals that are independent of the event tradition. However, events are also used by the media, government and business to take readings of the climate of multiethnic, multicultural and economic relations. This process may be referred to as event barometrics. That is, the media use of the event as a barometer of general social and economic relations. The event ceases to be only a process with objectives defined by event planners. It also becomes an instrument for measuring the health of the city, the region or the nation.

For example, the UK's Notting Hill Carnival, which is Europe's largest cyclical outdoor festival, is no longer regarded as simply a celebration of Afro-Caribbean culture and the Notting Hill community. It has become a barometer of the state of national, particularly, multiethnic relations. The event started in 1959 as a response to troubled race and youth relations. It was designed to unify London's multiethnic community. It also incorporated various subcultural influences, most notably a hippy festival known as the London Free School. From small beginnings, the event now attracts 1 million visitors and, during the weekend of its duration, blanket media coverage.

The event is promoted as a celebration of multiethnic, multicultural West London. However, because it also highlights and dramatically expresses difference it has developed into a national power-play of racial, generational and sub-cultural diplomacy and sub-politics. The event has a long history of episodes of intermittent youth and racial violence. In 1976 rioting left 100 police officers and 60 carnival-goers requiring hospital treatment. The event has grown into a barometer for tensions between the local community, multiethnic Britain, the police, the Mayor of London and government.

In 2011 the event was held against the backdrop of serious rioting in Britain's cities.[1] There were fears that the event would be postponed.

Eventually, it went ahead, but with double the normal police presence. This brought allegations from event planners and festival participants that the number of police was provocative. Although there were incidents of violence they were sporadic and limited, the overwhelming media and community response was that the 2011 Carnival was a success. Because Notting Hill was relatively trouble free, the media portrayed it as a symbol of national healing.

The privileged position of the Carnival in this respect was used by event planners to highlight long-standing problems of under-funding. The Notting Hill Carnival relies upon voluntary labour. It has always been run on a shoestring. The resignation of the core event planning team was intended to highlight funding problems and pressurise official authorities, notably the Mayor's office, to provide secure sponsorship. In terms of crowd attraction and event barometrics, Notting Hill has become too big to fail. The festivities are a measure of the state of the nation, especially in respect of youth matters and race relations. Even if intense media coverage is confined to the duration of the Carnival, the event is judged to have more durable consequences in achieving social integration.

The Notting Hill Carnival is by no means the world's only example of this. Knowles's (1995) account of the Stratford Shakespeare Festival in Canada (which was launched in 1953) observes that the event has a recurring history of being used to highlight extraneous debates about Canadian nationhood.

This brings us to the question of the nature of event consciousness. It is oddly neglected in the event literature, which tends to presuppose only positive audience reactions, is cagey about the duration of effects on social consciousness and is not directed to elaborate the multiple meanings that audiences bring to events. We will come to consider the question of event consciousness in Chapter 7 of this study. But before coming to that point, another question must logically be brought into play: what are the roots of event attraction? For the issue of attraction is the mobilising device behind the generation and display of event consciousness.

Note

1   The rioting was a dislocation of social order, but despite the police clamp down, it was no threat to the state. The riots were dominated by looting. Controversially, looting might be defined as consumption without money. The 2011 UK riots were driven by consumer culture not an opposition to the state.

7

WHY ARE WE DRAWN TO EVENTS?

That there is a buzz about events and event management can scarcely be doubted. Live Aid (1985) was a global event that generated enormous media coverage and, for many people, remains revered as truly life-changing. Event management is regularly described by advocates as 'vibrant', 'relevant' and 'essential' to 'contemporary life' (Arcodia and Reid, 2004: 5; Bowdin et al., 2011). Events automatically signify vigour, excitement and revitalisation. Gallup (1988: xii), writing of the local and national impact of the Salzburg Arts Festival, documents a variety of observed and purported event-related social and psychological features:

> The Festival lasts for about five weeks a year, roughly between the end of July and the end of August. The quiet provincial city comes alive with the sound of music and theatre, the excitement of the crowds, the packed hotels, restaurants and cafes, the elegance of the visitors from all over the world.

These outcomes are oft-repeated in the professional event literature. Whether they be single-issue or cyclical in nature, events carry strong connotations of anticipation, pleasure, festivity and emotional uplift. The desire to see stellar acts in sport, music, business, academic life and other sectors of performance, or mix in gatherings of like-minded people, is mirrored by the keenly felt anticipation of departing momentarily from life routines and performing various rituals of transcendence.

The overtones of non-conformity and dissent are also important. Single-issue events are portrayed as stateless, direct action solutions to management problems that governments and corporations have botched. Events carry intimations of equality, shared responsibility, kinship and social inclusion. These qualities are highlighted by the PR–media hub which, for example, presents the Olympics as a celebration of fraternity and arts events such as the Edinburgh International Festival as jamborees that respect the family of humankind.

The popularity of events in contemporary life is reflected in the expansion of event training and provision. In the UK, there are over 68 event-related undergraduate courses and 20 postgraduate courses. This pattern is paralleled in the USA, Ireland, Germany, the Netherlands and India (Bowdin et al., 2011: 40). The rapid rate of growth has eroded student recruitment patterns in more established fields of study, especially leisure and recreation.[1]

Indeed, it is commonly accepted that there is now something quaint and old-fashioned about the latter. It is depicted as becalmed in debates about 'traditional' ideas of 'adequate state provision', 'social improvement', 'gender equality' and the defence of the principle of a 'just settlement for all' based in a partnership between the state, business and the people. These questions do not figure prominently in professional events literature. Events are portrayed as expressing the real needs of communities and pragmatically addressing moral and organisational issues. By implication, traditional systems of leisure, health and recreation are associated with donatory systems of provision based in bureaucratic principles of public funding through taxation and state administration. Against this, the philosophy of event management is an emotional combination of 'direct action' and 'people power'. Even large-scale corporate events carry the ideological baggage of 'listening to the consumer' and 'helping consumers get the best possible service'. By and large, questions of wealth redistribution and transforming the basis of public ownership and control are handled as if they belong to a bygone age.

Event management is, in fact, part of the neoliberal revolution in government. Its origins in the hospitality, leisure and tourism industries precede the New Right era of Margaret Thatcher, Ronald Reagan and their successors. Market logic in the age of large-scale urban-industrial organisation and mass communications recognised events as a major social mechanism of fundraising, moral regulation and performative labour, using play and leisure as resources to solve social and economic problems.

The neoliberal argument is that the market is a superior type of organisation to government. According to this logic, there is an iron law which holds that the state is inevitably the prisoner of social interests. In the period between 1945 and 1980, liberal and conservative concerns focused upon the cost of state regulation and the power of labour to influence the distribution of central wealth. It was contended that the postwar state was too interventionist and organised labour had grown overpowerful. The result was the stifling of enterprise. By the 1980s, the neoliberal revolution drove through a series of measures designed to deregulate the market. These included curbing the power of trade unions, privatising nationalised assets, reducing taxes on enterprise, permitting deindustrialisation, limiting workers' rights and abandoning the commitment to full employment. The market was to be set free and through this, the people too were to be liberated.

There are, of course, many objections that can be made about this line of reasoning. Not least the peculiarity of the proposition that the market is free. In view of what we know about social inequality and the concomitant disparity in power relations that enable markets to be rigged – the sub-prime lending arrangements that allowed some banks to achieve super-profits before the economic crash in 2008 is a case in point – this is beyond parody. However, now is not the place to delve into the many paradoxes of free market liberalism (but see Harvey, 2005; Judt, 2010; Stiglitz, 2010). Suffice to say that liberal logic in this respect is a major ingredient of contemporary event management. For the neo-liberal renaissance of the 1980s is the historical context in which this approach to resource management gained ascendancy in the leisure and voluntary sectors.

Event management presents itself as a *stateless solution* to public problems. It portrays its function as an impeccable media-savvy, popular response to achieving social inclusion and building effective responses to international emergencies. On the whole, statecraft is stereotyped as being incapable of optimally handling these issues. The preferred route of resolution is media communication and people power.

The *popular, inclusive* nature of events as high value stateless solutions to public ills is paramount in event mentality. Some form of market incentive system and deregulation are presupposed. All of this is adorned in the rhetoric of 'people power'. People are described as 'refusing to take it any more', 'seizing power' and 'making a stand'. The proposition that the man or woman in the street has the power to solve global problems is dubious. For it misses out the many stages of mediation and representation between the people and a set of policies. However, the language of equal inclusion, empowerment and 'everybody counts' is part of the event mainstream.

There is a powerful, unparticularised new broom quality about event cognition. It is as if leisure and recreation studies go hand in hand with the dying world of the clipboard, sellotape, blu-tak and the biro. In contrast, event management belongs to the new world of the lap-top, wi-fi, the mobile phone and the Cloud. Why should events be linked so strongly with anticipation, pleasure, festivity, inclusion and excitement? Why should the market and deregulation be presuppositions of most types of event intervention? And why should event planning seem to be so practical and modern, while state planning seems so grey and old-fashioned?

From the earliest days in human history carnival, feasts and festivals have been associated with exuberance, transgression and transcendence (Bakhtin, 1968; Stallybrass and White, 1986). To this day the celebration of carnival and mardi gras entails public role reversal, boundary busting and status levelling (Gaudet, 1998: 34). Carnival culture suggests connections with levels of reality that go beyond common or garden metrics of time and space. The Carnival in Rio and the Mardi Gras in New Orleans and Sydney use exhibitionism, samba, masks and transgression to express non-conformity. They aim to transport individuals from living social consciousness in a bubble of existence to universal themes and trans-personal identity. In this way, anthropologists argue, they symbolise the presence of transcendence and the eternal (Forsyth, 2001; Lowell Lewis, 2000; Turner, 1987: 76).

Global events certainly enlist many aspects from what we might call primordial systems of festivity and transcendence. But whereas these systems rely upon the treadmill of custom, global events harness the communication network to allow events to go global. Single-issue and cyclical events are portrayed as modern televisual spectacles that offer a departure from routine, instant social networking and intimations of a bigger reality *for the world.* The media portray single-issue and cyclical events as catalysts of life-affirming exhibitionism, festivity and transcendence. In the case of global cyclical events such as the Olympics and FIFA World Cup, excitement, festivity and anticipation now even encompass the pre-event bidding process through which nations compete to host the games. The build-up to the bids and the unfolding of strategies are now enlivened with colourful pageantry of bidding rituals and fervent media coverage. Hosting a single-issue or cyclical event has become an emblem of metropolitan and national prestige, with all of the implications of glamour, status and cohesion that come in its train.

The links between exhibitionism, transgression and events are associated intimately with the suspension of authority and control. Single-issue events like Live Aid (1985), Live Earth (2007) and the Haiti Relief Concert (2010) and cyclical events like Burning Man City are portrayed as representing the will of the people and proffering direct solutions to human problems. This is associated with dismantling barriers, overcoming reserve and combining productive resources. Even corporate events like cyclical company meetings that involve the whole workforce encourage workers to take the gloves off, avoid pussy-footing, put issues frankly to the bosses and exhibit unity (Bowdin et al., 2011).

The twinning of events with a community of common interests is especially strong. Events are associated with dissolving social hierarchy, overturning barricades and giving a voice to the little man or woman. In Live Aid (1985), Live 8 (2005), Live Earth (2007) and the Haiti Relief Concert (2010), the division between superstars and the network public is symbolically replaced with *team-world* consciousness. Bono, George Clooney, Julia Roberts, Angelina Jolie, Brad Pitt, Madonna, Al Gore and Jay Z are all in it together with us in the call for the relief of misery, the end to dictatorship, the establishment of global justice, or what have you. Although global event communication is based in the global media network, the relationship between celebrity activists and leaders is strenuously accented as *unmediated*. It is not just that Bono and Sir Bob Geldof stand shoulder to shoulder with us, they proclaim themselves to be in the same boat, stricken with common worries about global injustice and hunger, and earnestly in favour of a better future for all. The communication network is presented as merely a tool to achieve universally agreed ends. Through it, stars share their thoughts about the troubles in the world, act informally and in other ways bring the network public into their confidence in a common cause.

The lynch-pin of this relationship is the expression of altruism, empathy and responsibility towards others who are less fortunate than ourselves, whether they be the starving in Ethiopia or victims of terror in Darfur. Events allow ordinary citizens to vicariously perform an heroic role in challenging domination and torture everywhere.

This exploits and develops customs of hospitality and sharing, but crucially, it transmits them through the communication network. Celebrity culture has developed systems of *syndicated fraternity* aimed at network publics to personalise and augment the lustre of stars. Syndicated fraternity uses the star as a brand to build global interest and involvement (Rojek, 2012). Event planning uses the same strategy, often in partnership with global celebrities, to publicise and promote the event concept. The atmosphere of social inclusiveness is all-encompassing as the strong pledge allegiance to the needs of the weak and the persecuted. Hence, events are not just about coming together to solve common problems, they are about the social recognition of community and difference and the acknowledgement of being either 'modern' or in some sense, past it.

Cyclical corporate meetings involving the whole workforce give the same stress to inclusiveness, partnership and involvement. For example, it is emphasised that everyone is engaged in 'the business' and the business is greater than any individual or group. The value of the business in adding service to the customer is likewise emphasised. Challenging questions of the profit motive and exploitation are conveniently ignored in preference to accentuating the value of the corporation's activity in fulfilling consumer wants.

The Professionalisation of Events

In the last two decades immense strides have been made in the professionalisation of the event industry (Arcodia and Reid, 2004). Specialised knowledge, objective principles of competence and binding protocols have been introduced and consolidated into official training programmes. Professionalisation involves the delineation of dedicated fields of expertise and codification of essential standards of practice.

Getz and Wicks (1994: 108–9) outline the key professional content issues in the event management industry as follows:

- Knowledge of history of events.
- Competence with organising event types.
- Knowledge of event supply and demand factors.
- Event leadership styles.
- Competence in event goal setting.
- Knowledge of operational factors.
- Competence in event marketing principles.

In terms of event training key content issues draw upon a mix of eclectic traditions.

Among the knowledge base and investigative traditions involved are history, cultural geography, audiovisual, organisation studies, drama, economics, sociology and business studies. One might suppose that because event managers award such high status to quantitative metrics – notably the cost-benefit analysis of events, planning, designing, marketing, overseeing, risk management and evaluation – that the academic origins of the field of study primarily lie in economics and business studies. In fact, these disciplines are indirect influences. Event management modules figure in business studies and economics degrees and many business studies and economics departments employ dedicated specialists. However, this reflects the current prominence of events in social and economic life rather than an evolutionary relationship proper.

The academic roots of event management lie much deeper in hospitality studies, leisure and recreation studies and tourism studies. Events management modules developed as a sub-branch of these older, established disciplines. However, since the 1990s, the expansion of event management courses in the academy has been swift and apparently all-conquering. Event management is now the market leader in innovative training programmes in the leisure, sport and tourism industries.

In accounting for the rise of global events, the professional event industry literature is mostly naive and ingenuous. In general, it presents what amounts to a reprise of the old Whig version of history.[2] That is, expansion is explained almost wholly in economic and progressive terms as a reflection of rising levels of disposable income, growing corporate affluence, the ethical maturity of modern business leaders, the greater transparency of global problems achieved by communication power and an awareness of the marketing power of events in boosting civic cohesion and national pride (Bowdin et al., 2011). Events are thus explicitly twinned with rising affluence, greater consumer choice, stateless solutions, community enhancement and increased freedom. In a word, events are presented as part of the process of making the world a *better* place. This translates into a cost-benefit approach to events which tends to privilege benefits over costs. For example, Hall (1989) groups the impact of events under four headings: social and cultural, economic, political and environmental.

According to Hall (1989), the positive social and cultural effects of events include the sharing of experience, revitalising traditions, affirming community, increasing social cohesion and enriching cultural experience. With respect to economic impacts, he mentions the multiplier effect in increasing investment and tourism, higher tax revenue, job creation and enriching local and national infrastructures. Coming to political impact, he lists generating international prestige, increasing public awareness, cementing responsibilities and rights and increasing local and national pride. Finally, with respect to environmental impact, Hall (1989) mentions showcasing the environment, producing models of best practice, urban renewal and transformation.

It is true that Hall (1989) goes on to provide a balance sheet of costs. However, these are exclusively confined to questions of event logistics and immediate social consequences. For example, among the economic negative impacts, he lists financial mismanagement, financial loss and exploitation. Similarly, under social and cultural negative impacts he mentions community alienation, bad behaviour, substance abuse, loss of amenity, pollution, noise disturbance and destruction of heritage.

This largely progressive account concentrates upon technical and operational issues. The question of the relationships between event management and the civic regulation of those sectors of the populations who become homeless, unemployed or are disadvantaged in other ways by events and the wider topic of using event romance as a tool for social ordering are not addressed. The technical, logistical bias is reinforced by content issues in professional event management training. Although the historical roots of events in carnival, festivals and 19th-century trade exhibitions are acknowledged, there is a conspicuous absence of systematic attempts to locate the phenomenon in broader questions of power, civic regulation and social ordering. To the extent that these attempts exist, they reside in the more deeply rooted and critical social science disciplines.

The Exhibitionary and Performance Complexes

Yet when one scrutinises the event industry field from these established perspectives, event management does not really seem either distinctive or new. Maurice Roche (2000, 2002) traces event culture back to the international expositions (1851–1939) and the consecutive emergence of public culture. He maintains that the success of the Great Exhibition in London (1851) was emulated in metropolitan centres as a business opportunity for entrepreneurs and a means of expressing civic pride and boosting the local economy through tourism. Already the multiplier effect of events was appreciated, i.e. in attracting sponsorship, metropolitan and government investment and flocks of visitors to contribute to the local economy. The Expo movement included staged games and international sporting events (Paris 1900, St Louis 1904 and London 1908). They provided the catalyst for the revival of the Olympics, which had fallen dormant since Ancient Greek times. According to Roche, events arose through the acknowledgement of new responsibilities of citizenship that reflected and reinforced the revolutions in communications and transport. He invites us to regard them as mechanisms for defining and redefining modern civic identity. 'Take pride in your Event' was translated into the exhortation to take pride in yourself.

In contrast, Tony Bennett (1988), following Foucault's cast of thought with respect to surveillance and discursive moral regulation, refers to the emergence of an 'exhibitionary complex' in the 19th century. That is, the use of organised spectacle as a device for building a public culture of conformity and consent. The emphasis here, *à la* Foucault, is upon the use of the spectacle as a means of affirmative discipline. In other words, taking pride in your event is not ultimately about self-liberation, but capitulation to moral regulators. By opening up a collective incident or emergency to the general public (rather than the rich elite) and making it a topic for all, ordinary people developed a sense of pride and self-confirmation in issues hitherto 'privately' managed by the state and corporation. By identifying with the generosity and munificence of the state, the people take it upon themselves to administer policing roles, in respect of emotional restraint, national obedience and group identity, that were formally the reserve of the public bureaucracy. Pride in the event therefore becomes a branch of moral regulation, no different in principle from schooling or policing. Thus, exhibition space operates finally to reinforce social hierarchy and engineer consent.

Roche (2002: 23–4) prefers the term 'performance complex' and relates it to the increasing prominence of visual culture in public life. The display of consent is the means of conveying personal status and acquiring the regard of others. Event participation is an arena of emotional regimentation and performance. It provides a stage for social affirmation and self-gratification. Participating in the event is therefore a means of adding a new dimension to the presentation of the self.

The authors are not quite splitting hairs. The concept of exhibition implies organised spectacle and the compliance of audiences to predetermined goals devised and implemented by exhibition planners. Roche accepts that these elements were part of the international expositions and global sporting events. However, he regards them as symptoms of a wider need for performance and display that gradually characterised an important part of modern public culture. So rather than events being imposed upon the general public as a means of organising conformity, the appetite arose, as it were, spontaneously, *from within*.

Both authors argue that the development of these phenomena was central to the rational recreation movement which sought to use organised play and programmatic education as mechanisms of cultural pedagogy and discipline. Bennett wants us to see exhibitions as instruments of discipline designed ultimately to produce docile bodies. In contrast, Roche comes to the question of discipline via the work of Erving Goffman (1959, 1971), Michel Foucault (1975, 1981) and Judith Butler (1990, 1997). That is, with an appreciation of the importance of visual culture, theatricality and embodiment in modern public life. For Roche, expositions and international sporting events are more truly participatory than they are for Bennett. In addition to discipline and pedagogy he sees them as occasions for crowd display and performance.

In their own contrasting ways Bennett (1988) and Roche (2000, 2002) do a good job in clarifying why events have become prominent in modern public culture. Event culture has spawned an event industry, bound by principles of professional practice, which has grown rapidly since the 1990s. However, its roots lie in the exhibitionary and performance complexes which are intertwined with much broader, deeper processes of industrial emotional governance and moral regulation. This train of thought is not adequately developed in the professional events literature.

Events exploit and develop older traditions of impression management. Writers in urban studies comment that while events are strongly associated with urban regeneration, social integration and cultural transformation, they present a 'sanitised' version of culture rather than an expression of cultural life in all of its 'multiplicity', 'multivocality' and 'complexity'. A common aspect of this is the bracketing out of the less 'palatable' elements of cultural experience, e.g. crime, inequality, racism, housing, illness, death and police brutality (Johansson and Kociatkiewicz, 2011). Providing a largely progressive reading of events is unsatisfactory because it obscures the connection between the expansion of this industry and the rise of neoliberalism and communitarian philosophy.

Sanitisation is an aspect of event planning and management that was anticipated in the critical literature on the society of the spectacle (Debord, 1967; Kracauer, 1995). This critical perspective regarded events as above all exercises in social control. Modern technologies of representation allow events to be presented in such an affirmative, warm light that they compel the network public to submit and stifle criticism. The aim of the event in the society of the spectacle is to divert majority attention from questions of popular agitation, mobilisation and resistance. The spectacle addresses the illusory community, often in ways that are memorable and satisfying, but in the end leaves people isolated and disaggregated. On one hand, global events are the affirmation of humanism, since they 'do not allow man to wither away'; on the other hand, they make the incidents and emergencies that give rise to events impenetrable and ultimately contribute to self-estrangement, since they neglect to address the underlying structures and processes that precipitate and post-date them (Kracauer, 1995: 83).

Communitarianism and Event Management

Management initiatives and social movements bear the birth-marks of their times. Global event management is characterised by an alliance between populism and the market. In addition to the influence of neoliberalism, it owes much to the communitarian movement of the 1980s which privileged the notion of responsible citizenship over questions of economic inequality and political injustice. Since we have already touched upon the relationship between events and neoliberalism, I will concentrate here upon the communitarian influence. Communitarianism identifies political agency with reformism rather than revolution. As such, it forms an easy alliance with propagandists of the market since it dismisses class-based solutions in favour of a version of pluralism that defines collective responsibility and problem solving with a sort of DIY activism.

Communitarianism is an eclectic philosophy drawing on some aspects of conservative and liberal elements interlaced with strands of *narodnik* sentimentality and anti-government protest.[3] At the same time it rejects purely market solutions to problem solving on the grounds that they inevitably lead to social division. One of the most powerful iterations of the communitarian way of thinking is Etzioni's (1993) *The Spirit of Community*. In order to clarify how event management stands in relation to communitarianism it is useful to re-examine the main features of Etzioni's argument.

Communitarianism is a revivalist social movement with strong traditional roots in American society. It started in the early 1990s as a protest against the alleged moral decay and fragmentation of American life. In a foretaste of event vocabulary it calls upon ordinary decent people not to take it any more and to stand up and be counted. In this case, social reaction is not called upon so much on account of an urgent, international emergency but more by the misdirected drift of society. Invoking the founding fathers, communitarianism urges Americans to cast aside empty materialism and intrusive government and restore community values. Etzioni (1993: 248–55) condemns the Left for social engineering in schooling, welfare and sexual inequality. For him this has resulted in a society wherein people recognise rights but not responsibilities. However, he is no apologist for the Right. He maintains that the unfettered market produces unacceptable levels of self-interest, greed, violence and careless hedonism.[4] He calls for a revitalised form of activism, based upon a middle path championing moral regeneration and the restoration of civic virtue. His motto is 'don't get mad, get going' (Etzioni, 1993: 249).

Event management shares the spirit of proclaiming that the conventional Left and Right traditions are exhausted. Communitarianism is populist and based in civic action. So is event management. Both hold the conviction that stateless solutions are better answers because they spring directly from the will of the people. Both privilege activism. 'Get going' is the message of Live Aid, Live Earth and the event management movement in general.

However, activism is only empowering if it is rooted in firmly based analysis of means and ends. Communitarianism, and a strong strain within the philosophy of event management, encourages the sort of passionate emotionalism that prevents you from seeing the wood for the trees. Because both define conditions in terms of emergencies, incidents and urgent solutions, the responsibility to act precedes a viable plan for action. The result is often the mistargeting of resources and the creation of excessive ideals of goal achievement and redemption that in the long run, almost always, end in anti-climax. Because both prioritise action over accountability or programmatic, year-on management and investment. Activism becomes an end in itself. It is celebrated as an intrinsic social good and in some cases shades over into outright narcissism.

This brings us to an extremely important question: the nature of event consciousness. It is an interesting subject to address because event managers claim to know how the public think. Market research and opinion polling are routinely used to provide data collection that is the basis for post-evaluation event analysis. However, these data are not generally expressed in terms defined by the audience. On the contrary, they are framed in terms set by event organisers and clipboard researchers. The next chapter turns to examine the distinctive qualities of event consciousness with a view to considering how big is the gap between the claims of event managers and the behaviour of event participants.

Notes

1   Leisure and recreation departments have been rather subdued about the threat posed by event management.
2   The Whig version of history presents it as an inevitable march of progress.
3   The term *narodnik* refers to a middle-class, socially conscious populist movement in Russia in the 1860s and 1870s. The *narodniks* regarded the peasantry as the revolutionary class. As such peasant life was glorified. The later Bolshevik movement rather ridiculed *narodnik* enthusiasms, bracketing them with bourgeois woolly-mindedness.
4   Communitarianism is essentially a conservative, revivalist movement. It did not so much seek to examine the imposed values of the state, rather it sought to appeal to essentialist so-called 'nationalist' values.

8

WHAT IS EVENT CONSCIOUSNESS?

Event consciousness may be defined as an orientation to global problem solving that privileges high profile disaggregated, discontinuous populist responses over fiscal, reformist or revolutionary solutions.[1] The term is mainly applicable to celanthropists, the PR–media hub and the audience to which they cater. Obviously, clients and executives have a systematic and continuous interest in event initiatives, post-event fund distribution and project management. In contrast, the activities of the PR–media hub are weighted to maximise immediate publicity equipped with a major social impact pay-off and encourage fund accumulation.

In general, they aim to focus global event consciousness upon a trio of issues: the rationale for the event (natural disaster, protest against social exclusion, green house gas emissions, celebrations of fellowship, as with the Olympic spirit), the programme of attractions and the stated action points arising there from. The last may take the form of medical relief, project aid or social investment programmes (as with cheap housing and associated infrastructural benefits packaged with global cyclical event bids such as the Olympics or the FIFA World Cup).

Event consciousness offers stateless solutions to global social and environmental crises. Globalisation highlights the inability of national governments to manage global risks arising from climate change, terrorism, nuclear catastrophe and economic meltdown. The world is regularly presented by the media as existing in a state of perpetual emergency. As public confidence in national institutions to manage global threats has receded, the personal has been projected to the forefront of public life (Furedi, 2004: 54). Event consciousness connects every caring, feeling person to global concerns. It postulates that the individual is a capable, competent agent in a world dominated by ostrich-like government and vulture corporations. The fundamental presupposition is impeccably humanist. Namely, that the individual can make a real difference to global affairs.

Embedded in this philosophy is a complex understated emotional complex of compassion addressing the contradiction between the plight of victims (of poverty, hunger, natural disaster, pollution, imprisonment, torture, the suffering of the Earth itself, etc.) and the complacency of the better off who are stereotyped as going about their business in an envelope of selfish indifference to global suffering. Live Aid, Sport Aid and Live Earth exploited and developed awareness and giving as pass-cards of emotional literacy. This system of belief lavishes a sense of righteous unity and uncompromising resolve upon the crowd in the stadium and network public behind the campaign. What is not often commented upon is the element of judgementalism and self-approval that also flows through its veins. By definition if you choose not to be aware and do not give, you are part of the problem.

In principle, there is nothing wrong with prevailing upon individuals to care and act in order to make a difference to poverty, hunger, global pollution and the enforcement of human rights. However, there is a thin line between individuals making a difference and *the* individual making a grandiose personal pact to save the world. The latter has more to do with ego management than global problem resolution. The element of megalomania in global event management is apparent in the public deportment of celebrity figureheads who situate themselves before the public as nobly saving the hungry in Africa, ending poverty, banishing war crimes and ending global warming. The emotional baiting in event publicity often produces astonishing acts of self-aggrandisement in the guise of helping 'humankind'.

The Make Poverty History (MPH) campaign in 2005 developed the tagline: 'think globally, act locally'. This is high in emotionalism (Nash, 2008: 172–3). It builds a powerful sense of fraternisation (we are all in it together) and identity (we can act 'as one'). But it is not a genuinely compelling *strategy* because it fails to build a viable structure of transformative politics capable of transferring meaningful economic and political power from the industrially advanced world to the developing economies. Indeed, in some ways, it reinforces old, discredited colonial presumptions since it implies a gulf between the developed world that has progressed and the developing world that, by implication, languishes in a stupor of poverty, want and misery (Moyo, 2010).

The division between the developed and developing world is a false dichotomy. The developed world is not, as it were, poverty-proof; while conversely, the developing world is not wholly poor. The reality is more complex. The distribution of actual wealth does not follow neat geopolitical boundaries. The trans-global elite are not confined to the metropolitan centres of the West. On the contrary, the flexibility and global reach of elite power presupposes mobility and multiple HQs.

The emphasis in the Live Aid and Live 8 events on the plight of the developing world, renders the poor in the economically developed world as forgotten citizens – as Bob Dylan's outburst in support of struggling Mid-Western farmers on stage in Philadelphia at the Live Aid (1985) broadcast sought to publicise.[2] In linking events to incidents and emergencies, event consciousness obfuscates the geopolitical dynamics of inequality. Even when post-event funding spreads money more widely than the emergency that precipitated the event, majority opinion sees everything through the lens of the original emergency. This is a tribute to the potency of the PR–media hub which fixes images of emergency as the symbol of event action. But the symbol has the awkward effect of casting an unhelpful halo around separate aid initiatives that derive from the original event publicity and fund accumulation. By distorting majority opinion, events make it more difficult to achieve adhesive, lasting solutions to world hunger, pollution and injustice.

Event consciousness prefigures one-stop, big bang solutions to global problems. In privileging and exhibiting immediate, heartfelt emotions over engagement with the context in which these emotions are nourished and exchanged, the understanding of event consciousness pushes meaningful reform off the rails. The spontaneity and depth of emotion is disarticulated from questions of global power and invisible government.

Events are settings to which most people commute from habitual life. For a week, a day or an afternoon the cares of the work routine are left behind. It is going too far to attribute bad faith to the majority of attendees. Some participants are energised by the event to maintain continuity with the event philosophy and the event agenda. However, the majority commute to this philosophy and agenda in the same way that people commute to work and leave the obligations of work behind at clock-off time. If this is not the case, why does the world still face problems of hunger, injustice, pollution and much else besides?

The drift towards event commuting is also part of event consciousness in company meetings. Since the company event is generally held off-site, participants naturally relate to it as a 'treat' or an 'awayday'. Off-site events translate organisational protocol into a different register. The provision of free food, access to gym or pool facilities and a 'free drinks' float at the bar contribute to a sense of 'time off'. Events symbolise the 'break', but it is always an empirical question if the break achieves real organisational reorientation.

In humanitarian global event planning a more nuanced set of considerations come into play. One of the most egregious mistakes that follows from obscuring the question of context is that events are typically portrayed as *emergencies*. Because of this, events are associated with crisis management rather than the result of deep-rooted economic, social and political *structural* inequalities.

The prominent, publicity-grabbing involvement of celebrities, who, as a category, are depicted by the PR–media hub as living on the frontier of existence, intensifies the association between events and emergency by highlighting the exotic exceptionalism of events and the high profile status of those who respond to them.[3] Metaphorically speaking, the audience is encouraged to follow these celebrity pied pipers to the frontier of human experiences of poverty and hunger and empathise with these issues. They are minded to do this not only because they are subject to images of suffering, want and risk but also because they are aware of being conducted thereto by exotic, revered creatures who themselves are situated on the frontier.

To go further into this, as a social form, celebrities are understood to 'live on the edge', to take career and health risks from which the rest of us flinch. As such we assume that they must be familiar with a range of artistic reactions to questions of need, extremity and misery that are not in the band-width of ordinary people (Rojek, 2012). In this sense, the frontier existence of the celebrity, with its staple features of risk, incident and emergency, mirrors the frontier existence of the poor, the homeless, victims of torture, etc. Although the polarities of wealth and influence between them need hardly be elaborated, emotionally speaking, both the extreme position of the celebrity and the emergency of the victim occupy the same space of *frontierism* which contrasts with the so-called predictable, tepid, emotionally restrained life of the mass.

Event publicity explicitly demands that the crowd and the network public at home take risks, to put their money where their mouth is, to step out of their life bubble and *get involved*. The willingness of celebrities like Bono, Bob Geldof, George Clooney, Angelina Jolie and Madonna to put themselves on the line provides attractive role models for agents of publicity. Stars risk media vilification for being seen as pampered 'big citizens' who do not really know what they are talking about, and opposition from the state and voluntary sector as inadequate economic agents of global relief. This contributes to the romance of charity because it presents celanthropists as champions who, by their example, encourage the people to play the part of heroes. It is as if the people alone can provide the solutions to problems that stump state highbrow civil servants and fox corporate CEOs.

In this and other ways, event consciousness works through transparent but frightfully crude lines of social inclusion and social exclusion. The culturally aware, being defined as of good heart and clear conscience, are placed on one side, aligned with the powerless and those in want; on the other side are the brain-blind and selfish, preoccupied with their narrow interests and ignorant of the relationship between the consequences of these interests and the fate of the planet.

The attribution of powerlessness and want to entire continents creates as many foes as friends. Understandably, many Africans take exception to Western metropolitan, pampered superstars like Bono, Sir Bob Geldof, Oprah Winfrey and Madonna taking it upon themselves to speak 'for Africa' (Easterly, 2007; Moyo, 2010). Beyond this, it is also risky to draw simple lines between those of good heart and those of bad faith in the economically better-off countries. Cultural distinctions are seldom so neat and clear cut. Profound tactical and strategic errors derive from insufficient ethnographic and theoretical regard in this respect.

Event consciousness falls in train with the principles of mass psychology described so cogently by Moscovici (2010). Above all, the event programme creates an appealing facade of noble, heroic leaders and offers a string of designer-based activities that provide a catalyst for the expression of repressed emotions through festive participation geared to engineer composite but ultimately conformist reactions. The imagination of the crowd and the television viewer at home is seized by 'exaggerated arguments', 'spectacular examples' and 'gripping short cuts' (Moscovici, 2010: 99). In the digital age the reduced importance of face-to-face discussion, the dispersal of the crowd and the authority of network power elicits syndicated forms of unity. Global togetherness is orchestrated by media network corporations who set banners of social recognition (of social problems, possibilities, threats, etc.) and adumbrate an agenda of action. The most striking thing about this togetherness is its *mediated* character. To quote Moscovici (2010: 195) again:

> One might wonder how people who neither see each other, come into contact with each other nor affect each other can be associated. What link is established between people when they are at home reading their paper or listening to their radio and all spread over a very wide geographical area? The answer, of course, is that they form a public and are subject to suggestion, because each one of them, at the same time, is convinced that he is sharing an idea or a desire with a large number of his fellows.

So much for the logic of 'illusory communities'! When emotions go through so many layers of processing and refinement it raises the question of who owns them.

Intrinsic to Castells' (2009) model of communication power is the capacity of network interests to marinate network publics so that they eventually latch on to a preferred outcome and lubricate this as 'common sense'. In the digital age, establishing common ground is the precondition for forming the illusory community. Network power has formidable capacity to pitch people into this or that course of action, because it controls the bulk of global data upon which personal action and performative labour rely.

At the global level, event consciousness is usually founded in the conspicuous involvement of network power and celanthropists. It always presupposes intensive PR–media involvement. The techniques it employs include games, comedy, music, drama, play and other festive elements to elicit a general sense of fun and transcendence. TV documentaries and strike-up-the-band interviews with event figureheads are also important instruments in the PR–media tool-box.

The urgent demand for direct responses is bolstered by media-genic images of intense suffering and acute want that legitimate the 'short cuts' in reason to which Moscovici (2010) alludes. Occasionally, emergencies are portrayed as the result of deep-seated tendencies in society that should be eliminated by a sequence of celanthropic events. The Make Poverty History and Fair Trade campaigns are examples. More commonly they are presented as acts of God or quirks of nature, which conveniently removes the obligation to seek tangible social and economic causes.

Throughout, an MTV level of comprehension and debate, based around 'exaggerated arguments', 'spectacular examples' and 'gripping short cuts', mostly prevails. Advocates and activists might say that this style of communication is the most efficient means of making an impact and achieving results. But since when has exaggeration been successful in yielding balanced conclusions and prudent initiatives? The danger is that in acting rashly, resource distribution becomes leaky, with a portion of funds intended for good causes draining away for other purposes. As we shall see presently, this accusation is made prominently by critics of the distribution of the global revenue, believed to be £150 million, generated by the Live Aid event in 1985.

Event consciousness directly relates programmes of attractions to crisis programmes of action. However, the logic between the two is seldom subject to robust public enquiry. Post-event evaluation exercises into the practical consequences of events in producing positive relief outcomes and engendering global activism are usually confined to the event executive and held *in camera*. Centre stage are event symbols, emotive appeals to care and to act, celebrity endorsements, television coverage, acting out the part of global heroes in public, the polish of corporate and government support and, of course, the artistic and social merits of the programme of event attractions.

Global events fuse the rhetoric of activism with orchestrated *camaraderie*. This is intensified by the presiding sanitised message that meaningful care and action can be activated simply by buying a ticket for a concert or sports tournament or texting a charitable donation through on your mobile phone. This *works* in terms of generating public awareness, majority sympathy and raising funds. However, it does next to nothing to prevent the root causes of the problems that precipitate emergencies on the event horizon.

Despite appearances, most human catastrophes do not really arise from fate or the hand of God. Most acts of nature can be anticipated and handled more effectively by adequate, planned, year-on, coordinated investment measures and prudent monitoring. Events like Live Aid, Sport Aid and Live Earth raise funds for campaigning and limited coordination and funding of relief programmes. However, their ultimate value is publicity (Easterly, 2007; Moyo, 2010; Sachs, 2010, 2011).

To the extent that this raises social consciousness about global questions it is laudable. However, a big problem with global event management and the event consciousness which it generates is that they prioritise the event over the chain of causes that engender the human problem that is the event's *raison d'être*. This puts the cart before the horse. Global event management pours concentration upon suffering, want or the desirability of universal fellowship and depicts them not as symptoms of larger questions pertaining to power, inequality and injustice but as acute problems that sprout up in random isolation from deeper questions of power and domination. Even when the attempt to relate human problems to larger questions of power, inequality and injustice is made, the lines become quickly blurred by event glamour and the paraphernalia of celebrity publicity. In some cases the agenda risks being appropriated by canny publicity seekers pursuing separate ends. As we shall see presently, the celanthropists behind the Make Poverty History campaign found their message diverted and appropriated by organisers of the G8 summit in Gleneagles (2007) who required a 'big joined-up question' to publicise their event and gain the attention of the world's media.

Of course, it would be an error to infer that event management is about a sort of resigned acceptance with respect to bigger questions of the geopolitics of global power and economic inequality. Such questions can hardly be avoided. Famine in Ethiopia, genocide in Darfur and social exclusion from participation in the Olympics and other sports tournaments are rightly challenged by event celanthropists, but they are mostly addressed as either separate or detached from the *events themselves*. Event consciousness focuses social awareness upon the immediate incident or emergency behind the event and the nature of the event programme above the economic and political sequence behind the emergency.

This has led some commentators to be scornful of the radicalism of modern event celanthropy. For example, William Easterly (2010) contends that celanthropy lacks the means to rise above *technocratic* responses to global problems. Events can generate resources and alleviate some aspects of global emergencies without addressing the more complex question of root causes. This is the modern equivalent of fiddling while Rome burns.

Thus, Bono and Bob Geldof condemn the privileges, hypocrisy and waste of the G8 leaders and George Clooney denounces the complicity of Western core powers with the dictatorial regime in Sudan.[4] However, they do not agitate or combine for economic and political retrenchment based around the subversion of G8 domination. By subversion here is meant the overthrow of G8 hegemonic domination, the rejection of G8 leaders who act as apologists for global inequality and pollution, and the reallocation of resources in the name of global distributive justice.

To some extent, this is understandable. The benign use of G8 power is the objective to which Bono, Geldof, Clooney and others set their formidable skills of people power and communication. At the same time, fundamental, irreversible fiscal tightening upon G8 corporations and populations together with bundled wealth redistribution would do more than all of the global events in human history put together to make a significant contribution to persistent questions of hunger, needless disease, poverty and greenhouse gas emissions. A 10% increase in personal taxation in the wealthy countries or a 15% tax on corporation profits and executive bonuses over an agreed threshold would go a long way to make a difference to most of the popular causes that events promulgate.

The Event as a White Elephant

That, by and large, modern celanthropists do not pursue the logic of critical political economy aggravates the likes of Easterly (2007: 7–10; 2010) on the grounds of relevance and realism. He suggests that event consciousness produces a white elephant – big publicity, the arousal of deep emotions of care and a programme of action that merely tinkers with underlying problems and diverts attention from the question of the power structure of the global economy.

By way of illustration, the Make Poverty History (MPH) campaign was built around a radical, far-reaching agenda of trade justice, debt cancellation and global justice (Brassett, 2008: 325). It was instrumental in persuading the G8 Gleneagles Summit (2005) to undertake to double financial assistance by pledging to assign an additional $50 billion per year by 2010 to foreign aid; while $1 billion per year of debt was cancelled for 18 of the most indebted nations. The campaign called upon the EU and USA to drop illegitimate or unpayable debt and stop maintaining harmful tariffs and subsidies while bullying poor countries into opening their markets.

At the time of the Gleneagles G8 communique this was portrayed as a watershed in relations between the economically advanced world and the emerging and developing countries. For the first time, partly through the efforts of celanthropy, advocates like Bono and Geldof and the MPH campaign, the better off were providing meaningful commitments to the emerging world. It has not quite turned out like that.

For the record, by 2011, according to the Organisation for Economic Cooperation and Development (OECD), G8 aid was $10 billion short of what was promised at Gleneagles. The EU provided only 60% of what was pledged in 2005. Of the $25 billion earmarked for sub-Saharan Africa only $11 billion was delivered. The OECD estimates a 40% shortfall partly due to the refusal of some ministers of finance to allow for the effect of inflation (Elliott, 2011). The failure of the G8 to maintain pledges on expenditure underlines the weakness of voluntary groups who have no real powers of enforcement and rely upon moral force to win the day.

The inability of global event management to move from the romance of charity to the logic of political economy imposes insurmountable limits upon the transformative power at its disposal. Easterly (2007: 7–10; 2010) and Sachs (2010, 2011) contend the result of event management is piecemeal technocratic reform rather than fundamental system change. By this logic, what is revealing about event consciousness is not the questions it asks, but the questions it passes over in monkish silence.

Why does the demand to relieve third world hunger and poverty halt before demanding the dismantling of the exploitative social, economic and political apparatus that makes hunger and poverty persist? For it is widely agreed that this apparatus is the root cause of the problem. What leads us to pay for the relief of victims of genocide though one-off charity donations rather than agitating, combining and acting to overthrow the brutal regimes that rule by torture, jail, the whip and the rifle and dismantle the collusion of Western powers which supports these regimes? How can we deplore environmental pollution while defending the freedom of families to own three cars, allow sports utility vehicle (SUV) production to thrive for all who can afford it, insist on the right to have unlimited air travel and resist tax hikes to pay for subsidised public transport?

Event consciousness is about a battle for the heart not the mind. It revolves around an unbalanced, emotive fixation upon 'incidents' and 'emergencies' to the exclusion of fully addressing the geopolitical issues that precede and post-date them. Typically, it extracts events from causal chains, defines them as 'abnormalities' or 'acts of God' and fastens upon a strategy of immediate relief rather than strategic structural retrenchment. On the whole, an assessment of the historically human-made conditions that trigger events is either veiled or excluded outright.

Because of this events are capable of only a tactical, technocratic response to global problems. Wider strategies of geopolitical realignment, that would genuinely 'feed the world', 'stop green house gas emissions' and 'make poverty history', are left in limbo. The result is that event consciousness cannot usually go beyond a crisis response. A geopolitical strategy of fiscal discipline, power realignment, intercontinental income redistribution and monitoring is massively underdeveloped.

Some commentators go further. Global event management is denounced as producing the explicit ideological effect of prioritising subjective responsibility over imperialism in explaining third world poverty and obscuring the operations of multinational corporations, the International Monetary Fund (IMF) and the World Bank in entrenching the development gap (Moyo, 2010). By privileging individual action and voluntary donations over the collective assault on hereditary privilege and institutionalised power, global events reinforce a neoliberal approach to government (Sivandan, 1990: 22).

We can go deeper into the issues involved by examining some case studies of single-issue event impact and post-event project evaluation. By so doing we can see more plainly how event consciousness lavishes publicity and generates excessive single-issue outbursts of emotionalism which create a white elephant that actually makes it harder to achieve effective system change.

The two cases that will be examined in the following chapter are the use of events to criticise official impact management initiatives to Hurricane Katrina (2005) and accountancy irregularities and fund appropriation for military ends of Live Aid money by the Mariam government in Ethiopia and Tigray rebel interests. This discussion paves the way for a more pointed analysis of the use of politics to appropriate events which takes up Chapter 11 of this book.

Notes

1   Event consciousness is above all an emotional reaction to social and economic questions. Emotionalism is explicitly exploited and developed by event manners and managers. Event management is an appeal to the heart above the mind.

2   Dylan gave an impromptu speech suggesting that *some* of the Live Aid cash should be diverted to help bankrupt farmers in the Mid-West. Dylan's bracketing of the plight of the starving in Ethiopia with farmers who were defaulting on their mortgages in the Mid-West was widely seen as ill judged and objectionable.

3   Elsewhere I have argued that superstars are located at the extremes of human existence (Rojek, 2012). They have access to wealth, political influence, sexual possibilities that far exceed ordinary experience. This condition of being situated 'on the edge' translates to the identification of superstars with those who are, globally speaking, at the bottom of the file. This carries over into the self-appointed role of humanitarian superstars as Good Samaritans and saviours.

4   At the same time, Clooney is refreshingly honest about event consciousness. The Not On Our Watch (NOOW) website carries a clip of him declaring, 'frankly, our team of policy wonks and super nerds could use an injection of MTV style' (notonourwatchproject.org; accessed 11 January 2011). The clip also carried news that NOOW's 'Satellite Sentinel Project' designed to track abuse in Sudan would be joined by MTV and mtv (the corporation's 24-hour college network) to amplify satellite tracking findings and provide analysis.

9

WHAT DO SINGLE-ISSUE EVENTS DO?

This chapter examines two types of single-issue events to explore three questions. How are single-issue events used to expose the policies of official institutions? What tactics are used to deny arguments that single-issue events do not achieve their official ends? How do events challenge official narratives and expedite resistance and opposition? The case studies are meant to be indicative, not exhaustive. The point is to develop a picture of events that is more realistic than the one-sided, progressive view generally advanced in the professional events literature. The case studies focus on two examples in detail. Indeed by focusing on the political and economic machinations that precede and post-date events I am deliberately challenging the laudatory, worthy, over-consensual ethos that, for my money, characterises the professional event literature.[1]

The first examines the use of a fundraising event aimed to provide relief for the devastation caused by Hurricane Katrina (2005). This is worthy of attention because it illustrates how events can expose official cover-ups and politicise audiences. States and corporations do not have a monopoly over the use of communication power to influence cognition. The Concert for Hurricane Relief (2005) embarrassed government officials by providing an unscripted critique of public underfunding in the Mississippi delta region which was allegedly based in racism and profiteering.

The second example addresses what is arguably the most famous humanitarian global event of the last half century. Namely, the Live Aid (1985) concert for famine relief in Ethiopia. This high profile event garnered such a bouquet of media praise that criticism of post-event fund distribution was stifled and made to seem ill mannered. Event organisers met allegations of fund misappropriation with heated scorn. Yet academic research reveals a more complex picture. I have labelled the two case studies considered here as examples of event exposure and event denial. Let us consider them in turn.

Event Exposure

Perhaps the largest public cost of privileging a tactical over a strategic response in event culture is the implication that catastrophe and disaster are *abnormal* features of the human condition caused by extraordinary natural or unpredictable forces. This was how the official PR–media hub at the federal level in the USA and at the local level in Louisiana tried to legitimate the public handling of the devastation caused by Hurricane Katrina. The staunch official line, which admittedly became harder to sustain after the emergence of a counter-culture of popular resistance and media criticism, was that Katrina was a natural catastrophe that no-one could have predicted. Further, official relief agents were said to be hampered by the foolish obduracy of local people in stubbornly clinging to their flooded homes. As a rider, it was insisted that official budgeted state resources were fit for purpose to deal with the tasks of emergency relief and reconstruction. On this reckoning it was nature that had caused the problem, but the ignorance of those worst affected that turned a natural disaster into a national tragedy.

Quantitatively speaking, there is no dispute about the human cost of Katrina. The hurricane left at least 1557 dead, 10,000 stranded, 430,000 homes damaged, 140,000 homes destroyed. The economic cost was estimated at $125 billion (Aldrich and Crook, 2008: 379).

It is now generally accepted that the loss of life and economic devastation was significantly worsened by ineffectual hazard mitigation at city and federal levels (Brinkley, 2006; Kellner, 2007; Trotter and Fernandez, 2009). In particular, the authorities are castigated for being heedless of Met Office warnings of extreme weather. Additionally, over a long period, neoliberal policies of deregulation had allegedly led to the poor maintenance of flood defences and little investment in drainage systems in low-lying areas. Decades of under-investment shackled the ability of the Federal Emergency Management Agency (FEMA) and local authorities to launch effective responses when the walls of the Mississippi levee were breached (Freudenberg et al., 2009). The US government is held to have performed at a 'sub-optimal' level in handling the emergency. This is now widely explained in terms of over-confidence, hubris, insensitivity to repeated warnings and 'wishful thinking' with respect to existing politics, practices and structures of hazard mitigation. In addition, and crucially, after 9/11 government policy placed strategy and budgetary responsibility to deal with the protection of the US homeland and the fight against terrorism at the head of its agenda. This diverted funds from investment in non-terrorist hazard mitigation which was judged by government officials and the PR–media hub to be of lower publicity value and risk evaluation (Parker et al., 2009).

Worse, in some circles conventional wisdom now maintains that disaster and alleged risk management in the city were freighted with unacceptable racist undertones. Suffering, want and homelessness were concentrated disproportionately in black areas of the city. This is because the black population occupied the flood prone lower 9th Ward from which, for at least two generations, middle-class and working-class whites had fled for the suburbs. Although 80–90% of the city was flooded, and white housing suffered immense destruction, the black population experienced greater distress because many were too poor to have effective transportation, insurance cover or anywhere else to go (Atkins and Moy, 2005: 917). According to Allen (2007: 466–7) more than 105,000 city dwellers did not have a car during Katrina's evacuation, nearly two-thirds of these were African-Americans; and almost half (44%) harmed most grievously by the flooding were African-Americans.

Official and popular media accounts of the deaths, homelessness and destruction initially whitewashed issues of racial and class inequality. Instead they fastened upon alleged personal failings. To wit, 'stragglers' only had themselves to blame for their misfortune. They were denigrated for ignoring official warnings and evacuating at, allegedly, a snail's pace rather than promptly as conditions demanded and government officials urged.

In some sections of the media and government the dispossessed and homeless were referred to as 'refugees' rather than fellow citizens. Analysis of photo and TV coverage in New Orleans reveals the presence of racial stereotypes with repeated images of black Americans appealing to white helpers to afford comfort, grant aid and other forms of civil assistance (Kahle et al., 2007). This reinforced historical plantation-style stereotypes of the black population as indolent and passive and whites as resourceful and active (Scheper-Hughes, 2005: 3).

Furthermore allegedly there is reason to believe that the authorities used the emergency as an excuse for the realisation of long-standing ambitions of demographic spatial redistribution and the elimination of low cost housing in the metro area. For the non-propertied class the consequences of Katrina have proved more adverse than for home owners.

FEMA provided aid to the propertied, awarding rent subsidies during the clean-up and renovation process. It was a different story for the non-propertied. After the flooding, public housing units remained boarded up. The authorities unilaterally created rubbish tips of private possessions. Within two years, 4600 of the publicly subsidised housing units in New Orleans were demolished and $1 billion was committed to property developers to introduce 'mixed use' residences. By 2008 it was estimated that only one in three rental units in the metro area would be rebuilt with publicly funded recovery assistance.

Drawing upon the work of Naomi Klein (2007) on the shock doctrine, Adams et al. (2009) allege that this is a classic case of 'disaster capitalism'.[2] That is, the disruption caused by the emergency was exploited by officials as a pretext to hatch long-laid plans to evict the poor from New Orleans along racial lines. The 'natural' catastrophe of flooding was appropriated as the catalyst to redefine downtown property values by replacing low cost housing with luxury condos and mixed housing schemes.

The argument that the post-hurricane restoration programme in New Orleans is a classic case of vulture capital looking after vulture capital is supported by analysis of the allocation of renovation funding. While federal resettlement money was closely rationed, corporations were awarded lucrative clean-up and reconstruction contracts. For example, Halliburton was awarded $124.9 million to repair Navy yards, pump water out of the city and assist the Army Corps of Engineers to restore utilities. Similarly, Bechtel was awarded a series of closed door contracts to supply low grade housing in the form of temporary trailer accommodation situated on the metropolitan perimeter. The Defence Contract Audit Agency later audited the contract and alleged that Bechtel had levied bills doubling the amounts for corrective and preventative maintenance on trailers. This produced an estimated $48 million loss to taxpayers in the shape of over-payments. Additionally, the company was criticised for improperly estimating costs of services and failing to comply with federal acquisition regulations (Waxman, 2006).

Coming back to the question of pre-emergency failings, under-investment in adequate drainage systems and flood-wall protection is interpreted as the result of 'pork barrel politics' that, over many decades, privileged private gain over public benefit (Burby, 2006: 181). The response of the Bush administration was symptomatic. According to Scheper-Hughes (2005: 2), Republican Party spin doctors, headed by Karl Rove, consistently dismissed the disaster as a mixture of forces beyond human control and attributed the huge death and homelessness rates to human fecklessness.[3] Specifically, they reiterated that Katrina was an act of nature and that the individuals who suffered most had no-one else but themselves to blame for ignoring government warnings to flee from danger. The Republican whitewash stereotyped local Democratic officials as inept and alleged that they mismanaged rescue teams. A thinly veiled subtext was the implied obduracy of those (mostly black, poor) inhabitants who were too slow to evacuate themselves and their families.

The Katrina emergency produced a robust reaction to official accounts that the catastrophe was, plain and simple, an act of nature. Cultural events designed to produce relief for the bereaved and homeless disputed official readings. The organised benefits in response to the Katrina disaster are a striking example of events performing the role of challenging official bumble-dum and raising critical consciousness. By exposing the myth that the Katrina event was a natural catastrophe, these benefits pointed to structural inequalities in event presentation. The event which politicised the emergency to best effect was the Concert for Hurricane Relief (2005) telecast on NBC, MSNBC, CNBC and Pax, featuring Faith Hill, Wynton Marsalis, Aaron Neville, Mike Myers, Richard Gere, Leonardo Di Caprio, John Goodman, Glenn Close and Kanye West. It included an unscripted outburst from West denouncing the President and his administration for 'not caring about black people'. The benefit generated $50 million and was watched by 8.5 million viewers. But as we shall see, West's anger about federal hypocrisy attracted the lion's share of post-event publicity.

Other benefit events, such as the one-hour telethon Shelter from the Storm, which was transmitted on six major US channels featuring artists including the Dixie Chicks, U2, Sheryl Crowe and Paul Simon performing live in TV studios in Los Angeles and New York, and the MTV, VH1 and CMT broadcast aid telethon ReAct Now: Music and Relief, featuring Green Day, the Rolling Stones, Coldplay, Elton John, the Foo Fighters, John Mellencamp, Kelly Clarkson and Pearl Jam, were received with the respectful *bonhomie* that is a standard feature of modern event management and event consciousness.

But Kanye's remarks stirred up a hornet's nest that for a while would not die down. For the unmistakable implication of his remarks was that the federal and local levels of government deliberately under-invested in flood hazard mitigation in the city. Kanye implied that the reason for this was that the main victims of any emergency were likely to be the relatively powerless, electorally insignificant inner-city Afro-American community.

Research by Sweeney (2006) unearths a depressingly familiar divide in the social reaction to West's statement. Conservative, patriotic America objected to the black rapper for raising the head of politics in the midst of a national catastrophe. Some took the view that he was trying to set himself up as 'a latter day Martin King Junior', expressing awkward truths that polite society would rather not face.

In contrast, the marginalised and the progressive supported West for speaking what they took to be the plain truth about colour blindness in a society that complacently stresses the 'facts' of meritocracy and equal opportunity. Government officials continue to insist that race is a red herring in respect of the Katrina emergency and its aftermath (Loven, 2005). They peddle a message of individual responsibility for personal conditions of life. By confronting the hypocrisy of this view, West is deemed to have performed a service to the country. Yet there are problems with this upbeat conclusion.

The Hurricane Katrina benefit throws the profound limitations of event consciousness into stark relief. West's accusation of government manipulation of the truth and relative disinterest in the suffering of African-Americans in US society was obviously connected to the implication of a bigger historically based problem in American life. To pursue the Martin Luther King analogy, what West is saying is that the Civil Rights Movement has failed to overcome deeply embedded racist stereotypes.

Hurricane Katrina was, indeed, a force of nature. However, the severity of the loss of life and economic devastation were human-made and reflected power differentials in class and race in American society. Yet while the links with the political economy of injustice and inequality are alluded to in mainstream event consciousness they are seldom elucidated. Instead the topic is sidelined by the emotionalism that typically turbo-charges the philosophy of emergency crisis management as the be-all of intervention. What really matters is bringing all hands to the deck to help the unfortunate folks in New Orleans *now*, rather than pursuing the more publicity-shy task of exposing the obscure, and sometimes deliberately concealed, manacles of power that made a bad situation worse.

This event form of reactive management is not based upon careful planning and balanced resource distribution. On the contrary, it prides itself upon automatic, unreserved impassioned responses. Typically, instant relief, rehousing, food, heat, clothing, water and medical supplies are at the forefront of action. The point is not that these requirements are insignificant. On the contrary, they are essential parts of any relevant major disaster relief programme worthy of the name. However, unless they are integrated with a holistic, strategic approach to events which does not rely on crisis goodwill but is based at state and non-government levels in systematic, informed reconnaissance and resource distribution which is fit for purpose, they run the risk of misallocating resources and failing to solve the problems that they are publicly designed to address. At their worst, they distract social consciousness from the real causes behind disaster and tragedy in national and global life.

Event Denial

The most famous example of a global event acting as a catalyst, inflating emotions and offering an unprecedented set piece for catharsis, mass emotionalism and exhibitionism is the Live Aid (1985) concert organised by Bob Geldof and Band Aid. This was a truly mediagenic, global event. It took the form of a 16-hour marathon of headline acts performing in

London and Philadelphia, broadcast live to 160 countries. Live Aid was the first event of its kind through which the global PR–media complex by virtue of the appropriation of media channels drilled home the message that the whole world is watching. Geldof himself claimed that the telecast was watched by one in two of the world's population. Live Aid preceded the age of the internet and lap-top/mobile phone culture. In short, it was the first wired-up, global event of the satellite era, communicating the message that 'team-world' has the power to get things done.

Appropriately, the origins of Live Aid were based in a BBC TV report on famine in Ethiopia. The footage of sick and dying victims of hunger gained widespread global media coverage as a human catastrophe that should never have happened. Later Geldof was interviewed about his reaction to Michael Buerk's BBC report. His off-the-cuff comments set the tone of indignant emotionalism that defined the publicity idiom for the whole Live Aid campaign:

> The overriding emotion was one of deep shame. Shame on those who have been picked to live. Shame on those who have been condemned to die because they couldn't even give their children life. Shame on those [famine relief] choosers because nobody should have to play God. And shame on the viewer because it's, in effect, our murder. Because we see what is going on, and we do nothing.

Note the emotional and psychological impact of defining, at a stroke, the affluent societies as 'murderers' based on the unexamined pretext of universal inaction. It is a controversial and unsubstantiated remark that reaps a big dividend in publicity but risks conflating personal ignorance of states with inaction and uses it as a precept to condemn a whole system of moral conduct. It might be said that this is a questionable form of criticism and an untenable form of intervention (since it assumes that everyone, all of the time, must be aware of what is really going on in the world – if they are not, they are, *a priori*, 'guilty').

At any rate, Geldof's refusal to be passive led him to persuade the world's music superstars to give free performances in a live worldwide telecast to generate public donations and push state and corporate sponsorship for famine relief. It is now widely forgotten that at the time both Britain and the USA refused to give state funds to Ethiopia (Trilling, 2011). Geldof saw this as a case of the moral derogation of the West. Instead of shrinking away from the problem on the grounds that it is too big for any individual to change, or leaving relief to multilateral voluntary aid agencies, Live Aid effusively and defiantly cultivated a populist 'can do' attitude. It endeavoured to move the ground in public opinion from regarding famine in Ethiopia as Africa's problem, to recasting it as a problem for one and all. There was an undeniable romantic, Musketeer quality about the Live Aid campaign. Unequivocally, the participants saw themselves as possessing the moral high ground despite having no elected or institutional power. Undoubtedly, this sense of superiority provided much of the fuel that motored the event to a high altitude in media ratings.

Notwithstanding this, one must insist that participation was overwhelmingly emotional in nature and that this produced tunnel vision about the relationship between means and ends. To wit: most backers and participants in Live Aid were resolute about the glorification of personal action while, at the same time, remaining awfully vague about the true dimensions of apathy and indifference in the network public. The part that inadequate education, misinformation or, for that matter, the absolutist claims of celebrity culture played in imprisoning the imagination of the latter was ignored, in preference to the emotive judgement that if you are not with us you are against us.

Moreover, most in the Live Aid camp were woolly about the means of distributing the money raised to the hungry and entertained at best a sketchy idea of the political situation in Ethiopia. The vast majority were oblivious to tribal and religious distinctions in Africa and knew less than zero about the capacity of the international criminal gangs and cartels and their role in the illegal seizure and trafficking of aid resources targeted from the economically advanced countries to recipient populations in the emerging and developing world.

Furthermore, Live Aid renewed old and difficult ideas about the *white man's burden*. Instead of trying to understand the culture, economics and religion of the people in Ethiopia, and by extension in all of Africa, on their own terms, Western categories and models of progress were imposed upon them. For example, the lyrics of the Band Aid song 'Do They Know It's Christmas' portrayed Africa as a dry, barren, godless, poverty-stricken place in which nothing grows (Elavsky, 2009: 384). Distinctions of religion (in a continent in which so many Muslims live), polyvalent culture, multi-varied politics and uneven economic development were scarcely addressed. Instead the values of the West were presented as the only realistic solution to Africa's problems. It was as if the continent was understood to be a place 'lacking in politics' or at least a place in which politics of the 'wrong kind' were practised (Repo and Yrjola, 2011: 53; Yrjola 2009).

Live Aid was buoyed along on a tide of exuberant emotionalism and extravagant exhibitionism. Questions of post-event financial allocation, auditing and accountability were instantly labelled as secondary to the imperatives of giving and acting. Again, appropriately for such a telegenic event, the accent was not merely upon giving and acting but crucially, upon being *seen* to give and to act. Public *display* was an essential feature of the event. The ritual of recorded mass assembly in London and Philadelphia, and the rhetoric of the world viewing network public emoting in conformity at home was designed to be cathartic and unifying. However, it was, of course, based in mere presumption since no-one in the Live Aid management team truly knew what people at home were doing during the 16-hour telecast. Rapt attention and growing intimacy with the suffering of Ethiopian victims were the *assumed* telegenically approved, stage-managed domestic responses. They were presented in the TV studios as facts. But the reality of the domestic attention span and meanings produced by the telecast have never been elucidated.

We know from studies of the emotions that constancy and focus upon events are not often maintained. When we are angry, when we cry or laugh the emotions come and go and are seldom coherent for long. Even when we appear to be in the grip of one emotion such as anger, other conflicting emotions like shame and embarrassment are not far from the surface (Katz, 1999). So presupposing an audience response on emotional grounds is as risky as constructing a political programme around a monolithic emotion. However, it does have undeniable publicity value in boosting media interest in a good cause.

The presumption of team-world unity from the start suggests that showmanship was not confined to the stars. It was always intended to extend to the crowd and to the network public at home who were loosely defined as being 'with the band'. This reinforced the overwhelming populist sense of justice and self-righteousness that was the hallmark of the campaign.

Kenyon (1985: 3) has correctly described the politics and morality of Live Aid as 'intricate'. The mixture of a politics organised around altruism with an economic approach based in the propensities of the market produced awkward positions and uneasy alliances. Medieval theologians warned against confusing charitable acts with self-gratification (Heal, 1984). Live Aid raised the same issue. There is reason to believe that this moral dilemma was swept under the carpet by the 'indiscriminate endeavour to exploit the sense of well being' encouraged by event planners (Kenyon, 1985: 3).

Certainly, the public relations consequences surrounding the event were complex and conflicted. Live Aid show-cased itself as responsibly seizing the technology of show business and diverting it from a fixation on fame and personality to raise the profile of the anonymous and powerless in famine-stricken Ethiopia. The hungry child not the rock idol was meant to be the star of the show. However, because it drafted in superstars and wanna-be superstars in pursuit of this end, and used the technology of show business politics to represent them to the public, the results were decidedly mixed.

Geldof himself repeatedly bemoaned the cult of personality in the task of aid campaigning. Nonetheless, he participated in TV interviews, chat show appearances and soap box fundraising campaigns that inevitably magnified his public image as, in effect, a saviour. It is all very well for him to justify this now as the only way to generate media interest and gain hard currency for those at risk in Ethiopia. To be sure, the pretext for this goes wider than his own attempts at self-justification. As we have already noted, Bernays (1928) clearly identified the leader as fundamental in effective public relations. The psychological appeal of acting on behalf of humankind, which is a common feature of the celebrity personality construct, is well understood. It would be unwise to allow Live Aid selfless piety to be the only or even the dominant moral reading of the event.

Likewise, the performers that Geldof shepherded to the bill underplayed the question of the publicity dividend that the live telecast broadcast presented to their careers. Today, it is commonly accepted that U2 and, particularly, Queen (fronted by the flamboyant showman Freddie Mercury) seized the day, and vastly multiplied their respective box office appeal. While it would be overstating the case to propose that this was a motive behind their involvement, there can surely be no quibble that it was one result of the proceedings that went beyond the question of relief for the starving in Ethiopia.

Live Aid mixed the ethos of a global party in which every performer was determined to shine, with the pious, humanist urge to feed the world. It was a televisual marriage between ludic and moral energy. For a day, it produced an unlikely, slightly awkward, embrace between superman and everyman. It is no wonder that the show business format to·relief produced tension and friction among many aid workers who felt that the Wembley and Philadelphia performance stage eclipsed the painstaking groundwork in areas of relief management that went unheralded and worse, largely unnoticed by the affluent societies.

Live Aid was honoured for generating publicity and hard cash for the plight of the Ethiopian poor. The event produced $40 million (£30 million) in cash, although in a subsequent interview Geldof upgraded this figure to £150 million, presumably reflecting the additional income generated by recording sales (Ecclestone, 2011). Be that as it may, it can be argued that the real contribution was not financial but changing the mindset of the better off on the question of their responsibilities to the poor. Live Aid set the bar for team-world caring and acting as a taskforce to solve global problems. Global politicians could ignore the publicity about the event and the opinion of the electorate at their peril. In this sense, Live Aid galvanised the then G7 countries to acknowledge that poverty is a destabilising force in the global economy. This resulted in renewed budgetary commitments by the G7 to close the development gap. However, to this day, Live Aid is criticised by aid workers for squandering resources on camera-friendly relief opportunities rather than addressing the deep political, economic and agricultural transformations in infrastructure that could provide the key to permanent change.

To return to the event itself, the run-up to the telecast programme and the day of live broadcasts were permeated with a spirit of transcendence. For those who could not get a ticket to the Wembley or Philadelphia shows, transcendence pulsated from the television set at home or the handset radio. The organisation and management of the event were presented as an implacable, heroic, people's revolt against apathy and indifference.

Live Aid was the forerunner of contemporary celanthropy culture in which celebrity rock superstars act as big citizens with an unwritten brief to save the world and play is recast as productive labour in global problem solving. Geldof and Band Aid presented themselves as the mouthpiece of popular opinion and used this unelected and, it must be added, largely unaccountable, status as the basis for energetic advocacy and global activism. After Live Aid the notion that you can make a real difference to hunger in Africa or other emergencies from your balcony garden in Battersea, the roof of your condo in Brooklyn or Potts Point was born. John Lennon imagined a future in which there are 'no possessions'. Live Aid created the illusion of no barriers between superstars and everyman in the bigger battle to help Ethiopia.

The public was left with the comforting impression of a momentous event and a job well done. However, with the passage of time this rosy picture has been challenged. Enquiries into post-event Live Aid fund allocation raised some awkward questions. Most notoriously, in 2010 a BBC report alleged that 95% of Band Aid and Live Aid money destined for Ethiopian famine relief was expropriated by rebels in Tigray to buy arms. Bob Geldof responded vehemently by insisting that 'not a single penny of aid money' sent via Live Aid had been diverted into rebel hands to buy weapons and assist in recruitment programmes. The PR–media hub surrounding him issued supportive, ferocious denials. Geldof went on the front foot accusing the BBC of a 'total collapse' of editorial standards. Eventually, after an internal investigation the BBC issued a public apology conceding that their reports had been misleading.

However, the historical record is not so clear cut. Band Aid's own field director in Ethiopia, John James, is reported as estimating that between 10 and 20% of the organisation's relief funds were in fact diverted to rebels to buy arms (Gilligan, 2010).

It is ironic that Geldof felt compelled to defend Band Aid and Live Aid from BBC allegations of terrorist theft. For the greatest misdemeanours were actually committed by the hard-line Communist Ethiopian government led by the dictatorial Colonel Menguistu Haile Mariam. Mariam headed the largest standing army in Black Africa (Vallely, 1985: 12).

Before Live Aid his government was publicly accused of imposing draconian policies of food relief in Tigray and Eritrea. The regime is now known to have manipulated food shortages in order to cement its control over the rebellious northern provinces (Trilling, 2011). Its public record had more to do with seizing military advantage and maintaining domination than administering relief (Polman, 2010). The Ethiopian government oversaw the distribution of Live Aid cash. It also applied its ample power to impose strict restrictions on media coverage and other forms of public record with respect to fund distribution.

Suzanne Franks (2010) recounts the military junta's appropriation of cash to buy arms, the diversion of food to feed the army, the use of aid to boost military recruitment and the rechannelling of aid money into forced population resettlement programmes. Live Aid allegedly was aware of the use of relief money in the resettlement programmes but, according to a leaked minute from one of the meetings, took the view that the priority lay in sending relief to Ethiopia and help 'as best it can', rather than become embroiled in trying to change the infrastructure of the system (Franks, 2010: 54). But this gets things back to front. Where is the sense in throwing money at a problem if the infrastructure cannot deliver the resources at its disposal for the benefit of those in want and misery (Easterly, 2007, 2010; Theroux, 2006)? It renews the force of the argument that Live Aid was an essentially ethnocentric response which showed no deep interest in engaging with Ethiopian and African traditions and infrastructure (Repo and Yrjola, 2011).

There is no credible doubt that the Mariam government was corrupt. Part of the relief funds supplied by Band Aid were used for ends that were the exact opposite of those intended by donors. As Franks (2010: 55) concludes:

> The tragedy is not only that aid was diverted – plowshares turned into swords – but that the aid potentially increased the suffering of the people. The fighting went on longer and was more widespread because aid was used to fuel the supply of weapons and pay for the war effort.

While the BBC report contained allegations that have since been publicly retracted, Geldof's emotive response is impugned by many aid commentators as blinkered and over-defensive.

For our purposes, the issue is not who is right or wrong in this well-publicised dispute. Evidence exists to support both sides. The issue is the use of emotionalism and exhibitionist blanket denials as a line of first resort – the business of presenting yourself as totally right and casting your critics as totally wrong – which characterised and distorted the dispute from the start. This reflects the qualities of emotionalism and exhibitionism in event consciousness to the life. It is not only a matter of digging in and not backing down. It is a matter of visually displaying these characteristics to others.

Geldof's post-Live Aid claim that 'not a penny' of the money raised by Band Aid was embezzled for military purposes, to say nothing of the separate question of resources accumulated for self-interest or organised criminal ends, was reminiscent of the holier-than-thou publicity that surrounded the entire Live Aid event. Live Aid was an imaginative response to a case of grotesque, needless human suffering. However, in adding its shoulder to the wheel to confront the emergency, it regularly made use of hyperbole and unsupported claims. Involvement in the cause was a pretext for blowing any contrary opinion, even of a moderate sort, out of the water. The images of starving children in Ethiopia turned Live Aid supporters into unelected sheriffs of pop culture, acting as grassroots 'big citizens' of those who supposed themselves to be the good folks and turning a vigilant, indignant eye on bandit power. This simplistic Wild West outlook supported hyperbole about the whole of humanity which was justified at the time, even by critics, as being in the service of a greater cause. The Live Aid event was admirable. But it was also, it must be said, imbued with a 'have it every which way' rhetoric which blended whole world deliverance with spurious ritualistic incantations of worthiness.

One example of this is Geldof's absurd claim that one in two of the world's population watched the Live Aid telecast. In 1985, as today, nothing like 50% of the world's population own a television set. Even the notion that 50% have regular access to television is dubious.

The same is true of his pious version of Live Aid as a selfless contribution of the famous who were presumed to be pampered superstars by the media, acting faithfully to feed the world and do all manner of good. Live Aid was not a fairy godmother's Christmas convention, although from the publicity campaign of the day you might be forgiven for thinking the opposite. Think again: the Christian ideal of charity is based in the principle of virtuous living, respect of the blessings bestowed upon the fortunate and the readiness to selflessly discharge obligations to the needy and poor (Heal, 1984: 66). There is no question that this was an aspect of the proceedings of Live Aid. However, the nature of show business means that personal aggrandisement was also an integral part of the emotional and exhibitionist mix. Again, the mixture of moral and ludic energy is not a marriage between like and like. The self-appointed task of feeding the world inevitably leaks into self-aggrandisement.

Leaving aside the use by some stars of the live telecast to revive or enhance box office appeal, Bob Dylan's performance was infamous for using the event as a soap box for what is, in essence, a parochial question in American politics. 'You know while I'm here, I'd just like to say', he declared from the Philadelphia stage, 'that I hope that some of the money that's raised for the people in Africa – maybe they can just take a *little* bit of it, maybe one or two million of it, maybe, and use it, say, to pay the mortgages on some of the farms that the farmers here owe to the banks.' This was widely interpreted as a case of all too familiar, erstwhile American introspection about geopolitics and world hunger delivered from the mouths of one of the most feted of its counter-culture heroes. Putting the needs of Africa behind the needs of American farmers facing bankruptcy in the Mid-West was regarded as a tasteless comparison which did not match like with like.

But looking back it was hardly inconsistent with the flurry of emotive, wayward, unsupported over-the-top remarks made during the event about transformative care, decisive action, the better off changing their ways and the world moving towards a new compact about feeding the hungry.

Unequivocally, Live Aid demonstrated the capacity of communication power to accumulate funds for global emergencies and provide an arena for humanitarian impulses. It resulted in project initiatives in Ethiopia and Africa that have been of value and are ongoing. Nonetheless, Elavsky (2009: 384) is surely justified in his observation that the publicity was 'short lived' and further, that the magnetic glamour of the event turned the spotlight away from the pre- and post-emergency failings of elected government officials in addressing global poverty. A typical feature of event consciousness is that it is dependent upon media communication power. Media agendas have no long-term interest in preserving event consciousness. Shifting media agendas mean that caring about Ethiopia and acting 'for Africa' quickly become yesterday's news.

More tellingly there is a real danger that responses driven by an emotional, self-righteous sense of worth can make things worse by throwing money at the wrong issues and easing local and multilateral pressures to engineer regime change and infrastructural reform that are the root cause of the emergency. A demand to 'act now' from the West is often prominent in event responses to a global emergency and therefore at the heart of event consciousness. But headline figures of the cash raised or the size of the world audience are not in themselves evidence of the value of the event to those in peril. System change requires careful strategic planning and the implementation of objectives. Live Aid excelled at publicity and the generation of funds. However, it is vulnerable to the criticism that it was an event without a strategy for aid distribution that was fit for purpose.

Single-Issue Events: Costs and Benefits

Global events draw upon emotionalism, exhibitionism and catharsis as expressions of personal disinterest. 'We' are all in it together when we 'join up' to put an end to poverty, stop pollution, quell torture in Darfur, save Africa, feed the world or more prosaically show up for the annual company meeting in which the well-paid people who run the show sermonise about adding value to the 'end user', proselytise low cost charity contributions and stress that 'we are all in it together'.

But public display introduces separate questions of exposure management, particularly for celanthropists and celebrity figureheads who, when all is said and done, put themselves forward as the unelected, largely unaccountable representatives of the people and seek to persuade others to follow their lead. Trust depends upon consistency. The public display of trust at global events is communicated around the world, often in the form of live telecasts. It is clearly jeopardised when awkward facts about what appears to be selfish personal practice come to light. When this happens, trust is endangered. The public comes to feel that they have been sold a pig in a poke.

The repercussions of this for event management cannot be easily contained or managed. Pre- and post-event exposure management of famous participants as well as financial accumulation, programme management and fund distribution are now *de rigueur*. Post-event distribution of funds may compromise the single-issue event concept. Inconsistency between public performance and private practice frequently poisons credibility. This may weaken the impact of event sequels and make celanthropists and celebrity figureheads appear like charlatans. The same network of communication power that promotes events can be turned against them to expose allegations of mismanagement and hypocrisy. The attempt by Sir Bob Geldof to deny fund leakage to the Communist government and rebel groups in Ethiopia lacks credibility because there is allegedly substantial contrary evidence that funds were misappropriated.

Professional and academic event literature tends to present pre- and post-evaluation in terms of producing technical feedback to improve individual events and contribute to the industry's pool of knowledge. The focus is upon quantitative cost-benefit analysis, measurement of impact factors, evaluation of the connection between events and tourist expenditure and medium- to long-term output effects for the community (Bowdin et al., 2011). Because this literature has not developed a robust critical perspective it does not typically go beyond the issue of technical feedback for event sponsors and managers. The questions of the meaning of events for programme participants and audiences and the context of power and inequality in which events are located are underdeveloped.

Yet the question of subjective meaning is central to participants. As the Concert for Hurricane Katrina Relief demonstrates, official meanings can be forcefully challenged by subjective narratives. Kanye West's outburst expressed what a lot of people were privately thinking. The live nature of event broadcasting means that event planners are unable to guarantee that the event concept will be confirmed. Event concepts can be challenged because individuals and groups bring different subjective meanings to bear in considering them. The challenge of event planners is to win hearts and minds over to the event concept. Kanye West hijacked this strategy to air much more uncomfortable questions about racial inequality and justice that metropolitan, state and national public administrations underplayed.

Because single-issue events are usually based in an incident and emergency they provide communicative loopholes that steer cognition away from the event to larger issues of domination, subordination, representation and ideology. The impact of an event is not just measured by the metric of whether you enjoyed the speeches, the propaganda or artistic performances. It fans out to the relationship between events and judgements of much broader relationships having to do with issues of justice, equity, responsibility, trust, power and the government of modern emotions.

Events are designed to confirm these qualities in public settings. It is for this reason that, in the opening chapter of the book, I described them as mechanisms of moral regulation. This twinning of events with moral regulation raises connections between event management, performative labour, the control of spectatorship and modern civic social ordering that rumple the feathers of professional advocates like Getz (2005) and Bowdin et al. (2011) who tend to see events automatically and overwhelmingly as a public good.

From the standpoint of event sponsors and managers the *raison d'être* of events is that they reinforce and magnify predetermined ethical and business requirements. Thus, Live Aid and Live Earth (2005) were viewed by their backers and handlers as, respectively, raising consciousness about poverty and pollution. Corporate sponsorship of these events was designed to build the brand by associating it with these lofty objectives.

All of this is reversed if it turns out that the meaning which audiences bring to events is separate from ethical or business considerations. For many attendees the event concept is incidental to having a good time. Recent empirical research by Bengry-Howell into music festival attendance makes grim reading for celanthropists and event managers (cited in Tickle, 2011). It indicates that for many, event consciousness privileges escapism over ethical considerations or awareness of the link between event sponsorship and business branding. Brands and causes may position themselves in event culture, but be neutralised by the euphoria of event consciousness.

For example, in the 1960s and 1970s alcohol corporations quickly appreciated the value in sponsoring pop music festivals. However, in 2006 the Advisory Council on the Misuse of Drugs and Alcohol submitted that sponsorship of festivals attracting under-18 year olds ought to be banned. Following this, with some notable exceptions such as 'T in the Park' sponsored by the Tennents lager company, beer companies, like Tuborg Lager, have pursued the lower key option of monopolising 'pouring rights' at festivals. What Bengry-Howell found when he interviewed festival goers is that many did not register a solid connection between the event and the brand. They did not care about the brand or pouring rights. Rather the main attraction of festivals for them was providing an alternative to unemployment or dissatisfying work.

There are separate conceptual and analytical dangers in tying event consciousness too closely to work. It repeats the mistake of an earlier generation of leisure theorists who postulated that some forms of leisure should be considered primarily as reactions to work (Parker, 1983; Wilensky, 1960). The error here is to assume that work is the central life interest for individuals and groups. This cuts off other fruitful ways of reading event consciousness such as an affirmation of counter-culture, a search for belonging, a desire for freedom, an exercise in transcendence and of course the articulation of narcissism and self-gratification.

Notes

1   The lack of a critical edge in the professional event management literature was a big impetus in making me want to write this book. The inexorable trend in this literature is to accentuate the positive. Events are portrayed as eliciting social integration, building kinship and creating a sense of transcendence. At its worse, this side of event management literature seems to me to be little more than a bluffer's paradise.
2   Klein's (2007) book seems to me to be one of the best things published in the study of society over the last five years. Just as the concept 'self-perpetuating prophecy' caught on because it elegantly refers to what we already know on the level of common sense, the notion of the shock doctrine shows how politicians and management engineer radical change.
3   Rove was a legendary Republican political consultant whose public relations skills were crucial in the rise of the New Right in the USA.

10

WHY ARE EVENTS SO EMOTIONAL?

The question of why modern men and women are attracted to express emotions strongly through event consciousness is complex. Not least because it begs a number of related questions, each of which is complex in its own right. Why should an emotional response be preferred to a rational one? Why have global events become catalysts for the articulation of private emotions? What psychological and social forces make event exhibitionism a marker of personal integrity? Why is it so crucial for people to record events? What precisely are they articulating and commemorating?

It is apparent that something has happened of late to make events a more prominent feature of social consciousness. Twenty or 30 years ago judgements about political responsibilities and social compassion were intertwined with the transformative politics of political parties and pressure groups. Events suggest the presence of a new politics, one which is no longer beholden to parties, parliaments or electoral systems, but works instead at the *personal* level – Beck's (1992) 'sub-politics'. The emotional content of events is strong not only because ludic energy is aroused by the event entertainment programme. The expression of direct action to address global problems also draws upon the sentiment of people power taking over from the inadequate responses of the state and corporations to global problems.

However, for the most part audiences engage around representation in a *gestural economy* to signify solidarity, commitment and action. The aspects of gestural economy important here are the aggregate of social markers that convey identification with a cause, a policy or some other form of collective undertaking. In the context of event relations, gestural economy may take the form of a highly public pledge of money, an emotive outburst against 'the rich', extravagant support for corporate values or a five-year plan and so forth. As one might expect in a culture so saturated with visual stimuli, the primary means of address is representation. This signifies a change in the politics of social activism.

When old style social activists used the term 'the personal is political', they meant incorporating the struggle against inequality and injustice as continuous characteristics of personal identity. Old style activists regarded the fight against domination and ideology to be unflagging and requiring, if necessary, total commitment. Undoubtedly, there are echoes of this in event relations. The Make Poverty History campaign urged people to make the war against hunger and poverty central to lifestyle design and practice. Be that as it may, the discontinuous, disaggregated nature of global events encourages an attitude that *representation is resistance*. The discharge of personal and collective emotions is concentrated in the event and its immediate aftermath. The event concept heightens social consciousness but does not appear to solidify it for a durable time frame. As with the media reporting of events, event consciousness appears to be episodic and discontinuous.

This raises concerns that event planning by itself is incapable of achieving more than a short-term commitment to the presiding event concept. Further, the attempt to renew the vigour of the concept through subsequent global events may be popularly regarded as overdoing it. Certainly, it is widely agreed that compared to Live Aid (1985) the popular response to the Live 8 (2005) event was lack-lustre. One reason often given for this is compassion fatigue.

The new social activism has come to maturity in the digital age. Event consciousness is intimately entwined with the programme schedules of media corporations. So it should be no surprise that it has given birth to the idea that *representation is resistance*. Display and representation are at the core of gestural culture. They enable participants to convey complex social, economic and political messages of criticism and reconstruction in a lapel badge or T shirt slogan. In most cases what is missing is the old style activist readiness to engage in continuous, direct mobilisation, organisation and action. The *representation* of the corruption of power is different from the dismantling and overthrow of corrupt power. Historically speaking, event relations have not broken out of this impasse.

Of course, it can reasonably be objected that they do not need to. The logic of old style activist politics was based on faith in common collective experience, with class, gender and race usually figuring as the three central foundations of resistance. While it is hardly the case that these foundations have evaporated today, there is widespread consensus that they do not have the same general purchase in personal politics. They are now mediated and refracted through new institutional pathways and patterns of association which privilege representation as the central means of expression. Let us go into these issues a little more deeply.

Criticism and Public Space

The old dominant explanation of how popular culture elicits social trans-formation was supplied by Jürgen Habermas's (1989) theory of the public sphere. It portrayed transformation in terms of the emergence of a free, informal public space in which civic problems were addressed. Via this means the democratic role of the press was first conceived and the system of political parties established. In order to understand how different things are today it is worth recalling the cardinal features of Habermas's thesis.

For Habermas (1989), the potential for democratic change initiated 'from below' derives from the historical development of new spaces for public discussion that emerge as urban-industrial society prospers. In coffee houses, meeting rooms, squares and other public settings, issues relating to 'the good society', that cannot be resolved via inherited, dominant cultural traditions, are aired and debated. Habermas uses the term 'the public sphere' to refer to the aggregate of public space. He sees it as a precondition for democracy and human rights. Its corner-stones are tolerance, the recognition of multi-diversity (of values and opinions), and respect for free speech. It is not enough for the public sphere to recognise personal liberty and pluralism. Habermas (1996) maintains that the good society also requires normative procedures that defend free speech, respect majority opinion and guarantee that the exchange of opinion will be treated fairly. The emergence of a free, popular press is central to these ends.

Democracy demands that different individuals and groups have equal access to the public sphere, their rights are treated with universal respect and their views are subject to the judgement of majority opinion. This, in turn, requires the development of a free electoral system, politi-cal parties and pressure groups. For through these means, believes Habermas, the will of the people is translated into public policy.

In addition, democracy requires a robust public sphere. Preconditions of this include imposing legal restraints on the powers of the military and corporations, ensuring that political parties are not subject to the manipulation of corporate interests, guaranteeing the impartiality of policing and protecting the freedom and authority of the law. These pre-conditions are met when society is organised around a liberal political culture, habits of personal freedom, a free press and an egalitarian sys-tem in which class privilege plays no significant part (Habermas 1996: 487; 1998: 384).

This comes close to what Popper (1968) understood by 'the open society'. It is part of the Enlightenment tradition which privileges rational thought, the free exchange of ideas and opinions and submits that objective standards can be applied to determine the justice of rational arguments. Both Habermas and Popper grant that it is difficult to find objective standards, yet each maintains that this does not obviate the search for them. For to do is more progressive than submitting to the rule of blind habit, metaphysics or dogma.

The case for the public sphere (and the open society), then, is based in the vindication of rationalism as the optimal means of resource distribution and ethical judgement in modern society. It recognises universal rights, acknowledges free speech and guarantees the independence of the social institutions necessary to maintain democratic order (the legislature, political parties, a free press and the civil service). But there are problems with Habermas's argument.

Most seriously, the realism of this account has been repeatedly questioned. From Marxist and feminist perspectives the independence of social institutions is inherently doubtful. Class distinctions, the privileges of male and ethnic power render ideals of egalitarianism and free speech unlikely. Without the transparent confirmation of these conditions, Habermas's defence of the public sphere and democracy slides into the water. For the precondition of a healthy public sphere, namely, universalism of human rights and respect for majority opinion, are not guaranteed.

Other objections have been made. Habermas's account of the public sphere assumes high levels of activism, motivation and involvement by ordinary men and women. Like John Dewey, his comprehension of democracy assumes that ordinary people have a zest for organised (pressure group and party political) politics and the necessary spare time to devote themselves to questions of organisation, agitation, education and the defence of free speech. It is probably true that, in a normative sense, the majority of ordinary people subscribe to these principles. Yet this is very different from proposing that a state of continuous practical involvement applies (Bernstein, 1998).

For example, we know that large numbers of eligible voters do not turn out in national elections. In the UK 83.9% of the eligible population voted in the 1950 General Election; in 1974, the figure was 74%; in 2001, 59.4%; in 2005, 61.4%; and in 2010, 65.5%.

In the USA the rate of decline for turnout in presidential elections is also just under two-thirds of the eligible voters. In 1952, 63.3% voted; in 1976, 53.5%; in 1988, 50.11%; in 2008, 51.2%. Bill Clinton was elected on 49% of turnout. True, the election of Barack Obama in 2008 saw a reversal in this trend, with a turnout of 57.7%. However, as the first black presidential nominee of the Democrats, Obama's campaign attracted intense media coverage .

In the European Parliament elections the rate of decline is even steeper. In 1979, 61.99% voted; in 1984, 58.98%; in 1989, 58.41%; in 1994, 56.67%, in 1999, 49.51%; in 2004, 45.47%; and in 2009, 43% (www.europarl.europa.eu).

The conclusion is inescapable. If over one-third of the eligible electorate regularly refrain from participating in general and presidential elections the mandate for democratic decision-making is flawed. In theory, democracy requires the full participation of the electorate as the precondition of the health of the good society. In reality, it tolerates substantial detachment from political participation.

Additionally, Habermas's understanding of the public sphere assumes direct democracy in which people have a concrete say in policy formation and accountability. In reality, what the West has produced is representative democracy in which the majority are represented by elected individuals such as senators, congressmen and women or members of parliament. The gap between the representative and the majority is compatible with all sorts of anomalies. In addition, the power of the communication network, which is dominated by media multinationals which are only superficially accountable to popular will, means that issues and choices are routinely framed to achieve readings and courses of action favoured by elites. As we saw in the discussion of moral regulation and performative labour (pp. 29–30; 31–4), network power is not disinterested. Rather, it seeks to frame responses to strengthen private ownership and control.

Habermas's view of democracy is therefore attacked by critics as a straw man since it refers to a theoretical rather than a real state of affairs. The inference is that events such as Live Aid and Live Earth show that people are deserting or withdrawing from official political institutions. They do not chose to make the rational decision to elect political candidates to represent them in the official institutions of public opinion, namely Parliament, the Senate and the House of Representatives. They abstract themselves from a system that it is in their best interests to support and refine through active participation.

Prima facie, this may seem irrational but in fact it is a perfectly rational course of action based upon the conviction that representative democracy is incapable of truly capturing and pursuing the interests to which it is bound. Instead people who are disenchanted with the established system of democracy pursue various forms of direct action which exploit the power of network communication to attain popular ends.

Doubtless, Habermas would accept much of this criticism. Yet his emphasis upon democracy as a learning process means that, for him, the solution is as plain as a pikestaff. Since people do not behave rationally to exercise their democratic freedoms fully, it is incumbent upon society to educate them so as to persuade them to act responsibly in the future. Through schooling and media campaigns, the public should be urged to take official political institutions more seriously and participate in them. A rider to this is that the institutions must themselves be reformed to ensure more transparency and a truer fit between majority opinion and representation.

To the charge that this solution is beside the point, since society has not achieved the prerequisites of egalitarianism that democracy requires, Habermas responds that the correct answer is to use legislation to reform social institutions to militate against the power of class, gender, race and ethnicity. This is consistent with his defence of liberal political culture and advocacy of rational thought and language to achieve social transformation and validity claims.

However, in reaffirming the privilege of rational thought and language as instruments of social transformation, Habermas is again accused of wearing rose-tinted spectacles. For the conviction that rationality and language define the inheritors of the Enlightenment tradition is held to be misplaced. A variety of arguments are used to elaborate the point. Most importantly, Habermas is accused of failing to appreciate the significance of the emotions in human motivation and resource allocation (Antonio, 1989; Wellmer, 1992). The communication network presents data in an emotional way. Stories are portrayed in an adversarial fashion to highlight conflicts and dramatise opposition. This makes for good television and popular journalism. It is no surprise that these tropes carry over into everyday life through performative labour.

When people rationally take the view that things cannot be fundamentally changed in society because the powers governing them are recognised as being too formidable, *representation* becomes the cultural plane in which dissent, contrarian opinion and opposition are primarily expressed. Events allow those who are generally powerless to act out repressed emotions in taking the bull by the horns and making a difference. Displaying and acting out become political statements. They are hugely bolstered of course by media representation. By way of evidence consider global media coverage of the Occupy campaign of 2011. By way of analytical justification: what did the Occupy campaign do to abolish or reform the habitual practices of global, let alone vulture capitalism?

The Janus Face of Event Life Politics

All of this is of great moment in the task of trying to achieve a sound understanding of events. For events attempt to fuse ludic and moral energy to produce direct solutions to problems that the established system of democracy is deemed unable to fix. That there is a strong, performative dimension to this can be in little doubt. It is not enough to give to the Make Poverty History campaign, one must also be *seen* to give. It does not suffice to attend the company annual meeting, one must be witnessed to attend, preferably through a recording of some kind. Participating in events is not just making common cause with others, it is making a personal statement about who one *is* or the manner in which one would ideally wish to be seen. Event management combines the urge to reach out with the compulsion to display the image of empathy and heroism. Self-gratification is a significant, and mostly, entirely unacknowledged component in event consciousness. The wish to help, to relieve and to demonstrate belonging may be genuine, but it is infused with the psychological desire to be publicly recognised as acting in ways that confirm credibility, competence and social impact.

Perhaps this strong desire to be recorded and witnessed has something to do with the apprehension that global events truly are illusory communities. The itchy feeling that 'team-world' is a shibboleth for something that does not really exist is managed by taking a mobile phone photograph to show that one is really there. It is as if, by establishing one's physical presence in the event setting, the loose, emotional sentiments of solidarity and unity behind the event are confirmed. For a picture cannot lie.

This is solidified by positioning celebrities as figureheads for grand causes. For the audience acquires the glamour and impact of the star through association. The heroic role that celebrities play in modern culture as role models and unofficial life coaches is adapted as an open intervention to step in where the footfalls of national governments and corporations fear to tread. Hence, the powerful connection between events, personal integrity and transcendent goals. Celebrity figureheads hot-wire popular passions through the PR–media hub and communication network to address global emergencies and social injustice. It has been noted many times that underlying this political response is a general sentiment that national governments are either inept in global management or are outright bankrupt. Several commentators refer to a shift in politics that requires a reconceptualisation of Habermas's notion of the public sphere (Crossley, 2003; Merrifield, 2011; Routledge and Simon, 1995).

Event participation implores people to engage in stateless types of direct action to achieve transcendent goals. This moral energy has spilt over to engender an event counter-culture which involves trespass, street protests and riots to achieve political objectives that are regarded to be fudged or understated by event planners. The G8 summit in Genoa (2001) involved protests from a crowd of 200,000, widespread acts of civil disobedience, including the torching of vehicles, multiple arrests and the death of one activist during police clashes. Anti-capitalist protests have become a standard feature of G8 summit meetings. These forms of protest reject the organised, institutional boundaries of democracy as too limiting and explicitly demand wider forms of global, extra-parliamentary intervention. They operate on a different terrain, namely that of lawless reaction to public ills.

This is a sub-branch of stateless solutions, but it is an important unofficial accessory. The organisers of lawless reactions are well aware of the publicity dividend in using violence and civil unrest as forms of protest. Events are the articulation of stateless solutions to social, political and economic problems and their prominence in the media has supported the development of an ancillary counter-culture of lawless activity. The emergence of both in recent years implies that there is something amiss with the theory of the public sphere.

Habermas (1987: 392) himself recognises the emergence of a new type of politics that he calls 'sub-institutional'. This is a type of life politics that is expressed in and through culture rather than via official economic and political organisations like trade unions, pressure groups and political parties. Rather than look to members of parliament, shop stewards, or business leaders to solve problems, they seize media communication networks to galvanise messages of popular resistance. They do not *replace* the institutions of democracy, but they do call these institutions to account for being unable to optimally manage public issues. They constitute a public space which is becoming ever more enmeshed with digital technologies of recording and communication, in and through which protest is organised and identity is articulated and witnessed.

I want to call this hinge between acting and being seen and recorded as acting as the Janus-face of event life politics. By Janus-face I mean the twinning of believing in a cause (moral energy) and doing good with performative labour and gestural economy that displays participation and is motivated by personal gratification (ludic energy). In highlighting this duality I wish to fix in the mind of the reader the proposition that the twin elements of emotionalism and exhibitionism are integral to events. Event participation is not simply about launching stateless solutions in the public sphere, it is also the corollary of modern communication networks in which display, performance, recording and gratification are integral components. Intricate dramatic motifs and stylised behaviours are used to provide critical counterpoints with habitual practices that bolster the self (Kapchan, 1995: 479). The heroic performance element expands when it comes to global events in which celebrity figureheads are portrayed as the unelected sheriffs of the people taking on the business of solving emergencies that national governments are widely condemned to fudge or ignore. Meaning is not elaborated and nuanced in this system it is telegraphed through blunt, emphatic messages. Representation *is* resistance and gestural culture enables you to tell who your real friends and true enemies are *at a glance*.

What does it mean to submit that events presume performance and self-gratification? In writing of the performative dimension in anti-corporate globalisation protests, Juris (2008: 62) distinguishes between mediated and embodied levels of action. According to him, protests are, at one and the same time, social landscapes in which activists communicate their messages to a network public (mediated action) and personal spaces in which belief and conviction are expressed (embodied action). Protests and events are therefore not just collective responses, they are personal statements carrying nuanced meanings for participants and observers.

I wish to take over Juris's proposition that protests involve a duality of embodiment and mediation and extend it to events. I do so because I maintain there is more to events than the face-value expression of unity, generosity and solidarity in response to a crisis, emergency or cyclical commemorative act. Our need to develop events as stateless solutions is the manifestation of the psychological urge for a certain kind of personal life politics to be articulated and witnessed, preferably digitally, since this produces an instant record and affords automatic, weightless communication about the otherwise intangible nature of the human soul. We seek personal gratification in displaying ourselves and being recognised by fellow supporters, as 'one of us' or people of 'selfless courage and conviction'. Bold and uncompromising responses to global emergencies provide opportunities for people to twitter posts designed to convey personal worth and self-affirmation. Identifying oneself with virtuous circles of charity, and being recorded as doing so, invigorates the self and produces positive waves of self-righteousness. This is often presented as plain and simple altruism. That is, people take it upon themselves to act without self-interest to resolve injustice and emergencies that victims are unable to overcome. But the more one looks into altruism and the field of events, the less straightforward and simple it becomes.

Event Altruism

'Altruism', writes Richard Sennett (2003: 135–6), 'some biologists argue, is programmed into human genes. Like other social animals, we would perish if we did not cooperate, if we did not give as well as take.' However, as Sennett (2003: 136–41) goes on the observe, it is naive to view altruism and empathy as entirely innocent. The Christian tradition of charity (from the Latin term, *caritas*) identifies the gift as not only an expression of generosity but as a brick that builds 'the good person'. In traditional society the Christian economy appreciated the blessings bestowed upon it by God and in return was willing to discharge obligations to the unfortunate. Caring for the poor was one of the foremost obligations. It was acknowledged to be the duty of all godly men and women (Heal, 1984: 66–7).

In an indifferent universe, the gift expresses moral worth and virtue. For Christians, it articulates closeness to God and contact with the holy. By means of the gift we transcend the irritating confines of self-interest and participate in the revelation of the goodness of the soul. Our acts also provide witness to this goodness, bringing us into alignment with theological conviction and conferring prestige in the sight of our fellows.

Does this mean that altruism is always bogus? That is, do humans never act selflessly in the interest of others? In fact, a good deal of empirical evidence exists to support the view that human beings are capable of pure altruism. For example, Kristen Monroe (1991) demonstrates that a group of rescuers acted on behalf of endangered Jews during the Nazi terror, over an extended period, despite risks of ostracism from family and friends and mortal punishment by the state. She demonstrates that people act cooperatively without the urgency of personal advantage.

However, Galston (1993: 119–20) notes that generalising the experience of one group or class to apply to the entire human species is inadmissible. Moral diversity means that there are wide variations in moral capacity. For this reason he holds that it is dangerous to extrapolate an 'is from an ought'. In other words, the fact that humans ought to be altruistic is no guarantee that they will behave in this way.

Conversely, it does not follow that we should always assume the contrary, i.e. that humans are generally self-interested. For Galston (1993), selfishness/altruism should be regarded as a continuum between utter indifference to others and complete responsiveness, rather than an either/or dichotomy. That is, we can be altruistic and selfish at one and the same time. Perhaps, it is even appropriate to identify a drift between these. It follows that altruistic behaviour is influenced by social conditions and takes various forms. Galston (1993: 123) distinguishes three types of altruism:

- *Personal altruism*, that is selfless behaviour dedicated to closely affiliated persons, such as family and friends.
- *Communal altruism*, that is, selfless behaviour dedicated to persons or groups who are acknowledged to have shared characteristics, such as religious belief, political party membership, common ethnicity, etc.
- *Cosmopolitan altruism*, that is, selfless behaviour dedicated to persons with whom one has no personal or group ties, i.e. the human race as a whole.

Global events belong to the third category. They are a cosmopolitan response, expressed in the context of post-Westphalian international relations and network communication cultures that are part of a gestural economy, to dramatic images of want, misery and suffering. It is necessary to insist on the *mediated* character, because communication networks are pivotal in raising consciousness and mobilising action in network publics to support relief. Global event management would be impossible without the camera and transmission networks. The more mediated a social encounter, the greater the scope for manipulation and impression management, since more people are involved in persuading an individual to get a result.

I might be moved by images of homeless people in Haiti following the 2010 earthquake. When George Clooney hosts a telethon to support disaster relief I may make an online donation. But how can I be sure that charity is its own reward? By donating $100 or £100 am I acting altruistically, or do I wish to demonstrate my allegiance with a glamorous, committed Hollywood superstar and others who visibly give money in support of the cause that he is espousing? If my donation is entirely altruistic, why didn't I make it *before* the telethon? Moreover, since the problem of disaster relief in Haiti is continuous, should I undertake to make regular follow-up contributions? And if I think that this is going too far, am I in fact revealing a desire to be regarded as worthy and to experience the aura of self-gratification after a Hollywood superstar has prevailed upon me through television to demonstrate my humanity?

From the standpoint of some biologists this whole line of reasoning is a red herring. For if it is true that we are genetically programmed to be altruistic, the response to help and to be cooperative is involuntary. But if this is the case why do I not make a donation as soon as news of the earthquake in Haiti breaks? Why should the appeal by George Clooney during the live telethon persuade me that it is my humanitarian duty to give? And how come I do not continue to make donations until the misery and want caused by the earthquake come to an end?

Caritas is not a biological given in the human species. Cooperation may be genetically programmed, but so is aggression and personal survival. All are socially conditioned. Only a social element can explain the diversity and inconstancy in giving. If we were really driven by the biological drive to give and to help, our response to the earthquake victims would be instantaneous, constant and the telethon appeal by George Clooney would be neither here nor there. Because *caritas* is social it is layered with psychological and cultural stimuli that motivate personal responses.

The spiritual value of *caritas* is difficult to measure because it refers to a force that is tangible only via belief. But the psychological value of making an individual feel morally worthy and the social value in conferring prestige on a charitable act are transparent. You can't give unless, in the first place, you take. The gift is always a distributive act involving a surplus, since if you have nothing, you have nothing to give. The gestural articulation of emotion that occurs in global events is only partly a mark of humanitarian solidarity with victims or an exercise in self-gratification.

It also reflects personal guilt at complicity with what many observers refer to as 'the new imperialism' (Harvey, 2004; Mann, 2003; Nederveen Pieterse, 2008). This imperialism refers primarily to the domination of the rich over the poor, but it also encompasses the express train of capitalist accumulation which is heedless to environmental costs and sees endless accumulation as the only station stop worth travelling to.

Goodwill News in the Culture of Display

Giving and being seen to give are not synonymous. Without doubt, there is a deep-rooted and close relationship between them. However, to give is to act in a manner that is ultimately indifferent to personal gain. Conversely, to be seen to give is to issue a calling card that demands the donor be recognised as a person of merit, it aims to produce a positive social response.

In the digital age giving and being seen to give have moved into another space with a psychological and social payload that has no precedent. They are no longer private, local matters. Global events make them a topic for the attention of the world. Indeed, it goes somewhat beyond that, in as much as we feel the world is judging us if we don't act.

But what is this world? Where are its eyes and ears? How does it act? We respond to the omissions of invisible government to deal effectively with global issues by forming illusory communities. Through them we commute from the world of private interest, that we are compelled by the necessities of acquisitive life to privilege, into a public space in which the plumage of fraternity, selflessness and goodwill are prominently displayed. These illusory communities are temporary. Yet it is to their disapproval to which we pay heed and to their scrutiny that we respond. We are tied by invisible bonds which impose a greater sense of personal obligation as the event comes to pass.

I have called the majority of responses that are attached to this space 'gestural economy' because it does not generate forms of agitation, mobilisation and action against the central pillars of power. It is a form of representative response that is fully compatible with capitalism. Indeed, in as much as it supports a setting in which the exhibition of personal worth and the accumulation of cultural rewards are rife, it is an extension of the market system. An emotional response to inequality and injustice is a precondition for social transformation. However, it ends in an *impasse* unless it uses emotion to precipitate social reconstruction.

The disjointed, segregated character of events means that they seldom get beyond the stage of emotional impasse. Even the take-to-the streets protests in response to capitalism that Gorringe and Rosie (2008) and Routledge (2011) analyse are primarily emotional outbursts, attuned and heavily dependent upon media representation for social impact. They do not involve the concerted, committed seizure of economic, social and political power that is necessary to truly change the system. In them the creation of new popular assemblies, serious thought to a constitution defining their powers and responsibilities, new fiscal and public investment policies and arrangements for international trade and security relations are mostly absent or massively underdeveloped issues. It is not to question their validity or the integrity of campaigners and participants. Although one should quickly add, in parentheses, that these street protests are unlikely to be immune from the Janus-faced nature of events described above.

11

WHAT IS EVENT APPROPRIATION?

What does it mean to speak of 'event appropriation'? How can an event that is nominally organised for all of the people come to be perceived and experienced as sectioned off by a narrow enclave?

The case studies of four events (three cyclical and one single-issue), the Carnival in Rio, the Sydney Mardi Gras, FIFA event management of the World Cup and the Live 8/Make Poverty History campaign, are examined here to explore these questions. Again, my aim is to combat the laudatory, worthy, over-consensual ethos which, I maintain, dominates professional event management literature. Emphatically, I do not mean to be understood as saying that events always end in event appropriation. Rather, I wish to push the boat out towards a more multi-layered, nuanced perspective which does justice to the principle that events must be studied as *a field of contradictory relations*. They involve alliances and clashes between a plurality of interests. Some are manifest, some latent. For example, cyclical events require securitisation and infrastructural investment. I have already noted that this is the basis for lobbying by the security and surveillance complex to secure upgraded service provision contracts and for property developers to engage in real estate profiteering (pp. 56–7; 83–8).

The motivation behind events must not, therefore, be taken at face value. The importance of the multiplier effect in global events means that economic and political interests inevitably hatch and pursue business plans that exploit the event as an excuse to make electoral gain or huge profits. Event appropriation may occur before the formation of the event concept as a deliberate strategy of fulfilling invisible sectional interests. It reflects the huge resource aggregation that global events are capable of generating, not merely in the accumulation of charity funds, but network syndication rights and investment opportunities.

Structurally speaking, the denominator in most forms of event appropriation is the seizure of folk traditions and/or collective gatherings which were originated by the people in the name *of* 'the people' (Thompson, 1991: 6–15). The branding of athletics and football by, respectively, the IOC and FIFA into a multi-million dollar global business and the transformation of the Rio Carnival and Sydney Mardi Gras into global mega-events are cases in point.

The seizure of folk traditions or gatherings involves the commercialisation of time-honoured practice and the imposition of bureaucracy and policing. The commercial logic is that the economic value of traditional events is underdeveloped if the dominant organisational principle is the preservation and accumulation of cultural capital without the attachment of a monetary value. Folk traditions are therefore monetised. The outward aim is to increase resources for the people. However, the inner principle is to separate the ownership and control of events from their roots.

This does not go without costs. Adding commerce, bureaucracy and policing to ludic, festive events produces acute challenges and risks for event planners. Events which fail to confirm an idiom of spontaneous transcendence are experienced as abstracted from popular sentiment. If this translates into the popular perception of imposed entertainment or enforced corporate manipulation it exerts a counter-multiplier effect. In a word, it boosts event consciousness fatigue. Thus, Live 8 is widely regarded as failing to achieve the same lustre of transcendence as Live Aid. This is generally explained as a result of the public growing over-accustomed to, and weary of, Geldof's formula of celanthropy.

Event planners aim for public coagulation around the event concept. Deeper analysis reveals conflicting objectives between sponsors and network publics, performers and audiences, the city and the village, host populations and ethnic minorities, etc. Event appropriation involves the co-option of history, the obliteration of identity and the redefinition of space. The four case studies here investigate and elaborate these themes.

The Rio Carnival

Carnival in Rio dates back to the early 18th century. Its origins and traditions are obscure but most authorities on colonial migration agree that they stretch back at least to the commencement of the Christian age. They lie in the pre-Lenten festivities prior to fasting, penance and the feast of the Resurrection. But of course what makes Brazilian Carnival special is the miscegenation between European, native Indian and African (slave labour) traditions. The plantation economy established by the Portuguese brought ingredients of vodoo and magic from Africa and mixed them with local Indian traditions. Cultural, religious and social distinctions of ethnicity and class were grafted onto Christian religious origins.

Carnival in Brazil began as a colonial celebration of Christianity and moved to become, first, a regional cultural event, then a hallmark national cultural event, before developing into a *bona fide* global event with international TV syndication rights and all of the frictions that arise from the emergence of new enclaves of privilege that stand to gain culturally and financially from sponsorship and guaranteed network telecasting.

Carnival evolved into a celebration of Brazilian nationalism which symbolises the jubilant, egalitarian, amorous, Dionysian, harmonious, welcoming, intermingling of cultures and ethnicities. It is portrayed as representing the 'most appealing', 'unique' aspects of Brazilian culture (Sheriff, 1999: 3). But it also carries associations with liberation, jubilation, renewal, frankness, Bacchanalia, the grotesque and various other types of 'unleashed' excitement. Brazilian Carnival constantly outgrows the frame in which it is momentarily encased. Hence, its associations with vigour, wildness, exuberance, intoxication and perpetual growth.

Within Brazil, a mounting objection to the organisation of Carnival is that the inclusive national symbolism and international associations favoured by the Brazilian Tourist Authority neutralise ethnic divisions. Culturally, this is a sensitive matter for Brazilian intellectuals and government officials because multiculturalism is the central pillar of nation-building.

However, sectional interests of course prevail. For example, within Brazil there have been widespread allegations that the planning and run-up preparations for the FIFA World Cup (2014) and Olympic Games (2016) have involved bribery and extortion in the construction industry, state and national government and the tourist industry. But, for many Brazilians, to question the reality of multiculturalism in an event like the Rio Carnival is like raising a red flag to a bull. The event is portrayed as a celebration of Brazilian nation-building and multicultural harmony. Yet the study of Carnival reveals a more ambivalent picture.

Historically speaking, black participation in Carnival expressed ethnic solidarity. It was also revered by the black population for providing an honourable role which they took upon themselves to act as ceremonial advocates for the whole of Brazilian culture. In the most energetic era of Brazilian nation-building, the downtrodden regarded the organisation and presentation of Carnival as a significant group privilege. There were echoes here of an earlier theft.

In the early 19th century, European, mainly French and Portuguese, migrants attempted to usurp the energy of what might be termed 'prototypical Carnival' and redefine it in the language of the costume ball and its counter-culture. African and Indian roots were pruned or disguised. However, by the 1920s the native Indian and African traditions reasserted themselves. This reflected the turn of the century influx of natives to Rio looking for work. Samba culture became a mark of cultural assertion. In plain language it enabled those normally excluded from the discourse of power to become visible and represent the nation during the five days of revelry. Today, many black groups maintain that their traditional role as cultural ambassadors of the Brazilian melting pot has been stolen by more powerful, mainly white, elites. Since the 1980s, two major developments are thought to have contributed to this situation.

In the first place, black groups have been forced off the lead floats by richer, more powerful ethnicities. Carnival occurs throughout the city, with suburbs such as Santa Teresa boasting their own flavour of celebrations. However, most of the black festivities occur in streets where there are no TV cameras or supporting publicity. These groups do not have a world stage. The eye-catching, expensive costumes of the whites have captured national consciousness and global air-time. Into the bargain, the history and contribution of the culture of resistance, opposition and cooperation that black traditions embodied have been muffled or silenced outright. In effect, the grotesque play forms and images that signified exclusion and repression have been depoliticised and parodied by privileged groups. They have been turned into open play forms, stripped of their historical and ethnic roots and dispensed for the electronic eye of Western controlled media corporations. Of course, this is not a simple one-way process. It is in the nature of Carnival for different groups to read their own meanings into the event and to challenge media representations which provide a false image of the setting and its celebration. However, a clear and contentious trend has been the marginalisation of black participation.

Second, and by extension, the construction of Oscar Niemayer's *Sambodromo* (1984) stadium transformed the culture of Carnival by creating a showcase space for the lead floats. The more powerful ethnic groups hogged the most sought after display space in *Sambodromo* and attracted primary TV coverage. The less rich, mainly black and native ethnicities were forced back onto the streets. This reinforced the tendency favoured by the Brazilian Tourist Authority and TV corporations to produce images of Carnival that are guaranteed to be media-friendly to the global spectators. The balance between a genuine multicultural expression of Brazil and a cosmetic presentation of national culture shifted. TV producers decided that ludic energy, not moral energy, had greater air-time value. So political questions of the relationship between native and black ethnicities have been marginalised and glossed over in support of an idealised image of Brazilian nationalism.

This resulted in the emergence of a climate that was propitious to deracialised, depoliticised images of the festivities for global media consumption. Until 1984, larger *escolas de samba* shared loosely policed street space with smaller *blocos* in the pageant. With the opening of the *Sambodromo*, the stadium became the key setting of Carnival. The poorer *blocos* floats were relegated to the side streets and scheduled for the least TV-friendly days of coverage. The growing power of the Brazilian Tourist Authority and the broadcasting teams of international TV companies willing to pay top dollar for syndication rights combined to change the planning arrangements for the event. Although the event celebrates Brazilian nationalism, its global nature means that powerful corporate and media interests now exert a measure of influence on planning and broadcasting.

Traditionally, the presidents of the samba schools, known as 'the wise men of Carnival', plan and manage the event. They remain a focal point in determining the agenda and setting of the event. Their duties are extensive. Thus, they distinguish between 'permitted' and 'forbidden' activities during the Carnival period, oversee broadcasting and recording rights, set admission prices and manage the prize money awarded to winning schools and distribute government grant allocations (Queiroz, 1985). Critics allege that as slots in the stadium became more competitive, a structure of bribes, fees and informal 'understandings' emerged to ensure poll position for rich and prestigious *escolas* before spectators and TV cameras. *Blocos samba* and social criticism were marginalised in favour of dazzling images of floats that presented bland views of Brazilian multiculturalism. At the same time, ticket prices for the *Sambodromo* have grown beyond the reach of *blocos* communities. Poorer blacks, who traditionally regarded their contribution to be central, have found themselves sidelined.

Contemporary frictions also reveal older divisions in the event, which conflict with the images of inclusivity favoured by syndicated television corporations and the Brazilian tourist industry. What are these divisions?

The festivities of dancing, singing and play have three distinct roots:

1   The traditional *entrudo* (a Portuguese masked ball organised around practical jokes, laughter and ribaldry).
2   The Western European Carnival developed in Paris and Venice (which is regarded to be largely a bourgeois construction).
3   The street Carnival of lower class, black revellers known variously as *ranchos, blocos* and those other groups enrolled in the *escolas de samba* (Queiroz, 1985).

Entrudo, which is reminiscent of the comedy devices and tomfoolery recounted by Bakhtin (1968) in his classic work on European Carnival in feudal society, did not make significant use of music or dance forms. Similar patterns of mocking authority, water-fights and status levelling described by Bakhtin (1968) were found in Brazil. For example, Lowell Lewis (2000: 549) refers to the popularity of *entrudo* in the 19th-century Carnival. This game took the form of the benign pelting of citizens with projectile sand buckets filled with perfumed or noxious liquids. Today throwing beer at spectators echoes this practice. The incidence of mugging, fighting, sexual molestation and theft is higher during the week of Carnival.

The latent threat to social order resulted in gradual repression of elements that were perceived to be potentially turbulent by the authorities. From the 1840s, wealthy Europeans championed Parisian and Venetian Carnival forms, notably exclusive masked balls and dancing. In the process the *entrudo* form was partly outflanked. The play forms of the Western European Carnival tradition became ascendant. But this produced latent conflicts about colonial influence over the event and a struggle for a national range of symbols that would define Carnival.

As the 19th century progressed, industrialisation, agricultural labour and commerce swelled the metropolitan population of Rio. By the 1880s, the dances, percussion, tambourines, whistles and processionals of the black plantation economy population, groups known as *Congos*, *Cucumbys*, *Ze Pereiras*, *ranchos* and *blancos*, gained head-wind. According to Chasteen (1996: 41), by the 1890s the press used the term *samba* to describe the dance cultures associated with these groups. The *exuberance* of the samba play form, combined with images of political and ethnic resistance, boosted its popularity. By the 1930s samba was the dominant play and display form in the festivities.

Important research by Moura (1983) demonstrates that Carnival was not the only front for the advance of samba. During the first two decades of the 20th century the peripheral samba popular nightlife culture began to be penetrated by white bohemians and middle-class thrill-seekers. Multiethnic participation, notably from wealthier metropolitan elements and recent migrants from the northeastern state of Bahia, supported the expansion of the *Festa da Penha*, a traditional religious festival celebrated in October, into a more colourful, notorious event associated with promiscuity, vagrancy, theft and roguery. The celebration of these values, which samba 'defined' and which were, in turn, associated as defining the dangerous classes, prompted criticism from conservatives and police crack-downs.

Much disagreement surrounds the question of the origins of samba. The inflections and nuances of the form are hybrid, reflecting the contributions of many cultures and ethnicities. However, there is no real dispute that the local Indian and African roots, transported to Brazil via the slave plantation economy, were fundamental. *Batuque* (or *batucada*), which refers to the rhythmic drumming that features in the Afro-Brazilian religious ceremonies of *Umbanda* and *Camdomble* (and their Brazilian and New World progenitors), is widely regarded to be the template of contemporary samba (Sheriff, 1999: 11). The *escola de samba* refers to social clubs, centred upon samba and Carnival. The clubs attract people of all ages and membership has been traditionally associated with people from the lower socioeconomic strata. Club activities revolve around the planning, design and execution of samba dancing, heavy drumming, original music, lavish costumes and intricately decorated parade floats. All of this connects up with the *samba enredo*. That is, a theme song repeated throughout the Carnival parade. The size of samba schools ranges from a few hundred to many thousands (Zagal and Bruckman, 2005: 90–1). Traditionally, they practise a form of revelry organised around cultural and recreation purposes rather than the profit motive (Querioz, 1985: 2). The strong evocation of 'the people' and the voice of the marginal are central ingredients. By providing the poor with a hallmark stage for global consumption Carnival traditionally offered, and still offers, temporary restitution of status and prestige.

By the early 1960s, the organisational dynamics of Carnival groups from the poorer districts of the city began to change. Some of the leading *escolas de samba* began to raise revenue by encouraging communities of outsiders to pay a fee to join. In addition, they introduced a fee structure to cover participation in their entrance trials, pay their dancers and regularise their finances (Goldwasser, 1975: 65–82). According to Ribeiro (1981), in 1977 the majority of those attached to the big clubs earned between two and five times the minimum wage.

Commercialisation and professionalisation have produced a schism between the groups that have embraced 'modernisation' and those still run by family and community interests intent on providing nothing more than cultural and recreation entertainment for the people (Gaudin, 2004: 80). The development of hallmark status, which was partly engineered by the Brazilian tourist industry, intensified these divisions. 'Modernisers' are increasingly regarded by traditional groups as treating the Carnival as a media-grabbing spectacle, rather than a means to express the pride of the *pessoas humildes*, the humble people. The notion of a colour-blind society may be a national illusion. Any visitor to Rio quickly learns that the city has its *favelas* and ghettos. For a Western visitor at night, without a guide, these remain 'no go' areas. However, during the heyday of Carnival the idea of the melting pot was generally shared by Brazilian people. Breaking down barriers, eliminating prejudice and making all see the world with the same eye, were advocated as the gift of Carnival.

Privileged enclaves now have a commanding role in the economic management of the event. Fairly straightforwardly, this is now widely regarded as the appropriation and neutering of ethnic traditions of pride and resistance. But this disguises the earlier appropriation. Namely, the late 19th- and early 20th-century transformation of the protest aspect of Carnival into an unapologetic celebration of Brazilian nationalism (Hatcher, 1998: 315). It would be going too far to assert that black participation is repressed. Black ethnicities are included in the representations of Carnival sponsored and publicised by the Brazilian Tourist Authority and Brazilian business. However, the participation of the black population has been sidelined, and with it the history of racial struggle and achievement has been replaced with neutral, deracialised, depoliticised images of Brazilian multiculturalism.

The history of Carnival illustrates how event idioms can be ripped from their historical and ethnic contexts and redistributed by sectional interests to create new depoliticised, deracialised images fit for global consumption. The interest of global media corporations, wishing to maximise syndication and viewing figures, in soft images focusing upon TV-friendly communication data reinforces this process. Energy, amorousness and exuberance are portrayed as pre-ordained, eternal forces in the land mass now known as Brazil, severed from history and context. The ethnic and class tensions which Carnival exposes and dramatises are conveniently segregated from the picture. Instead, the TV-friendly images of Carnival are designed to enhance the power and influence of the new enclaves of prestige that promote the event.

The double appropriation is reflected in the five days of festivity, not least in the weakened glow of transcendence that the contemporary event is said to generate (Sheriff, 1999). However, the greater part of the domestic audience of consumers and nearly all in the global audience do not register political and racial tensions. Invariably, they are brushed out of the picture by event planners, managers and broadcasters. Of course the double appropriation has produced resistance and counter-action. To repeat: it is in the nature of Carnival for groups to read their own meanings into the event and to challenge official representations that are judged to be off the mark. However, since the construction of the *Sambodromo*, these forces have been in general, successfully muffled. Instead, Carnival is presented as a people's party that has eternal roots, an uncontentious history and represents the triumph of Brazilian multiculturalism.

The Sydney Mardi Gras

Cyclical events sometimes owe their origins to issue-based political objectives. Calendarisation provides a slot in which issues are commemorated, publicised and fortified. However, the higher the profile of these events, the greater the probability that the political message they carry will be diluted by commerce and the dynamics of general metropolitan or national politics. Event dilution occurs when the political issue that gave rise to the event produces parasitic offshoots which draw on the appeal of the event but diminish the strength of the original event concept. Typically, this occurs when the political issues that precipitated the event are incorporated into the normative order. When rights are formally recognised, the spur to mobilise and commemorate resistance and opposition is blunted. In the course of this the strong political message behind the original event concept may be neutered and sink into anodyne, all-embracing formulations, that lack precision and are ultimately vacuous.

The recent history of the Sydney Mardi Gras is a case in point. The origin of the event was a gay rights march in 1978. It had a strong political motivation. It was not a freedom fest, nor a vague general protest against authoritarianism. The ends of the march were quite coherent and pointed. It was conceived as a radical protest against gay repression and a demand for sexual recognition.

The intervention of the police, which resulted in 52 arrests, politicised the march. The development of Sydney Mardi Gras as a calendarised event was designed as a tribute to the struggle of 1978 and the articulation and defence of gay rights.

This extended to the recovery of gay and lesbian histories repressed by elected governments and the opening up of gay and lesbian space, which the authorities had hitherto marginalised. The Gay and Lesbian Sydney Mardi Gras was a political statement of sexual defiance and assertion. It was committed to a transformative ethic of gay and lesbian sexual liberation that defined itself against the strictures of heterosexual normative authority.

As the event evolved, it embraced bisexual, transgender, queer and intersex movements and values. From the goal of gay and lesbian liberation, the event ballooned into an all-encompassing expression of repressed and marginalised sexualities. Eventually, the range of non-heterosexual values was captured by the abbreviation GLBTQI (gay, lesbian, bisexual, transgender, queer and intersex). This widening of non-heteronormative interests retained a commitment to radical gay and lesbian liberation. The prefix 'Gay and Lesbian' to the Sydney Mardi Gras was indeed staunchly defended.

However, later generations of event planners argued that generational change compromised the growth potential of the event. Legal recognition of gay and lesbian rights meant that later generations were automatically tolerant of matters of sexual orientation. For younger people, being gay was not an issue. In effect, the radical politics of the Gay and Lesbian Mardi Gras was a victim of its own success. By raising the profile of gay rights and widening the span of tolerance and achieving legal recognition, the appeal of an event prioritising gay issues was diminished.

This is reflected in the chequered economic history of the event. In 2002 it went into administration following financial shortfalls. In 2009 sequencing problems separated the parade from the after-party by a week, resulting in a $A600,000 loss. However, these financial problems have been overcome. The Mardi Gras now injects $A30 million into the economy of New South Wales. For the gay and lesbian community, the Gay and Lesbian Mardi Gras is the premier national showpiece of gay rights.

This changed in 2011. The event management team announced that the 'Gay and Lesbian' prefix would be dropped from the 2012 parade and after-party. This was portrayed as a progressive development. The label GLBTQI was decried as an 'alphabet soup' which muddled the event concept. Post-1978 generations were said to be progressively free of the prejudices that motivated the original gay march. The new Sydney Mardi Gras would celebrate diversity and global rights. Thus, the post-2011 concept would be 'the right to be'. This was symbolised in the new logo of intertwined hearts symbolising 'infinite love' devised by Sydney's Moon advertising agency. While event organisers were careful to respect gay and lesbian sensitivities by insisting on the historical importance of the movement for sexual liberation, the new logo and event concept were blatant attempts to broaden the appeal of the concept for event sponsors and television broadcasting agencies (Munro, 2011).

What's in a name or logo you might say? Gay and lesbian interests are not ignored in the new Mardi Gras, rather they are being allied with kindred movements of resistance to build a general progressive statement of liberation politics. But this is tantamount to hitching a ride on the back of a movement for sexual recognition that had quite specific objectives. To propose that gay and lesbian rights have been won does not mean that these same rights must not continue to be defended or that the struggle to achieve them must cease to be commemorated. The Gay and Lesbian Mardi Gras provided the general public with a global image of the defence of gay and lesbian rights and a commemoration of the struggle to achieve them. This image is inevitably watered down in the new Mardi Gras which celebrates 'the right to be'.

What the Gay and Lesbian Mardi Gras did was to continuously remind the public that the right to be involves collective mobilisation, action and vigilance around specific rights issues. The political precision of the original event is forsaken and replaced with a more general, insipid message. Because they are divorced from politically specific ends, the 'right to be'/'infinite love' mantra risks being seen as meaning everything and nothing. The defence of sexual rights subsides into 'freedom politics'. But unless the ends of freedom politics are particularised, and the means to accomplish them specified, the effects of the event are unlikely to go beyond event consciousness. By taking the specific gay liberation politics from the forefront of the event and replacing them with a diffuse struggle for freedom, the event management team have redefined Mardi Gras as a hallmark spectacle with global broadcasting potential rather than a political protest which has continuing relevance to the defence of gay rights.

FIFA Event Management

Founded in 1904 and based in Geneva, FIFA controls and regulates the international agenda of what is arguably the world's most popular game. FIFA currently boasts 208 member countries. This is over a 400% increase since 1904 when it had only seven members. Through its control of the World Cup, FIFA is one of the premier global managers of cyclical events. The World Cup is a profit-driven cyclical event in which FIFA maintains strict authority over the regulation and quality of host-nation stadiums and sponsorship agreements (Cornelissen and Swart, 2006: 112).

At the time of writing, FIFA is mired in press allegations of bribery in the bidding process for the 2018 and 2022 World Cup. The two events were awarded respectively to Russia and Qatar. Soon after the announcement, Lord Triesman, the former chairman of the Football Association, accused four leading members of FIFA of 'improper and unethical behaviour' in the 2018 bid. Triesman maintained that the president of North America's football body CONCACAF requested £2.5 million to build a school and office complex in Trinidad for his support of the England bid. The head of the Paraguay FIFA executive was accused of requesting a knighthood in return for his vote to support the England bid.

An independent enquiry by *The Sunday Times* accused the president of the Confederation of African Football of being paid £$1.5 million to support the Qatar bid and the Oceania president asked for £1.5 million for an academy. At the time of writing these allegations are still under investigation. However, they were widely accepted as part of the backdrop to the summer pre-Olympic (2011) riots in London and other UK metropolitan centres. They contributed to the impression of super-profits for event planners and indifference to the plight of the unemployed, homeless and low paid in flagship event venues.

Nor, in respect of FIFA, are the criticisms of malpractice isolated. Within the sociology of sport there is a long history of criticism of the FIFA managerial cadre's conduct. For example, Sepp Blatter's entry in the campaign for the FIFA presidency in 1998 was widely reported to be built around connivance with Joao Havelange, the flamboyant, high handed Latin American president of FIFA who served between 1974 and 1998. Havelange had partly risen to power through a campaign to develop the game in underdeveloped football regions. In the build-up to the presidential vote Blatter borrowed Havelange's canvassing style by offering African nations financial assistance for football-related development (primarily through the Goal! projects) and endorsement of South Africa's (unsuccessful) bid as host nation for the 2006 World Cup. Critics were not slow to observe that the gesture went beyond an interest in globalising and democratising the international game. Not to beat about the bush, Blatter was accused of making campaign undertakings in return for votes (Darby, 2003: 11).

More damagingly, it was alleged that Blatter's eventual election was secured by payments of $50,000 to delegates from developing nations in return for their support (Campbell and Kuper, 1999; Hughes, 1998). In addition, $5 million of FIFA-allocated funds to the National Assistance Programme designed to provide technical and infrastructural assistance to the development of football in Liberia, between 1998 and 2002, was claimed never to have left the Zurich-based bank of FIFA. The electronic transactions were recycled back to private Swiss bank accounts held by African recipients (Armstrong, 2007: 237). Some observers have been prompted to see allegations of this sort as evidence that FIFA is an agent of the new imperialism, in which funds intended to redress inequality in sport and global society are syphoned off to construct 'personal fiefdoms' (Sugden and Tomlinson, 1998: 313).

FIFA has been described as 'a multi million dollar business operating under Swiss charitable association rules' (Jennings, 2011: 9). The ruling body's domicile in Switzerland is widely regarded to contribute to its reputation for a lack of transparency and accountability. For example, under Swiss law the legal charitable status minimises routes of disclosure about income distribution. This means, for example, that fundamental and legitimate issues of public interest, such as the salary of the president and the network of financial transactions, are *sub judice*. The dominant picture that emerges is of an international event management organisation veiled in secrecy and ruled by a cadre that is only partially accountable.

There is no doubt that the World Cup generates millions. Analysis of the Japan–Korea joint hosting of the 2002 FIFA World Cup reveals the scale and range of commercial interests embedded in the event that profited from the competition (Horne and Manzenreiter, 2004). Sales of JVC digital satellite TV sets were boosted 70% in the run-up to the FIFA World Cup (2002) in Japan. In the financial year before the tournament Fuji Xerox doubled sales of its high end colour copiers. Subscriptions to JPhone (Vodaphone's representative in Japan) and SkyPerfect TV! jumped dramatically prior to the kick-off. The official sponsor of the Japanese national team was Kirin beer. Sales of their specially brewed low malt Olympic brand were so successful that they exceeded targets by 400%. Adidas sold more than a million footballs and 600,000 Japan national shirts. Hotels, restaurants, bars and retail shops also benefited from the event. Between 31 May and 30 June 2002 482,000 foreign nationals entered Japan.

The event provided countless attractive opportunities for corporate branding and national prestige building which had little to do with adding to the fellowship of the World Cup. Rather the event and the global media publicity surrounding it were appropriated as marketing tools for sectional business and government department interests. The leading Korean electronics company Samsung spent US$100 million on global advertising to promote its mobile phone range, computers and DVD players. The official Korean World Cup sponsor, Korean Telecom, estimated that brand recognition increased by 95%. The opening ceremony, watched by an estimated 2.5 billion people worldwide, was employed by the Korean tourist industry and government to showcase Korean 'consumer nationalism' in which national culture and technology were favourably and prominently displayed. The Korean tourist industry reported 463,000 visitors during the tournament (Horne and Manzenreiter, 2004: 193–7).

Business appropriation of the World Cup mirrors tendencies in FIFA itself. The FIFA PR–media hub portrays the organisation as popularising and serving the cause of 'the people's game' (Walvin, 1975). Yet there is now a substantial body of evidence to suggest that an enclave in the governing body has deployed the bidding process for the World Cup as a bargaining chip to advance their own interests. The invocation of consensus and harmony provides cover for clandestine deal-making and power-brokering. In this way events are hijacked. Their significance as a global cultural celebration provides the means for business and political interests to make economic and cultural capital.

Another aspect of this process in the event field can be illustrated if we turn to examine Live 8 and the Make Poverty History campaign. This is an especially noteworthy example because the event committed itself to achieve economic justice for the developing world and was openly dismissive of political chicanery.

As we shall see, things did not quite turn out as intended.

Live 8 and the Make Poverty History Campaign

The Make Poverty History (2005) campaign was coordinated by the Global Call to Action Against Poverty (GCAP). It consisted of an international coalition of charities, trade unions, religious groups, campaigning organisations and celebrities. The Live 8 concert also involved considerable behind the scenes planning between the Band Aid Charitable Trust, the Prime Minister's Office, the Treasury, the Department of Culture,

Media and Sport and the London Parks Authority. In addition, global agreements for performance and live transmission were made. In addition, event planners negotiated sponsorship, rights deals and merchandise sales to cover the £11 million cost of the event (Street, 2011). The Live 8 intercontinental concert was timed to influence the deliberations on global aid scheduled for the G8 conference in Gleneagles, Scotland. It was designed to be the climax of the campaign, billed as a world party for global justice.

What was understood by the term global justice extended well beyond financial and trade questions. The GCAP agitated for far-reaching, irreversible, global transformation that included provisions to achieve nothing less than the elimination of present and future crimes against humanity, the promotion of democratic government, the establishment of accountable infrastructures, the end of discrimination against women, racial equality and the application of human rights.

Unlike Live Aid it addressed the structure of hunger and poverty and asked to be judged finally, under the optic of system change. That being said, there was no interest in seizing institutional power. The immediate aim of Live 8 was propaganda, i.e. to educate the public about the relationship between poverty and global power and to make G8 leaders cognizant of the political dangers involved in turning a deaf ear to the 'voice' of the electorate and world opinion.

Live 8 was a supporting series of 11 international shows, bringing together over 1000 musicians, telecast live on 182 television networks and broadcast on 2000 radio networks. The estimated audience was, as we have had occasion to note, 3 billion. Once again, Sir Bob Geldof played a leading role in the Live 8 organisation. With Bono, he was the celebrity 'face' of the event.

Although Live 8 occurred on the 20th anniversary of Live Aid, Geldof went to great lengths to insist that the 2005 concert should not be seen as Live Aid 2. The GCAP organisers recognised the sponsorship and publicity potential of events. However, the explicit objective of Live 8 was to apply publicity to exert dual leverage over the economically strong nations to formally acknowledge deep, new, irreversible social and economic obligations to those living in poverty. In other words, Live 8 aimed to raise event consciousness to precipitate system change. Indeed, Make Poverty History was widely portrayed as the prelude to a new form of citizenship in the West.

At the core was the wholehearted recognition of a new post-Westphalian vision of global cosmopolitanism (Nash, 2008: 168). This was woven around the explicit acknowledgement of extra-territorial financial obligations on the part of the G8 and global responsibilities on the behalf of ordinary citizens. Tacitly, in recognition of the limitations of the emotionalism, catharsis and exhibitionism of event consciousness, Live 8 and the GCAP pitched for renewable financial aid, debt reduction and trade reform packages. This was predicated in guaranteeing media vigilance in countries who are recipients of Western aid and building appropriate infrastructural auditing and policing frameworks. We shall come back to examine this vision in more detail later.

One organisational feature of the GCAP that must be highlighted at the outset is size. The coalition consisted of over 700 corporate and non-profit organisations (Elavsky, 2009: 386). To begin with, size was held to be an asset because it supposedly symbolised a groundswell of unity behind the agenda of social justice. However, as the campaign unfolded this interpretation became harder to sustain. Friction over strategy, tactics of activism and publicity made the GCAP open to the charge that too many cooks were spoiling the broth (Sireau, 2008).

This was exploited by the hosts of the G8 conference, who sought to redefine the 'system change' banner of the campaign into a more publicity-friendly, regionally specific, message, offering politically profitable photo-shoot and op-ed opportunities. Not to beat about the bush, as we shall see presently, the GCAP social justice campaign was hijacked by G8 hosts as a reprise of the Live Aid event, with all of the rich historical legacy of pop culture emotionalism, exhibitionism and *chutzpah* to 'save Africa' associated with Band Aid in 1985 (Harrison, 2010).

To be clear, the GCAP focus differed radically from Band Aid. It was not directed at an emergency or a region. It was aimed at the poorest 1 billion living on less than a dollar a day. The GCAP went to considerable lengths to publicise global poverty as a *normal* consequence of the present existing global system. Unnecessary poverty was the foundation of the demand for fundamental *structural* reform. Pragmatically, this boiled down to forcing the G8 to confirm that the poverty produced by the present system is 'morally unacceptable' and to accede to three concrete objectives (Harrison, 2010: 394):

- The authorisation of multiple debt write-off.
- The implementation of substantial year-on increases in aid.
- The regulatory reform of trade.

Aid, debt and trade were advertised as the cornerstones of the campaign. However, it is important to repeat that the justice agenda encompassed a range of human rights issues that was much broader and radical. It was committed to nothing less than the irreversible reform of the system of injustice between the rich and poor countries and the construction of a meaningful post-Westphalian construct of citizenship. The video and other forms of GCAP publicity rammed this home by presenting system change and global justice as a keystone of modern citizenship. However, as with the Live Aid proceedings, the question of what constituted world opinion was vague. The GCAP acted on the presumption that it was representing the world, but it was not accountable to any recognised electorate and the question of the basis of jurisdiction was murky. The much publicised march in Edinburgh in support of the campaign involved an estimated 225,000 people (Gorringe and Rosie, 2008: 693). At the time, GCAP organisers and publicists presented this as self-evident proof of popular support. However, a march is not a movement. Anti-capitalist protesters, local campaigning groups and seekers of spectacle brought different meanings to the march. It is unwise to claim solidarity without careful examination of the orientations of different groups (Routledge, 2011). The 225,000 were the only quantitative data provided to support the claim of a popular mandate. As stated, it is of debatable validity.

The lack of clarity about the justification of the claim to speak for the world was paralleled in woolly thinking about the precise social and financial objectives of the campaign. Although a new world order based in the recognition of political and social obligations to the poor was demanded, the fiscal and citizenship implications were not clearly spelt out. For example, none of the promotional material produced by the GCAP provided estimates of the consequences for personal taxation or national borrowing of debt write-off, increased aid and the regulatory reform of trade. Instead, Live 8 and GCAP publicity dwelt on the theme made familiar by Band Aid, that *'we' must do something.* Bold objectives marked public pronouncements, but there was imprecision about the fine details of redistribution, realignment and renewable responsibilities of cosmopolitan citizenship. Nowhere was this more apparent than in the question of the appropriate international machinery to ensure that any G8 reform pledges arising from Gleneagles would be honoured.

It is worth going into this in more detail because it implies that there may be insurmountable limits to event consciousness as an effective instrument of system change. Most commentators now agree that what happened at Gleneagles was a triumph of the political manipulation of GCAP social justice objectives by G8 leaders and their secretariat (Elavsky, 2009; Harrison, 2010; Payne, 2006). The final communique issued by Tony Blair, who hosted the summit, acknowledged that, 'it is in the nature of politics that you do not achieve absolutely everything that you want ... we do not simply by this communique make poverty history ... we do show how it can be done, and we do signify the political will to do so' (Blair, 2005). The communique went on to claim that the G8 achieved:

a firm consensus that this problem needs to be tackled, has to be tackled now, together with a dialogue for the future and a plan of action that brings on the one hand the major wealthy economies, including America, and on the other hand the emerging economies of China and India and other countries together. That ... is something to be proud of. (Blair, 2005)

But Tony Blair and Gordon Brown have been attacked by many commentators for using the MPH campaign for political capital. By manoeuvring publicity-friendly images of Africa as 'the real problem', they watered down the radical, transformative social justice agenda that the GCAP intended to apply to the world. This diverted public attention from the existing international institutions and wider context of the balance of power relationships behind aid, trade and debt which favours rich and powerful states. By projecting Africa as 'the problem', Blair and Brown encouraged support from liberals who object to poverty but prefer not to follow their thoughts beyond that point (Harrison, 2010; Payne, 2006).

That a degree of reform was achieved at Gleneagles is not in dispute. Moreover, any shift in favour of reducing the development gap is to be welcomed. The G8 pledged to commit to a collective foreign aid target of 0.56% of GNI (Gross National Income) by 2010 and 0.7% by 2015. However, what emerges most forcefully from an analysis of the G8 proceedings is the cautious mindset of many leaders to sacrifice growth for aid. This was reflected in the resistance of some G8 members to meet the GCAP demands in full. The majority of undertakings to deliver the reform of aid, debt and trade were hedged with bail-out clauses of various kinds. For example, the American delegation agreed to double US aid to Africa between 2004 and 2010, but refused to go beyond a 0.7% of GNI target. Canada refused to go beyond the 0.33% target agreed at the Monterrey 'Financing for Development' conference in March 2002. Within the EU, the German and Italian governments gave themselves latitude in honouring relief obligations by flagging that aid commitment would be subject to budgetary contingencies.

Moreover, some critics note that the principle of equitable distribution has not been observed in foreign aid. In particular, Afghanistan, Palestine and Iraq have been awarded disproportionate amounts of G8 funds for, respectively, reconstruction from the effects of war, infrastructural reform and debt relief (Payne, 2006: 926). In this way powerful members in the G8 are vulnerable to the allegation that they have used aid money to support political ends rather than the straightforward relief of the poorest in the world.

In addition the G8 has been criticised for sacrificing commitments on aid for growth after the economic recession hit economic performance in 2008 (Elliott, 2010). As I have already noted, the OECD has documented substantial shortfalls of delivery in G8 aid. If the pledges made in 2005 are adjusted for inflation, total aid should have risen by $60 billion (rather than the $40 billion actually achieved). The G8 fulfilled only 50% of its commitment to Africa – roughly a $15 billion increase in aid as opposed to the promised $30 billion (Sachs, 2010). An accountability review of aid performance delivered at the G8 summit in Deauville (2008) reported that in 2010 only the UK met the 0.56% target agreed at Gleneagles. France achieved 0.5% of GNI, Germany, 0.38% and the USA, 0.21% (Porter, 2011).

Turning now to the question of global citizenship. Arguably, this is a deeper issue than aid, debt relief and regulatory trade reform, because it seeks, through the PR–media hub to create space to engineer the consensual extension of citizenship beyond national borders. National citizens are called upon to recognise global obligations and responsibilities. Kate Nash (2008: 172) spells out the scale of ambition involved very clearly:

> The real task of Make Poverty History was to create a new imagined political community to put pressure on the cosmopolitanizing state from national and civil society. It was not just a matter of getting people to change their perspectives in order to agree with the particular proposals of the campaign and then to take action within the 'normal' frame of national politics. ... It was rather a matter of transforming the dominant frame of 'national interest' to conceive of justice more broadly, as concerning those with whom national citizens are connected *outside the nation.*

The spirit of emotionalism and altruism produced during the campaign by the GCAP PR–media hub was widely commented upon in the press and by the public. However, post-event history suggests that the imagined community was illusory. The MPH campaign did not succeed in making the majority understand themselves as part of global society, with strong interconnections with people living far away with whom, in other respects, they have nothing in common. This is not to say the social consciousness was not influenced by the MPH campaign or that Live 8 backfired. Rather, the high objective of making new citizens was not accomplished. If it had been, there would have been a firestorm of criticism and mass protests on the publication of OECD figures indicating that the G8 Gleneagles target had not been met by 2010. Instead, the news barely made the headlines and was relegated to the economics back pages of the dailies.

Additionally, there is an argument that because the MPH campaign and Live 8 used aid and debt machinery that had been invented by the West, the goals of wealth redistribution and social justice were fatally compromised. This machinery was so steeped in stereotypical presumptions about the 'advanced' West and the 'helpless' 'third world' that it prohibited the emergence of genuinely global citizenship (Yrjola, 2009). What then, was the significance of Live 8?

In typical forthright fashion Bob Geldof repudiates the argument that celanthropy, as embodied by the MPH campaign and Live 8, failed to learn from the mistakes of Live Aid. As he puts it, 'in purely financial terms: Live Aid: 150 million; Live 8: 50 billion per annum' (Ecclestone, 2011). However, he concedes that the campaign's PR–media hub did not succeed in getting the message across of the requirement for fundamental system change. The 'romance' of Live Aid was not replicated at Live 8, which perhaps implies that contemporary audiences now treat global mega-events like Live 8 with a degree of compassion fatigue. The law of diminishing returns has set in with too many local and global events clamouring for emergency relief.

Be that as it may, Geldof's readiness to let money do most of the talking is symptomatic of the event consciousness mindset. Complexity is sacrificed for banner statements and slogans. Unproven solidarity and unsupported popular mandates are presented by publicists as 'facts'. A dubious, unexamined contrast is drawn between the helpless and powerless and the vigorous and imaginative who act on behalf of 'the world'. Emotionalism and exhibitionism combine to make a charitable act inherently romantic. Who in their right mind is going to argue against '$50 billion per annum' for the third world?

In reality, many G8 delegates at Gleneagles did argue against this level of relief on the grounds that it constitutes an unacceptable risk to growth and, by implication, to the standard of living in G8 territories. Far from endorsing a mode of global citizenship, G8 leaders and their secretariats committed to limited, conditional relief packages that privileged existing geopolitical boundaries. As I have noted, according to the latest OECD figures, there has been significant default on these pledges. This takes nothing away from the achievements of the GCAP campaign and the Live 8 event in providing a measure of relief for the poorest 1 billion. However, it underscores the point that pledges have not been fulfilled. So Geldof's $50 billion headline is eye-catching, but misleading.

Larry Elliott (2010) maintains that the challenge of the global recession has led some G8 leaders to attempt a clandestine manoeuvre to reduce G8 relief commitments. Thus, the Gleneagles agreement has been reframed by some major participants from being a milestone to a millstone. In addition, this raises questions about the real nature of the political capital of the Gleneagles agreement. *Prima facie,* it was an undertaking of support for the poor and hungry and a recognition of limited global obligations. This made the electorate appreciative of their leaders and soothed their own conscience. However, Sachs (2010, 2011) and others have noted that inequitable relief distribution since 2005 has supported Western interests in Afghanistan, Iraq and Palestine. This raises the spectre that funding has been used to *consolidate* global domination by G8 powers rather than to address the dilemma of those who are most at risk.

Outwardly, the GCAP campaign and Live 8 publicity put the onus upon the world to act in order to eliminate poverty and hunger. In reality, the proceedings were founded upon the notion of a struggle involving a few clued-up, sympathetic, active people over the heads of an apathetic mass. The campaign publicity given to the 225,000 anti-capitalist campaigners who marched in Edinburgh pointed the finger at the majority who stayed at home, implicitly contemplating their navels. The division between an active few and an apathetic majority is a fatal defect in event strategy. Unintentionally, it sows the seeds of defeatism and despair because it neglects to determine effective methods of politicising the majority and caricatures entire continents as befuddled and helpless. The question of how power and control can be wrested from the institutions controlled by the dominant powers was fudged in preference for a propaganda war that makes for good television and big newspaper headlines. William Easterly (2007: 15) gets it right when he writes that, the main problem with the publicity for relief interventions like the Live 8 event, is that the people paying the bills are rich people,

> who have very little knowledge of poor people. The rich people demand big actions to solve big problems, which is understandable and compassionate. The Big Plans at the top keep the rich people happy that 'something is being done' about such a tragic problem as world poverty. In June 2005, the *New York Times* ran an editorial advocating a Big Plan for Africa titled 'Just Do Something'. Live 8 organizer Bob Geldof, said 'Something must be done; anything must be done, whether it works or not.' Something, anything, any Big Plan would take the pressure off the rich to address the critical needs of the poor. Alas, if ineffective big plans take the pressure off the rich to help the poor, there's the second tragedy, because then the effective piecemeal actions will not happen.

There are many lessons for event management from the GCAP campaign and the Live 8 event. Classical statements of public relations theory emphasise the importance of clarity of purpose (Bernays, 1923, 1928). At first sight, it might be said that the GCAP campaign and Live 8 fulfilled this to the hilt. The message of increased aid, debt write-off and the reformation of trade certainly got through to the public.

Deeper enquiry presents a different picture. The social justice aspects of the campaign left many people with the impression that bigger goals had been fluffed. Set against the objective of transforming social consciousness in the direction of global citizenship the G8 agreements on aid, trade and debt appeared like pyrrhic victories. The efforts of Geldof and Bono to stir a generation into the moral condemnation of poverty and encourage them to take the lead in global transformation failed to rise above what Nash (2008: 177) calls 'narcissistic sentimentalism'. To some extent this is inherent in event technologies of communication which privilege emotionalism, exhibitionism and apply mass events as catalysts to offload repressed feelings rather than as building blocks for planned system change. Narcissism goes hand in hand with display. So it is difficult to establish where self-interest ends and personal disinterest begins.

In the case of the GCAP/Live 8 campaign lack of clarity also reflects the large number of stakeholders involved. The coalition consisted of participants of different sizes and interests in poverty and inequality that spanned local, national and global levels. Although the coalition went to great lengths to produce the public impression of speaking with one voice, it proved challenging to reconcile the conflicting interests of members. This went to the heart of the concrete policy goals that the coalition presented to the G8. They were unbalanced. While it cost comparatively little for the G8 to increase aid and write off debt, trade justice was a different matter. Restructuring trade cartels in the economically advanced countries and introducing protectionism to shield enterprise in the developing world had direct implications for employment and growth. The reluctance of the G8 to fully go down that route demonstrates the limits of post-Westphalian models of global and cosmopolitan citizenship. In particular, although communication networks are global, local and national media reflect domestic interests that hinder the communication of transnational goal achievement. There are obvious practical, political difficulties for elected national leaders in providing relief for the anonymous billion living on less than one dollar per day, while enforcing domestic debt foreclosures and rationalising national welfare programmes. At the level of national government, the old adage, that 'charity begins in the home', is a matter of political expedience as well as kinship.

Live 8 also raised troubling and uncomfortable questions of the gap between public emotionalism and exhibitionism and private practice. How deep does the public display of charity marry up with charitable practice in personal life?

The issue was brought to a head one year after Live 8 when the media reported a tax avoidance scheme involving Bono that tarnished his reputation as a global Samaritan. In 2006 U2 Ltd moved part of their business relating to royalty earnings from Ireland to the Netherlands. This followed the decision by the Irish government to limit tax-free earnings for artists. Before this, all artistic earnings has been tax free. After 2006, artists were legally required to pay taxes on earnings over €250,000. Bono was widely portrayed as a hypocrite, preaching social justice in public, while practising 'tax efficiency' in private (Noah, 2006).

Now, tax avoidance is different from tax evasion. The former is legal, and is an established part of the international financial system, whereas the latter is illegal. The U2 Ltd tax avoidance scheme of which Bono was a part, was legally compliant. It merely involved switching operations from a tax regime that had become adverse (Ireland) to one that is friendly (the Netherlands). Notwithstanding the legality of the move, Bono's decision caused uproar in Ireland and censure from the global media. The singer was accused of trying to have his cake and eat it.

A bigger question than the inconsistency of a charity superstar is how deeply the audience and public networks connected to the Make Poverty History campaign and Live 8 were changed by the event. In the absence of empirical research one has recourse only to conjecture. But how many people do you know who were either aware of or remember the precise objectives of the Make Poverty History campaign? It is not so much that people are insincere or that they have the memory of a sieve. Rather, it is in the nature of modern media-based celanthropy to continually replace public awareness about one incident or emergency with another. The charity sector presents the world as being in a state of permanent crisis. Moreover, the structural causes of incidents and emergencies like famine, pollution or injustice are poorly understood. Humanitarian aid prefigures giving and caring over analysis and learning. Event management exacerbates this by glamorising giving and caring through high profile displays of charity that are broadcast and recorded by the media. The question is, how much good does this really do?

As we have seen, critics of Western aid programmes are not sanguine about the benefits of private celanthropy. Instead, they point to the necessity of firm agenda setting and concerted action to divest the rich of more resources and to redistribute the balance to the developing world (Easterly, 2007; Moyo, 2010; Sachs, 2010, 2011). Yet the history of the G8 Gleneagles agreement reveals the difficulties and pitfalls involved in turning aid policy into practice. Governments and multinational corporations are at the mercy of global economic conditions and the demands of their home electorates and customers. There is a tendency to play to the media gallery in presenting communiques and agreements as set in stone. When the story drops under the media radar the fine print of the balance sheet involved in delivering policy is typically sidelined by other incidents and emergencies.

Conclusion: Appropriation and the Society of the Spectacle

Event appropriation is related to the commodification, commercialisation, bureaucratisation and professionalisation of event management. As events expand from minor (local) to major (regional/national) and mega (global) levels the complexity of managing them increases and the rewards that they generate multiply. The downfall of cyclical events like the Sunset Junction Street Fair (Los Angeles) was related to the commodification and commercialisation of the event. This was popularly perceived as transforming the spontaneous, inclusive origins of the event by turning it into a paid spectacle with salaried management and surveillance staff providing cost control and public order. It is by no means an isolated example in the event field. Why?

In sociology there is an old rule known as 'the iron law of oligarchy'. Formulated and developed by Robert Michels (1962) in an attempt to explain the conundrum of oligarchies in democratic political parties, it is now applied more generally to the tendency for enclaves of domination to perpetuate in all structures of democracy. As the scale of events advances, there is a clear correlation with the emergence of oligarchies in the event planning and management teams. Even in projects strongly committed to the ideal of flat hierarchy, such as Burning Man City, there is a demonstrable tendency for a salaried, professionally qualified executive to emerge and monopolise issues of cost control, revenue distribution, publicity and public order.

The result is a separation between planners, providers and consumers. To repeat the observation made by Flyvbjerg et al. (2003: 5), the enlargement in event scale results in the exclusion of the majority from mega-project decision-making issues and concentrates power in the hands of the few.

The iron law of oligarchy was given an important twist by Guy Debord (1967, 1988) and his colleagues in the Situationist movement (McDonough et al., 2009). Their work on the society of the spectacle relates directly to the event phenomenon, yet is oddly neglected or ignored outright in most of the professional event literature. In a nutshell, they propose that societies built around mass communication demand the development and use of the commodified spectacle as a means of pacifying the population. Events are thus defined not so much as a modern axis of regulation, but as the means of strengthening consumption and delivering political control.

While it dramatically highlights the political and economic importance of the event spectacle, there are problems with the Situationist thesis. It maintains that the spectacle has dissolved the separation between truth and illusion so any notion of reality is now redundant. Event festivity is viewed, on *a priori* grounds, as parody (Debord, 1967: 154). Indeed, if one reads the Situationists closely, genuine event festivity is portrayed as an exclusively historical phenomenon. It has nothing to do with the society of the spectacle which demands spectators make gestures of wider transformation while leaving the essentials of the system of organised inequality intact. For the Situationists, the Paris Commune of 1871 fulfilled the requirements of a genuine festive event.

What are these requirements? We can answer the question most precisely by considering the primary features that the Situationists identify as marking the Paris Commune. This is the closest that they come to outlining the features of genuine festivity, i.e. an event and a form of society that is not subjected to the interests of capital but follows the dictates of human creativity and sociability (Debord et al., 2009). Four features are earmarked as decisive.

In the first place, they observe that the event was *leaderless*. Because of its spontaneity and short duration, the Commune never generated an oligarchy. It thus avoided the hierarchical divisions and power differences of inclusion and exclusion that characterise event appropriation.

Second, the Commune was based in the overturning of power relations in capitalist society. It involved the real empowerment of the oppressed. For a moment the workers acquired direct power. Upon this basis a series of legal decrees were issued aimed at the restitution of working-class rights that had been swept aside after the historic capitalist triumph over capitalism. These included remission of rents, separation of church and state, the abolition of interest on debts, the rights of employees to take over and run enterprises, wage equality for women and gender equality.

Third, the Commune contributed to the re-spatialisation of working-class life from the periphery of national culture to the core. The way of life of working-class people was no longer treated as insignificant. Instead, for the three-month period before the Commune was crushed, it occupied centre stage. It knocked aside what the Situationists called 'the petrified signs of the dominant organisation of life' (Debord et al., 2009: 170). The recolonisation of space formerly devoted to honouring the privilege of capital was regarded as an essential *material* contribution to liberate social consciousness.

Fourth, the urban revolution of 1871 was an *armed* revolution. The Situationists emphasise the severity of the assault against capitalist domination by the willingness of the Communards to take arms against the oppressive forces of capital. Armed struggle is presented as the precondition of genuine rebellion. The willingness to use arms and stake one's life in the cause of revolution is portrayed as the hallmark of an effective repudiation of what we would now call the gestural economy. There is a pointed contrast at issue between real, direct action and the *display* of real, direct action. The burden of the contrast is of course that the society of the spectacle has superseded real, direct action by turning resistance and opposition into representation and gesture.

The Paris Commune lasted for only three months. It was eventually defeated by the forces of the establishment. The reprisals were terrible. In one week, 20,000 Communards and suspected sympathisers were shot. As Anderson (2004) notes, this far exceeded the casualties in both the Franco-Prussian War and Robspierre's infamous 'Terror' of 1793–4. It was accompanied by mass deportations, jailings – often on flimsy pretences – and a general clampdown on workers' rights.

The Paris Commune has entered the mythology of the Left as prefiguring the progressive society based upon the free and full development of the individual. It was not the inevitable expression of the fate of history. Rather it was an opportunist strike that exploited the political and economic disarray that followed the Franco-Prussian War. Because the structural preconditions for the transition to post-capitalist society were not in place, the revolution disintegrated.

The Situationists comment critically upon its lack of preparation and the disorganisation of the Communards, especially in relation to seizing the resources of the banks and repelling the armed forces of the establishment. But what simultaneously outshines this, and underscores the characterisation of the Commune as a truly 'festive' event, is the Situationist recognition of the *audacity* of the events in the Paris spring of 1871.

When one looks at the likes of Getz (2005, 2012), Getz and Wicks (1994) and Bowdin et al. (2011: 87), with the casual references they make to event management producing 'celebration spaces', 'cultural and economic benefits', 'building community pride', 'increasing environmental awareness' and 'introducing new and challenging ideas', it is the question of the *audacity* of events today that comes to mind. This is also why, for all its unexamined rhetoric, the critique of Debord (1967, 1988) and the Situationists (McDonough et al., 2009) continues to be deeply relevant. For, not to beat about the bush, this critique asks bluntly, how can we get beyond the gestural economy? The answer that it provides would certainly unsettle and even incense the management of the Make Poverty History campaign and Live 8, the planners behind the 'right to be'/'infinite love' manoeuvres in the rebranding of the Sydney Mardi Gras and the economic and social interests in Brazil intent on maximising attendance and syndication of Carnival rights. For at the nub of it is a demand for direct and violent action to change the system.

It might be objected that this approach is amoral since it is predicated in the use of physical violence to achieve liberation. Many event managers would add that the argument confuses event management with social revolution. However, by the same token, flirting with 'making a difference' by holding rock concerts for relief and championing the romance of charity may be dismissed as ineffective, because it confuses ludic energy with moral energy.

The moral regulation of populations works best when individuals are persuaded that private acts of charity to address inequality and injustice are preferable to collective mobilisation and concerted action to transform the structural components that proliferate inequality and injustice. One reason why events have become so prominent and popular is that they offer a public forum for these private acts to be displayed and recorded. But this does not get away from, or go beyond, the profound reservations voiced by Debord and his colleagues in the Situationist movement about the shallow nature of event festivity in what they refer to as 'the society of the spectacle'. For the precondition of this society is based in organised inequality, which partly explains the correlation between the magnification of scale in event provision and event appropriation.

12

DOES EVENT MANAGEMENT HAVE A FUTURE?

The future of global event management is copper-bottomed. It answers to the human needs of compassion and transcendence. It is feted to prosper because it fits so snugly with the age of communication power and network publics. Few stateless solutions to global problems display a 'can do' attitude with greater gusto than the image of millions of ordinary people coming together and acting 'as one'.

On closer inspection, the numerical aggregate attributed to global events turns out to be a classic example of an illusory community. The dimensions and formations are imprecise, like the number of raindrops one observes through the windscreen wipers of a car window on the motorway. One has the feeling that it all connects, but exactly how, in what volume and to what purpose, is a mystery. The reports of the corporate media which, in most Western democracies, privilege entertainment over information and portray the global news as a string of disconnected episodes instead of links in a chain dominated by an interlocking global power network, contribute to public obfuscation (Curran, 2011: 114–15).

Nobody knows the size of the network public that connected to the Live 8 or Live Earth concerts. Nobody knows what percentage of the population was genuinely radicalised by the respective messages of debt relief, fair trade and anti-pollution. Nobody knows how powerful the Olympics are in building a durable global spirit of fellowship. Nobody really knows how many cents of Live Aid money were deployed effectively, and how many were expropriated by the military junta and Tigray rebels. But the traffic of language in event management points resolutely in the opposite direction.

The publicity that promotes global events choreographed by the PR–media hub is, overwhelmingly, a game of smoke and mirrors. It may be prudent to play this game to the hilt in order to win coveted air-time.

However, it does no service to the cause of accurate reporting or informed assessment. The massive goodwill that permeates global events is a tribute to the power of the romance of charity and the popular appeal of stateless solutions to incidents, emergencies and entrenched issues of inequality and injustice. The logic of political economy requires a more bracing solution.

The absence of this solution is more than a matter of the current strength of the Right and the accompanying disarray of the Left. There has been an important change in how we view political change and action. Doubtless, this reflects the pivotal importance of corporate/ state-sponsored media and the ubiquity of visual culture in global social ordering and moral regulation. What has happened is that modern psychology now routinely seizes upon representation as resistance and rewards symbolic gestures of opposition above direct political action.

Let those who doubt this turn to the public and police response to the Occupy movement against global capitalism in 2011–12.[1] At first, the tents in high profile urban spaces were tolerated. The Wall Street occupation was centred on Zuccotti Park a handful of blocks from the Wall Street stock exchange, while the London occupation occurred in St Paul's churchyard a stone's-throw from the London stock exchange. The public expressed sympathy with the case against the bankers and public opinion moderated police action. However, as the occupations became perceived as an unacceptable impediment to transport and tourism, the police applied tactics of mass arrests and enforced clearance. In some cases this resulted in the long-term securitisation of public space. For example, Wall Street intensified police presence and installed a network of metal barriers outside the approach and entrance to the stock exchange which acted as a *cordon sanitaire* between stock traders and potentially unruly elements. The spatial epicentre of the occupation, Zuccotti Park, was also cordoned off, with police guards manning the barriers.

Likewise, Metropolitan Police tactics in London sought to kettle protesters around the main site of occupation in the churchyard of St Paul's Cathedral while boosting police presence and erecting barricades in nearby Paternoster Square to act as a *cordon sanitaire* between the London stock exchange and the axis of protest. Once the occupiers became portrayed as 'unrealistic' in their demands, an 'obstruction' to transport and a 'threat' to tourism, they were defined by the authorities as a public nuisance and steps were taken to neutralise their influence.

Occupy did not challenge the citadels of capital. Arms and violence were no significant part of the movement. Rather, it was a peaceful protest that relied heavily on boosting social consciousness about the realities of economic inequality and power differences. Metaphorically speaking, it threw tomatoes and rotten eggs at the establishment (the propertied 1%) in the name of the 99%.[2] It was a symbolic gesture rather than an attempt to subvert power.

Global event management exploits and develops the principle that representation is resistance. It rewards votive behaviour, rather than direct (violent) action (since the focus is upon the event not post-event evaluation), and it promotes episode-driven exhibitionist energy to make incidents and emergencies *causes célèbres*. Further, it assigns ultimate value if these forms of practice are recorded. Although it portrays itself as spontaneous and inclusive, global event management is, in fact, stage-managed and closely codified. One of the signature messages that it conveys is that we are all in it together. When Bono tells us that 'every time I clap my hands a child dies in Africa' or Sir Bob Geldof rejects media reports that Live Aid money was syphoned off by military and rebel forces in Ethiopia by proclaiming 'not a single penny of Live Aid money went to military, bullets or anything else – 100% went to aid', the aim is to silence critics and create an overwhelming wave of glib unity among the media, the concert audience and network publics. However, what we know about the facts of charity votive behaviour and giving do not support a 'team-world' thesis. Take one of the most obvious issues that we have not addressed sufficiently before: event participation.

One of the nations that pride themselves most on their philanthropic impulse and, as a result, have embraced celanthropy with hearty enthusiasm is, of course, the USA. Here, households earning less than $25,000 per year donate an average of 4.2% of their income to charity; those with earnings in excess of $75,000 give away 2.7%. It need hardly be added that the personal sacrifice of giving from low income groups is disproportionately large. The rich receive tax breaks for charitable donations. The US runs an expanding scale of tax breaks so the level of personal relief rises the higher you are on the income scale (Warner, 2010).

International measures establish that the USA is the richest nation in the world. Yet the latest data supplied by the US Census Bureau report that 51 million people have incomes of less than 50% above the poverty line. One in three Americans (over 100 million people) either live below the poverty line or in the stress zone immediately above it (DeParle et al., 2011).

In common with most other Western capitalist democracies, the US fiscal system affords tax avoidance for the rich and penalises the poor. To put this into perspective, Warren Buffett (2011) – according to the Forbes Business Rich List (2011), the second wealthiest individual in the USA with a current net worth of $39 billion – in a refreshing *New York Times* op-ed piece, points out that his tax bill in 2011 was $6,938,744. While this sounds like a lot, Buffett notes that it amounts to only 17.4% of his taxable income – a lower percentage than any of the 20 people employed in his office. (Their tax burden ranged from 33% to 41%, with an average of 36%.)

These data, from official government resources, reveal something of the level of social and economic divisions in US society. They do not tell us much about the level of human suffering. How can we speak of a 'team-world' in the US humanitarian response to global incidents and emergencies when one in three US citizens live in a condition of poverty or near poverty? The team-world rhetoric of global event management disguises that humanitarian responses do not consist of equal partners. Worse, it calls upon the poor to sacrifice more than the rich, since a financial contribution from them erodes their income margin with disproportionate severity.

Turning now from the double standards of global event management, the corporate media and PR–media hub to the politics and economics of sacrifice, there is also something to be said about the mass psychology of giving, and the benefits it bestows upon donors. The balance of discussion in event management is heavily weighted towards the recipients of help. That is, the victims of emergencies and crises. What this ignores is the therapeutic rewards of the gift. We do not participate in events out of nobility, we participate out of *need*. Global event management exploits and manipulates a 'can do' attitude. It exhorts people to unleash their hidden power, get in touch with their inner selves, join hands 'as one' and launch 'team-world' against the incidents, emergencies, inequalities and injustices that are the moral blight of the planet. The spirit of 'doing something, 'doing anything', is presented positively, and is indeed akin to gifting. Yet the gift is not as innocent as it seems. For it bears the hidden hallmarks and expectations of cultural institutions (Douglas, 1990). As such, it is a calling card that represents one's perceived place in the social order. It adds to personal self-image and status. It says something about who you *are*.

The public exhibition of gifting makes us feel better about ourselves since it provides a tangible statement of both our compassion and the progressive nature of the society to which we belong. This explains why the future of global events is secure. When events are heralded in the media, and better, when they are broadcast, we feel a sense of transcendence which makes us briefly conscious of belonging to a bigger whole, a greater, pre-ordained unity.

But of course this unity is a veneer. It lacks the discipline of collective mobilisation, collective action and a vision of a compelling collective social, economic and moral alternative. All that events are capable of breeding is event consciousness. That is, a fragmentary, episode-driven, media-fuelled awareness of global problems. This is deeply connected to political passivity since it offers no effective structural challenge to the forces of invisible government in the global media and transnational elements of the state who run the show.

A much debated straw in the wind that has lately gained a good deal of coverage and acceptance as promising effective resistance and even system-breaking opposition is the mobile phone, the internet and cognate forms of digital communication technology. The media have credited this technology with acting as a catalyst for the so-called 'Arab Spring' of 2010–11 and regime change in Egypt, Libya and Tunisia and significant civil unrest in Yemen, Sudan, Iraq and Syria.

Similarly, police authorities have also noted the significance of social media like Twitter, Facebook and Meetup in the anti-capitalist Occupy movement (2011–12). The movement is credited with sparking protest marches and rallies in 900 cities around the world including Auckland, Tokyo, Taipei, Toronto, Oakland, Melbourne, Sydney, Mexico City, Paris, Rome, Madrid, Frankfurt, Hamburg and Zurich. Digital communication technology is credited with providing paths of communication that are comparatively insulated from police surveillance, and knitting together cooperative labour networks that act as salient anti-capitalist, anti-consumerist agents.

Respected commentators like Cornell West (2011) refer to the Occupy movement as a mould-breaking 'critique of oligarchy', a 'holistic movement' and 'a deep, democratic awakening'; while Manuel Castells (2011) has described the movement as a movement of 'the 99%' against unregulated informational-financial capital.

Perhaps, they want to detect the ghosts of the old Paris Communards (1871) in this new wave of popular unrest directed against capital. True, it lacks the Situationist desiderata for genuine festivity under capitalism of guns and armaments. However, it fulfils the remaining salient Situationist requirements of festivity, namely a flat hierarchy (no leaders), a revolt against capitalist rule and territorial re-spatialisation (the seizure of prestigious downtown sites adjacent to, or bordering, the financial cortex and transforming it into living space for the people, music and theatre spaces, a people's university, etc.).

All of this is loosely supported by wider, theoretical convictions that digital communication technology is bringing power to the people. How? By connecting the physically and socially disconnected in a symbolic universe of unity which cannot be effectively securitised by external forces. Policing is unable to deliver end to end monitoring of digital communication routes. Hence, organizations like Adbusters,[3] who are credited with fomenting the Occupy events, can channel agit-prop and engage in clandestine event planning operations, with negligible risks of detection. Digital communication provides the invisible cords that will, in time, enable global festivity among the 99% to spontaneously emerge. Thus, an optimistic reading presents the Occupy movement as the first iteration of a rising tide of popular festivity that will precipitate a new velvet revolution in the heartland of capitalism just as the popular revolt against communism in the 1980s and 1990s produced the peaceful collapse of state capitalism and the Arab Spring of 2011 usurped the rule of tyranny.[4]

Would that it were so. Without wishing to diminish the signifi-cance of popular disenchantment with finance and industrial capital-ism that the movement captured, or the obvious sincerity of the protesters, is it too jaundiced to maintain that Occupy is mostly a popular extension of a prankster form of event consciousness that relies upon 'staged authenticity' and the communication power of the media to telecast 'raw ego' over 'personality' (MacCannell, 2011: 24)? We live under the discipline of a gestural economy wherein the proof of the pudding is not just a matter of response. It is a matter of *rapid response*. Everything in the telecasting of incidents and emer-gencies and the public perception of events is front-loaded. It is the immediate, rapid action response that gets noticed and wins applause, not the painstaking monitoring and evaluation of questions of causal-ity and post-event resource distribution.

The outpouring of grief over 9/11, Hurricane Katrina (2005), the earthquake in Haiti (2010), the *tsunami* in Japan and the nuclear melt-down that it precipitated (2011) was truly global. We were judged by our immediate reaction to the burning towers, which most of us watched live on television. Engagement with American foreign policy and its role in generating militancy among Arab Islamic fundamental-ists was discouraged by communication power. It was in immediate, automatic gestures of compassion, often communicated solely through face work (a perplexed grimace, tears, a sigh) that our social worth as *relevant* people was evaluated. We were not judged upon plans to interrogate the justice of American foreign policy or provisions to reform anti-Americanism in the Middle East, Africa and Asia. Instead, the focus was on what 'they' had done to 'us'.

Global events seize upon this intense, widespread need to be recog-nised as a morally competent, *relevant* person. People who emote deeply and display an inner connection with incidents and emergencies are respected for their bravery and integrity. Caution is interpreted as inhibi-tion, and diffidence is identified with withholding (Furedi, 2004: 50). Culturally speaking, the accent is upon expressing yourself. This is what gives you credit to be noticed as 'a good person' and 'a caring individual'. It is no longer enough to keep these feelings to yourself. Representation is the key to social recognition and an important axis of self-esteem in managing a 'healthy' personality.

It is also lends itself to a currency of face-value impression management in which the motif of compassion and the gesture of action are infinitely adaptable, flexible resources. The cultural requirement to display emotion encourages performative labour in which affect is not just released but stage managed and dramatised. Global events provide a stage for emotional exhibitionism and a media-friendly symbol of a rapid action response. They bestow the front of self-esteem and purpose in conditions in which conventional interpersonal experience is often loaded with feelings of helplessness and powerlessness.

Yet they leave the questions of what causes incidents and emergencies, and why planning for them is not more efficient, permanently dangling in mid air. More profoundly, these questions are connected to deeper issues, having to do with structures of inequality, divisions of power, access to the forces of manipulation and the nature of invisible government that media-dominated, episode-fuelled event consciousness conspicuously fails to address.

The display of emotions has been a constant in human history. However, the application of global events to morally regulate populations is relatively new. It reflects the waning of nation-state power and the global expansion of corporate–state power. Events are now part of the policy software of invisible government.

The connections between celanthropy, media power and moral regulation are so ubiquitous and unquestioned by the public, that they deserve to be studied more widely. An orthodoxy of this type does not become embedded without meticulous preparation. The notion that high profile events can make a difference is presented as evidence of people power. Actually, it reflects neglect on the part of invisible government with regard to fiscal prudence, social investment, global justice and international corporate regulation. By benignly endorsing global events as 'can do' contributions, invisible government perpetuates global conditions of entrenched economic inequality and organised injustice.

It is not that global events are without economic, social or political value. They do make a difference. But in comparison with the scale of the global problems of disease, malnutrition, under-education, premature death and pollution, the difference is modest. At their worst they contribute to public opinion that meaningful action is occurring, while conveniently obscuring the question of the comparative *inaction* of the state–corporate behemoth in piloting equitable resource distribution and environmental security (Easterly, 2007; Moyo, 2010; Sachs, 2010, 2011). I maintain that the public has been softened up to accept this by the organised jeremiad against collective mobilisation and action, involving academics, politicians, communitarians and the PR–media hub, that has made conventional wisdom of the argument that market solutions to public problems are economically and ethically superior, and the whitewash that the corporate media simply mirrors reality. The portrayal of global events as part of a history leading inevitably to greater liberty and enlightenment is naive and superficial (Bowdin et al., 2011; Getz, 2005, 2012; Getz and Wicks, 1994). By the same token, to celebrate events as expressions of pure altruism, devoid of the trappings of self-interest, economic opportunism, political gain and social control, is to see them through a glass darkly.

The public profile of events caters to the psychological need for emotional exhibitionism and mobilises economic and political interests to engage in profiteering, moral regulation and event appropriation. But the roots of why this psychological need is now so insistent, and how it contributes to political passivity, lie beyond the event platform. The professional literature that surrounds it has shown little interest to date in exploring this territory. Instead it has contented itself with mostly laudatory lubrications of events as the utmost expression of decency, enlightenment and human worth. The romance of charity is all very well, but unless it is sympathetically entwined with scrupulous fidelity to the *ends* of charity and effective regulation it will keep the world forever captive in the grip of event consciousness.

Event consciousness has a preference for episode over structure, representation over analysis, indignation over reflection and a rapid action response over coordinated long-term transformation which would minimise the risk of incidents and emergencies facing the world and militate against widespread feelings of helplessness and powerlessness. There needs to be a change in the public mindset from identifying the froth of action along many fronts as contributing to meaningful social change to the renewal of a politics of structural transformation that will contribute to equitable resource distribution, social justice and global empowerment. The high profile of event management as part of a phalanx of social and economic strategies attached to a market-led, loosely communitarian philosophy provides a media-friendly message of positive action. Notwithstanding this, the perpetuation of global hunger, disease, under-education and environmental instability means that more and more people are posing the question of whether the game is really worth the candle.

Before we permit global events to occupy are hearts and minds with spurious sentiments of global unity and effective, decisive action let us pause to reflect upon the entrenched character of global inequality and the well-defended power structures that perpetuate it. True festivity lies in developing and communicating a clear idea of the real causes behind unrest and protest and a realistic vision of the future that soars above cheerful conformity. Only then will we stop the brutal, disfiguring global forces that lead to a child in Africa needlessly dying every time Bono claps his hands.

Notes

1   Occupy is a global movements against social inequality. It took the Arab Spring as a template for popular uprising. The immediate context for the emergence of the movement was the economic slump in the West which started in 2008 and the role of finance capital in generating social inequality.

2   The 99% was a crucial slogan in Occupy propaganda. It refers to an item in a Congressional Budget Office (CBO) report which notes that net income among the top 1% has almost tripled in the last 30 years (Pear, 2011).

3   Adbusters (1989) is a Canadian-based not-for-profit, anti-consumerist, pro-environment organisation. It presents itself as an anti-capitalist global network of artists, activists, writers, educators, entrepreneurs and pranksters. Among the practices of organised disruption that it favours are culture jamming (interrupting consumer conventional wisdom by exposing advertising and corporate manipulation) and re-spatialisation (the Occupy movement). There are clear parallels with the Situationist commitment to the tactic of *detournement* (standing the expressions of capital on their head). The derailing of conventional wisdom is presented in festive terms as producing celebration and a transcendent sense of unity. Adbusters takes over event ideology and makes the event a staple of the grassroots activism.

4   Interestingly, the Arab Spring had its own 'burning man' as a symbol of resistance and liberation (compared with the Burning Man City event). Mohamed Bouazizi, a Tunisian street trader, immolated himself in 2010 as a protest against municipal harassment. His suicide, conducted against the state, became the catalyst for the Tunisian revolution which in turn, inspired the wider Arab Spring.

REFERENCES

Adams, V., Van Hattum, T. and Enlish, D. (2009) 'Chronic disaster syndrome: Disaster capitalism, and the eviction of the poor from New Orleans', *American Ethnologist* 36(4): 615–36.

Aldrich, D. and Crook, K. (2008) 'Strong civil society as a double edged sword: Siting trailers in post-Katrina New Orleans', *Political Research Quarterly* 61(3): 379–89.

Allen, J. (2000) *Event Planning*. Toronto: Wiley.

Allen, T. (2007) 'Katrina, race, class and poverty', *Journal of Black Studies* 37(4): 466–68.

Anderson, B. (2004) 'In the world-shadow of Bismarck and Nobel', *New Left Review* 27: 85–129.

Andrews, D. (2006) 'Disneyization, Debord and the intergrated NBA spectacle', *Social Semiotics*, 16(1): 89–102.

Antonio, R. (1989) 'The normative foundations of emancipatory theory: Evolutionary versus pragmatic perspectives', *American Journal of Sociology* 94(4): 721–48.

Arcodia, C. and Reid, S. (2004) 'Event management associations and the provision of services', *Journal of Convention and Event Tourism* 6(4): 5–25.

Armstrong, G. (2007) 'The global footballer and the local war-zone: George Weah and transnational networks in Liberia, West Africa', *Global Networks* 7(2): 230–47.

Atkins, D. and Moy, E. (2005) 'Left behind: The legacy of Hurricane Katrina', *British Medical Journal* 93(3): 916–18.

Austen, I. (2010) 'Concerns as Canada balances protests and civil liberties', *New York Times*, 10.02.2010.

Austin, J.L. (1962) *How To Do Things With Words*. Oxford: Clarendon.

Baade, R. and Matheson, V. (2002) 'Bidding for the Olympics: Fool's gold?', in C. Barros, M. Ibrahimo and S. Szymanski (eds) *Transatlantic Sport*, pp. 127–51. London: Edward Elgar.

Bakhtin, M. (1968) *Rabelais and His World*. Cambridge, MA: MIT Press.

Bauman, Z. (2000) *Liquid Modernity*. Cambridge: Polity.

Baym, N.K. and Burnett, R. (2009) 'Amateur experts: International fan labour in Swedish independent music', *International Journal of Cultural Studies* 12(5): 433–50.

Beck, U. (1992) *Risk Society*. London: Sage.

Bell, D. (1976) *The Coming of Post Industrial Society*. New York: Basic.

Bennett, T. (1988) 'The exhibitionary complex', *New Formations* 4(4): 73–102.

Bernays, E. (1923) *Crystallizing Public Opinion*. New York: Liveright.

Bernays, E. (1928) *Propaganda*. New York: Ig Publishing.

Bernays, E. (1947) 'The engineering of consent', *The Annals of the American Academy of Political and Social Science*, 250(1): 113–20.

Bernstein, B. (1998) 'The revival of the democratic ethos', in M. Rosenfeld and A. Arato (eds) *Habermas on Law and Democracy*, pp. 287–305. Berkeley: University of California Press.

Binnie, J. and Valentine, G. (1999) 'Geographies of sexuality – a review of progress', *Progress in Human Geography* 23(2): 175–82.

Bishop, M. and Green, M. (2008) *Philanthrocapitalism: How The Rich Can Save the World and Why We Should Let Them*. London: A & C Black.

Black, R., Morris, S. and Bryce, J. (2003) 'Where and why are 10 million children dying every year?', *The Lancet* 361: 2226–34.

Blair, T. (2005) "British Prime Minister Tony Blair reflects on "significant process" of G8 summit'; at: www.g8.gov.uk.

Blyton, P. and Jenkins, J. (2007) *Key Concepts in Work*. London: Sage.

Bowdin, G., Allen, J., O'Toole, W., Harris, R. and McDonnell, I. (2011) *Events Management* (3rd edition) Oxford: Butterworth-Heinemann.

Brassett, J. (2008) 'Cosmopolitanism vs. terrorism? Discourses of ethical possibility before and after 7/7', *Millennium: Journal of International Studies* 36(2): 311–27.

Brinkley, D. (2006) *The Great Deluge: Hurricane Katrina, New Orleans and the Mississippi Gulf Coast*. New York: William Morrow.

Bryce, J., Boschi-Pinto, C., Shibuya, K. and Black, R. (2005) 'WHO estimates of the causes of death in children', *The Lancet* 365: 1147–52.

Bryman, A. (2004) *The Disneyization of Society*. London: Sage.

Buffett, W. (2011) 'Stop coddling the super-rich', *New York Times*, 7.08.2011.

Burby, R.J. (2006) 'Hurricane Katrina and the paradoxes of government disaster policy', *The ANNALS of the American Academy of Political and Social Science* 604: 171–87.

Burkitt, L. (2009) 'Proctor & Gamble will sponsor Winter Olympics', *Forbes Business Journal*, 31.08.2009.

Butler, J. (1990) *Gender Trouble*. New York: Routledge.

Butler, J. (1993) *Bodies that Matter*. New York: Routledge.

Butler, J. (1997) *Excitable Speech: Politics of the Performative*. London: Routledge.

Calhoun, C. (2001) 'Putting emotions in their place', in J. Goodwin (ed.), *Passionate Politics*, pp. 45–57. Chicago: University of Chicago Press.

Callinicos, A. (2006) 'Winding up Make Poverty History', *Socialist Worker Online*; at: http://socialistworker.co.uk(1988).

Callois, R. (1961) *Man, Play and Games*. Glencoe, IL: The Free Press.

Campbell, D. and Kuper, S. (1999) '$1 million "fixed" the FIFA poll, author claims', *The Observer*, 21.03.1999.

Carroll, J. (2011) 'The gift spigot was not open wide', *San Francisco Chronicle*, 29.12.2011.

Cashman, R. (2005) *The Bitter Sweet Awakening: The Legacy of the Sydney 2000 Olympic Games*. Sydney: Walla Walla Press.

Castells, M. (1997) *The Information Age*. Oxford: Blackwell.

Castells, M. (2009) *Communication Power*. Oxford: Oxford University Press.

Castells, M. (2011) 'Manuel Castells on Occupy London', You Tube broadcast posted by 'Voicing the City', 26.11.2011.

Chambers, S. and Costain, A. (2000) *Deliberation, Democracy and the Media*. Boston: Rowman & Littlefield.

Chappelet, J. (2006) 'The tale of three Olympic cities – forecast for Torni on basis of Grenoble and Innsbruck', XX Winter Games Symposium, Turin.

Chasteen, J. (1996) 'The prehistory of samba: Carnival dancing in Rio de Janeiro, 1840–1917', *Journal of Latin American Studies* 28(1): 29–47.

Chen, K. (2009) *Enabling Creative Chaos*. Chicago: Chicago University Press.

Clarke, M. (1982) *The Politics of Pop Festivals*. London: Junction Books.

Coates, D. and Humphreys, D. (1999) 'The growth effects of sport franchises, stadia and events', *Journal of Policy Analysis and Management* 16(4): 601–624.

Cohen, M. and Whelpley, M. (2007) 'Cooking for Burning Man', 8 August; at: http://video.google.com.

Cohen, S. (2001) *States of Denial*. Cambridge: Polity.

Collins, R. (2001) 'Social movements and the focus of emotional attention', in J. Goodwin (ed.), *Passionate Politics*, pp. 27–44. Chicago: University of Chicago Press.

Cooper, A. (2008) *Celebrity Diplomacy*. New York: Paradigm.

Cornelissen, S. and Swart, K. (2006) 'The 2010 Football World Cup as a political construct', *Sociological Review* 54(2): 108–23.

Corner, J. (2000) 'Mediated persona and political culture', *European Journal of Cultural Studies* 3(3): 386–402.

Corrigan, P. and Sayer, D. (1985) *The Great Arch*. Oxford: Blackwell.

Cottle, S. (2008) ' "Mediatized rituals": A reply to Couldry and Rothenbuhler', *Media, Society & Culture* 30(1): 135–40.

Crang, P. (1994) 'It's showtime: On the working of geographies of display in a restaurant in Southeast England', *Environment and Planning D: Society and Space* 12: 675–704.

Crossley, N. (2003) 'Even newer social movements? Anti corporate protests, capitalist crises and the remoralization of society', *Organization* 10(2): 287–305.

Curran, J. (2010) 'Entertaining democracy', in *Media and Society* (5th edition), pp. 38–62. London: Bloomsbury.

Curran, J. (2011) *Media and Democracy*. London: Routledge.

Curran, J., Iyengar, S., Lund, A.K. and Salovaara-Moring, I. (2009) 'Media system, public knowledge and democracy', *European Journal of Communication* 24(1): 5–26.

Darby, P. (2003) 'Africa, the FIFA presidency and the governance of world football: 1974, 1998 and 2002', *Africa Today* 50(1): 3–24.

David, M. (2010) *Peer to Peer and the Music Industry*. London: Sage.

Debord, G. (1967) *Society of the Spectacle*. Cambridge: Zone.

Debord, G. (1988) *Comments on the Society of the Spectacle*. London: Verso.

Debord, G., Kotanyi, A. and Vaneigem, R. (2009) 'On the commune', in T. McDonough et al., *The Situationists and the City*. London: Verso. (Originally published as 'The bad days will end', *Situationist International Anthology* 84 (1962).)

DeParle, J., Gebeloff, R. and Tavernese, S. (2011) 'Older, suburban and struggling, "near poor" startle the census', *New York Times*, 18.11.2011.

Deustschman, A. (2000) *The Second Coming of Steve Jobs*. New York: Broadway Books.

Deuze, M. (2007) *Media Work*. Cambridge: Polity.

Dimanche, F. (1996) 'Special events legacy: The 1984 Louisiana Summer World's Fair in New Orleans', *Festive Management and Event Tourism* 4: 49–54.

Douglas, M. (1990) 'Foreword', in M Mauss, *The Gift*. New York: Norton.

Douglas, M. and Isherwood, B. (1979) *The World of Goods*. New York: Basic.

Easterly, W. (2007) *The White Man's Burden: Why the West's Efforts to Aid the Rest Have Done So Much Ill and So Little Good*. Oxford: Oxford University Press.

Easterly, W. (2010) 'Lennon the rebel, Bono the wonk', *The Washington Post*, 12.12.2010.

Eby, D. (2007) 'Still waiting at the altar: Vancouver's 2010 on-again, off-again, relationship with social sustainability', report prepared for COHRE Expert Workshop on Protecting and Promoting Housing Rights in the Context of Mega-Events. Geneva: COHRE.

Ecclestone, D. (2011) 'Bob Geldof: Live Aid & Me', *Mojo*, 1.01.2011.

Edensor, T. (2001) 'Performing tourism, staging tourism', *Tourist Studies* 1(1): 59–81.

Eisenger, P.K. (2000) 'The politics of bread and circuses: Building the city for the visitor class', *Urban Affairs Review* 35(3): 316–33.

Elavsky, C.M. (2009) 'United as ONE: Live 8 and the politics of the global music spectacle', *Journal of Popular Music Studies* 21(4): 384–410.

Elliott, L. (2010) 'G8 summit communique drops Gleneagles pledge on aid to Africa', *The Guardian*, 4.06.2010.

Elliott, P. (2011) 'G8 accused of cover-up on broken aid pledges', *The Guardian*, 19 May.

Etzioni, A. (1993) *The Spirit of Community*. New York: Touchstone.

Ewen, S. (1998) *PR! A Social History of Spin*. New York: Basic.

Farrell, P. and Lundegren, P. (1991) *The Process of Recreation Programming*. State College, PA: Venture Publishing.

Fishkin, J. (2009) *When The People Speak*. Oxford, Oxford University Press.

Florida, R. (2002) *The Rise of the Creative Class*. New York: Basic.

Flyvbjerg, B., Bruzelius, N. and Rothengatter, W. (2003) *Megaprojects and Risk*. Cambridge, MA: MIT Press.

Food and Agricultural Organization of the United Nations (2010) *The State of Food Insecurity in the World*. New York: Food and Agricultural Organization.

Ford, L. (2007) 'So you want to work in . . . events management', *The Guardian*.

Forsyth, A. (2001) 'Nonconformist populations and planning sexuality and space', *Journal of Planning Literature* 15(3): 339–58.

Foucault, M. (1975) *Discipline and Punish*. London: Penguin.

Foucault, M. (1981) *The History of Sexuality*, volume 1. London: Penguin.

Franks, S. (2010) 'Why Bob Geldof has got it wrong', *British Journalism Review* 21(2): 51–6.

Freudenberg, W., Laska, S. and Erikson, K. (2009) *Catastrophe in the Making: The Engineering of Katrina and the Disasters of Tomorrow*. Washington, DC: Island Press.

Fruin, J.J. (1987) *Pedestrian Planning and Design*. New York: Elevator World Inc.

Furedi, F. (2004) *Therapy Culture*. London: Routledge.

Furlong, J. (2011) *Patriot Hearts: Inside the Olympics that Changed the Country*. Toronto: Douglas & McIntyre.

Fussey, P., Coaffee, J., Armstrong, G. and Hobbs, D. (2011) *Securing and Sustaining the Olympic City*. Farnham: Ashgate.

Gallup, S. (1988) *A History of the Salzburg Festival*. London: Weidenfeld & Nicolson.

Gallo, C. (2010) *The Innovation Secrets of Steve Jobs*. New York: McGraw Hill.

Galston, W.A. (1993) 'Cosmopolitan altruism', *Social Philosophy & Policy* 10(1): 118–34.

Gaudet, M. (1998) 'The world turned upside down: Mardi Gras at Carville', *The Journal of American Folklore* 111(439): 23–38.

Gaudin, B. (2004) 'The Micareta and cultural identity', *Latin American Perspectives* 31(2): 80–93.

Gellner, E. (1994) *Conditions of Liberty*. London: Penguin.

Getz, D. (2005) *Event Management and Event Tourism*. New York: Cognizant Communication Corporation.

Getz, D. (2012) *Event Studies*. London: Routledge.

Getz, D. and Wicks, B. (1994) 'Professionalism and certification for festival and event practitioners: Trends and issues', *Festival Management and Event Tourism* 2(2): 108–9.

Getz, D., Andersson, T. and Larson, M. (2007) 'Managing festival stakeholders: Concepts and case studies', *Event Management* 2(3): 103–22.

Giddens, A. (1991) *Modernity and Self-identity*. Cambridge: Polity.

Gilligan, A. (2010) 'Africans don't rate Bob Geldof, so why should we?', *The Telegraph*, 15.07.2010.

Gilmore, L. (2010) *Theater in a Crowded Fire*. Berkeley: University of California Press.

Goffman, E. (1959) *The Presentation of the Self in Everyday Life*. Harmondsworth: Pelican.

Goffman, E. (1961) *The Presentation of Self in Everyday Life*. London: Penguin.

Goffman, E. (1963) *Stigma*. London: Penguin.

Goffman, E. (1971) *Relations in Public*. London: Pelican.

Gold, J. and Gold, M. (eds) (2007) *Olympic Cities*. London: Routledge.

Goldblatt, J. (2008) *Special Events: Event Leadership for a New World* (5th edition). Hoboken, NJ: Wiley.

Goldwasser, M. (1975) *O palacio do samba*. Rio de Janeiro: Zahar.

Gorringe, H. and Rosie, M. (2008) 'The polis of "global protest"', *Current Sociology* 56(5): 691–710.

Graham, S. (2010) *Cities Under Siege*. London: Verso.

Graham, S. (2012) 'Welcome to Fortress London', *The Guardian*, 13.03.1012

Gregory, C. (1982) *Gifts and Commodities*. London: Academic Press.

Haahti, A. and Komppula, R. (2006) 'Experience design in tourism', in D. Buhalis and C. Costa (eds) *Tourism Business Frontiers,* pp. 101–110. Oxford: Elsevir Butterworth-Heinemann.

Habermas, J. (1987) *The Theory of Communicative Action, Volume 2: System and Lifeworld*. Cambridge: Polity.

Habermas, J. (1989) *The Structural Transformation of the Public Sphere*. Cambridge, MA: MIT Press.

Habermas, J. (1996) *Between Facts and Norms*. Cambridge, MA: MIT Press.

Habermas, J. (1998) *The Inclusion of the Other*. Cambridge, MA: MIT Press.

Hall, C.M. (1989) 'Hallmark events and the planning process', in G. Syme, B. Shaw, D. Fenton and W. Mueller (eds) *The Planning and Evaluation of Hallmark Events*. Aldershot: Avebury.

Hall, C.M. (2006) 'Urban entrepreneurship and corporate interests and sports mega-events: The thin policies of competitiveness within the hard outcomes of neo-liberalism', *Sociological Review* 54: 59–70.

Harrison, G. (2010) 'The Africanization of poverty: A retrospective on "Make Poverty History"', *African Affairs* 109(436): 391–408.

Harvey, D. (2004) *The New Imperialism*. Oxford: Oxford University Press.

Harvey, D. (2005) *A Brief History of Neoliberalism*. Oxford: Oxford University Press.

Hatcher, E.P. (1998) 'Performances, discourses and trial balloons: Negotiating change at special events', *Cultural Dynamics* 10(3): 307–23.

Hayes, G. and Horne, J. (2011) 'Sustainable development, shock and awe? London 2012 and civil society', *Sociology* 45(5): 749–64.

Heal, F. (1984) 'The idea of hospitality in early modern England', *Past & Present* 102: 66–93.

Hedges, C. (2010) *Death of the Liberal Class*. New York: Nation Books.

Hiller, H.H. (1998) 'Assessing the impact of mega events: A linkage model', *Current Issues in Tourism* 1(1): 47–57.

Hiller, H.H. (2000) 'Towards an urban sociology of mega-events', *Research in Urban Sociology* 5: 181–205.

Hiller, H.H. and Wanner, R. (2011) 'Public opinion in host Olympic cities', *Sociology*, 45(5): 883–91.

Hoberman, J. (1984) *The Olympic Crises: Sport, Politics and the Moral Order*. New Rochelle, NY: Caratzas Publishing.

Hochschild, A. (1983) *The Managed Heart*. Berkeley: University of California Press.

Hopkins, N. and Norton-Taylor, R. (2011) 'US officials worried about security at 2012 Olympics', *The Guardian*, 13.11.2011.

Horne, D. and Manzenreiter, W. (2004) 'Accounting for mega-events: Forecast and actual impacts of the 2002 Football World Cup finals on the host countries of Japan/Korea', *International Review for the Sociology of Sport* 39(2): 187–203.

Horne, J. (2007) 'The four "knowns" of sports mega-events', *Leisure Studies* 26(1): 81–96.

Horton, D. and Wohl, R. (1956) 'Mass communication and para-social interaction: Observations on intimacy at a distance', *Psychiatry* 19: 215–29.

Hughes, R. (1998) 'Blatter set to carry on where Havelange left off', *The Times*, 9.06.1998.

Hume, D. (2004) *A Treatise on Human Nature*. London: Penguin.

Jennings, A. (2011) 'Investigating corruption in corporate sport: The IOC and FIFA', *International Review for the Sociology of Sport* 1–12.

Jennings, W. (2012) *Olympic Risks*. Basingstoke: Palgrave Macmillan.

Johansson, M. and Kociatkiewicz, J. (2011) 'City festivals: Creativity and control in staged urban experiences', *European Urban and Regional Studies* 18(2): 1–14.

Judd, D. (2003) *The Infrastructure of Play: Building The Tourist City*. London: M.E. Sharpe.

Judt, T. (2010) *Postwar*. London: Vintage.

Juergensmeyer, M. (2003) *Terror in the Mind of God*. Berkeley: University of California Press.

Juris, J. (2008) 'Performing politics: Image, embodiment, and affective solidarity during anti-corporate globalization protests', *Ethnography* 9(1): 61–97.

Kahle, S., Yu, N. and Whiteside, E. (2007) 'Another disaster: An examination of portrayals of race in Hurricane Katrina coverage', *Visual Communication Quarterly* 14(2): 75–89.

Kapchan, D. (1995) 'Performance', *Journal of American Folklore* 108(430): 479–508.

Karamichas, J. (2005) 'Risk versus national pride: Conflicting discourses over the construction of a high voltage power station in the Athens Metropolitan area for demands of the 2004 Olympics', *Human Ecology Review*, 12(2): 133–42.

Katz, J. (1999) *How Emotions Work*. Chicago: Chicago University Press.

Keane, J. (2005) 'Journalism and democracy across borders', in G. Overholser and K.H. Jamieson (eds) *Institutions of Democracy: The Press*, pp. 92–114. Oxford: Oxford University Press.

Kellner, D. (2007) 'The Katrina Hurricane spectacle and crisis of the Bush presidency', *Cultural Studies-Critical Methodologies* 7(2): 222–34.

Kennelly, J. and Watt, P. (2011) 'Sanitizing public space in Olympic host cities' *Sociology*, 45(5): 765–81.

Kenney, M. (1998) 'Remember, Stonewall was a riot: Understanding gay and lesbian experience in the city', in L. Sandercock (ed.) *Making the Invisible Visible*, pp. 120–32. Berkeley: University California Press.

Kenyon, T. (1985) 'The politics and morality of "Live Aid" ', *Politics* 5(2): 3–8.

Klein, N. (2007) *The Shock Doctrine*. New York: Metropolitan Books.

Knowles, R. (1995) 'From nationalist to multinational: The Stratford Festival, free trade, and the discourses of international tourism', *Theatre Journal* 47(1): 19–41.

Kolakowski, L. (1982) *Religion*. London: Fontana.

Kozinets, R. (2002) 'Can consumers escape the market? Emancipatory illuminations from Burning Man', *Journal of Consumer Research* 29(3): 20–38.

Kracauer, S. (1995) *The Mass Ornament*. Cambridge, MA: Harvard University Press.

Kurtzleben, D. (2011) 'Japan's quake, tsunami among most costly of all time'; at: www.usnews.com.

Ladurie, E. (2003) *Carnival in Romans: Mayham and Massacre in a French City*. London: W&N.

Le Bon, G. (1896) *The Crowd: A Study of the Popular Mind*. New York: Cosimo.

Lee, C.-K. and Taylor, T. (2005) 'Critical reflections on the economic impact assessment of a mega-event', *Tourism Management* 26(4): 595–603.

Levine, M. (1999) 'Tourism, urban development, and the "world class" city: The cases of Baltimore and Montreal', in C. Andrew, P. Armstrong and A. Lapiere (eds) *World Class Cities: Can Canada Play?*, pp. 191–212. Ottawa: Ottawa University Press

Lewis, R. and Wappler, M. (2011) 'Junction's spirit lost in growth', *LA Times*, 26.08.2011.

Li, T. and Petrick, J. (2006) 'A review of festival and event motivation studies', *Event Management* 9(4): 239–45.

Linklater, A. (1998) *The Transformation of Political Community*. Cambridge: Polity.

Lippmann, W. (1922) *Public Opinion*. New York: BN Publishing.

Livingstone, S. (1998) 'Relationships between media and audiences: Prospects for audience reception studies', in T. Liebes and J. Curran (eds) *Media, Ritual and Identity: Essays in Honor of Elihu Katz*, pp. 237–55. London: Routledge.

Loven, J. (2005) 'Bush tours devastated Gulf Coast', *Associated Press Wordstream*.

Lowell Lewis, J. (2000) 'Sex and violence in Brazil: Carnival, capoeira and the problem of everyday life', *American Ethnologist* 26(3): 539–57.

Lunt, P. and Livingstone, S. (2001) 'Language and the media: An emerging field for social psychology', in W.P. Robinson and H. Giles (eds) *The New Handbook of Language and Social Psychology*, pp. 585–600. Chichester: John Wiley & Sons.

MacCannell, D. (2011) *The Ethics of Sight-seeing*. Berkeley: University of California Press.

Mackin, B. (2010) 'Seven arrested in Vancouver protest', *Toronto Sun*, 13.02.2010.

Mann, M. (2003) *Incoherent Empire*. London: Verso.

Martin, E.D. (1920) *The Behavior of Crowds: A Psychological Study*. New York: Harper.

Mason, G. and Lo, G. (2009) 'Sexual tourism and the excitement of the strange', *Sexualities* 12(1): 97–121.

McDonough, T. et al. (2009) *The Situationists and the City*. London: Verso.

Merrifield, A. (2011) *Magical Marxism*. London: Pluto.

Michels, R. (1962) *Political Parties*. New York: The Free Press.

Monroe, K. (1993) 'John Donne's people: Explaining difference between rational actors and altruists through cognitive frameworks', *Journal of Politics* 53(2): 394–433.

Moscovici, S. (2010) *The Age of the Crowd*. Cambridge: Cambridge University Press.

Moura, R. (1983) *Tia Ciata: A pequena Africa no Rio de Janeiro*. Rio de Janeiro: Fundacao Nacional de Arte.

Moyo, D. (2010) *Dead Aid*. London: Penguin.

Munro, K. (2011) 'Mardi Gras festival goes straight and loses the alphabet soup', *Sydney Morning Herald*, 18.11.2011.

Nash, K. (2008) 'Global citizenship as show business: The cultural politics of Make Poverty History', *Media, Culture & Society* 30(2): 167–81.

Nauright, J. (2004) 'Global games: Culture, political economy and sport in the globalized world in the 21st century', *Third World Quarterly* 25(7): 1325–36.

Nederveen Pieterse, J. (2008) *Is There Hope for Uncle Sam?* London: Zed.

Newman, P. (2007) 'Back the bid: The 2012 summer games and the governance of London', *Journal of Urban Affairs* 29(3): 255–67.

Noah, T. (2006) 'Bono, tax avoider', *Slate*, 31.10.2006.

Ong, W. (1982) *Orality and Literacy*. London: Methuen.

Owen, K. (2002) 'The Sydney 2002 Olympics and urban entrepreneurialism', *Australian Geographical Studies* 40(3): 563–600.

Parker, C.F., Stern, E.K., Paglia, E. and Brown, C. (2009) 'Preventable catastrophe? The Hurricane Katrina disaster revisited', *Journal of Contingencies and Crisis Management* 17(4): 206–20.

Parker, S. (1983) *Leisure and Work*. London: Allen & Unwin.

Payne, A. (2006) 'Blair, Brown and the Gleneagles agenda: Making poverty history, or confronting the global politics of unequal development?', *International Affairs* 82(5): 917–35.

Pear, R. (2011) 'Top earners doubled share of nation's income, study finds', *New York Times*, 25.10.2011.

Pine, B. and Gillmore, J. (1999) *The Experience Economy: Work is Theatre and Every Business a Stage*. Boston: Harvard Business School.

Pipan, T. and Porsander, L. (1999) 'Imitating uniqueness: How big cities organize big events', *Organization Studies* 20(1): 1–27.

Polman, L. (2010) *War Games*. London: Viking.

Ponsofrd, B. and Agrawal, J. (1999) 'Why corporations sponsor the Olympics', *Journal of Promotion Management* 5(1): 15–28.

Popper, K. (1968) *The Open Society and its Enemies: The High Tide of Prophecy: Hegel, Marx and the Aftermath* (4th edition). London: Routledge.

Porter, A. (2011) 'G8 Summit: David Cameron defends foreign aid spending', *Daily Telegraph*, 27.05.2011.

Poynter, G. and MacRury, I. (eds) (2009) *Olympic Cities: 2012 and the remaking of London*. Farnham: Ashgate.

Preuss, H. (2007) 'The conceptualization and measurement of mega sport event legacies', *Journal of Sport & Tourism* 12(3): 207–88.

Queiroz, M. (1985) 'The samba schools of Rio de Janeiro or the domestication of the masses', *Diogenes* 33(1): 1–31.

Randerson, J. (2006) 'World's richest own 1% of all wealth, UN report discovers', *The Guardian*.

Reid, S. and Arcodia, C. (2002) 'Understanding the role of the stakeholder in event management', Event Research Conference, UTS Sydney.

Repo, J. and Yrjola, R. (2011) 'The gender politics of celebrity humanism in Africa', *International Feminist Journal of Politics* 13(1): 44–62.

Ribeiro, A.M. (1981) 'Samba negro, espoliacao branca: Um estudo das escolas de samba do Rio de Janeiro', Universidade de Sao Paulo.

Roberts, K. (2004) *The Leisure Industries*. Basingstoke: Palgrave Macmillan.

Robinson, L. (2011) 'Legacies of the games: Did the Olympic glow last?'; at: www.playthegame.org.

Roche, M. (2000) *Mega-events and Modernity*. London: Routledge.

Roche, M. (2002) 'Mega events, culture and modernity', *Cultural Policy* 5(1): 1–31.

Rojek, C. (2010) *The Labour of Leisure*. London: Sage.

Rojek, C. (2011) *Pop Music, Pop Culture*. Cambridge: Polity.

Rojek, C. (2012) *Fame Attack: The Inflation of Celebrity and its Consequences*. London: Bloomsbury Academic.

Routledge, P. (2011) 'Sensuous solidarities: Emotion, politics and performance in the clandestine insurgent rebel clown army', *Antipode,* Online version: 1–29.

Routledge, P. and Simon, J. (1995) 'Embodying spirits of resistance', *Transactions of the Institute of British Geographers* 13: 471–98.

Rutherford, J. and Goldblatt, J. (2003) *Professional Event Coordination*. New York: Wiley.

Sachs, J. (2010) 'The facts behind G8 aid promises', *The Guardian*, 4.07.2010.

Sachs, J. (2011) *The Price of Civilization*. London: Bodley Head.

Sahlins, M. (1972) *Stone Age Economics*. Chicago: Aldine-Atherton.

Samarajiva, R. (2005) 'Mobilizing information and communications technologies for effective disaster warning: Lessons from the 2004 tsunami', *New Media & Society* 7(6): 731–47.

Samatas, M. (2007) 'Security and surveillance in the Athens 2004 Olympics', *International Criminal Justice Review*, 17(3): 220–38.

Sayers, S. (1998) *Marxism and Human Nature*. Abingdon: Routledge.

Scheper-Hughes, N. (2005) 'Katrina: The disaster and its doubles', *Anthropology Today* 21(6): 2–4.

Scott, P. (2006) 'St Bono the hypocrite?', *MailOnline*, 11.08.2006.

Sennett, R. (2003) *Respect*. New York: Norton.

Shannon, C.E.A. (1948) 'Mathematical theory of communication', *Bell System Technical Journal* 27: 379–23, 623–56.

Sharma, A. and Grant, D. (2011) 'Narrative, drama and charismatic leadership: The case of Apple's Steve Jobs', *Leadership*, 7(1): 3–26.

Shaw, C.A. (2008) *Five Ring Circus: Myths and Realties of the Olympic Games*. Gabriola Island, BC: New Society Publishers.

Sheriff, R.E. (1999) 'The theft of Carnival: National spectacle and racial politics in Rio de Janeiro', *Cultural Anthropology* 14(1): 3–28.

Sherry, J., McGarth, A. and Levy, S. (1993) 'The dark side of the gift', *Journal of Business Research* 28: 225–44.

Shin, H.B. (2009) 'Life in the shadow of mega-events: Beijing summer Olympiad and its impact upon housing', *Journal of Asian Public Policy* 2(2): 122–41.

Siegel, B. (2010) 'Playing host is hard to do: The allure of the world stage and shiny new stadiums', *World Policy Journal* 27: 59–66.

Silk, M. (2012) 'Towards a sociological analysis of London 2012', *Sociology*, 46(4): 733–48.

Sireau, N. (2008) *Make Poverty History*. Basingstoke: Palgrave Macmillan.

Sivandan, A. (1990) 'All that melts into air is solid: The hokum of New Times', *Race & Class* 31(3): 1–30.

Smith, D. (2010) 'Life in "Tin Can Town" for the South Africans evicted ahead of World Cup', *The Guardian*, 1.04.2010.

Smith, W. (2007) 'Cosmopolitan citizenship: Virtue, irony and worldliness', *European Journal of Social Theory* 10(1): 37–52.

Stallybrass, P. and White, A. (1986) *Politics and the Poetics of Transgression*. London: Methuen.

Stempel, J. (2010) 'Warren Buffett on donation spree, gives $1.93 billion to charities', *International Business Times*.

Stiglitz, J.E. (2010) *Freefall: America, Free Markets and the Sinking of the World Economy*. New York: Norton.

Strauss, B. (2009) *The Spartacus War*. London: Phoenix.

Street, J. (2002) 'Bob, Bono and Tony: The popular artist as politician', *Media, Culture & Society* 24(2): 433–41.

Street J. (2011) *Music and Politics*. Cambridge: Polity.

Sugden, J. and Tomlinson, A. (1998) 'Power and resistance in the governance of world football', *Journal of Sport & Social Issues* 22(3): 299–316.

Sweeney, K.P. (2006) 'The blame game: Racialized responses to Hurricane Katrina', *Du Bois Review* 3(1): 161–74.

Tassiopoulis, D. (2000) *Event Management*. Landsdowne SA: Juta Education.

Teigland, J. (1999) 'Mega-events and impacts on tourism', *Impact Assessment and Project Appraisal* 17(4): 305–17.

Theroux, P. (2006) 'Bono aid is making Africa sick', *Sunday Times*, 1.01.2006.

Thompson, E.P. (1991) *Customs in Common*. London: Penguin.

Tickle, L. (2011) 'The sound of escapism', *The Guardian*, 19.07.2011.

Touraine, A. (1974) *Post-industrial Society*. London: Wildwood House.

Trilling, D. (2011) 'The art of listening: Live Aid', *New Statesman*, 8.07.2011.

Trotter, J. and Fernandez, J. (2009) 'Hurricane Katrina: Urban history from the eye of the storm', *Journal of Urban History* 35(5): 607–13.

Turner, B.S. (2002) 'Cosmopolitan virtues, globalization and patriotism', *Theory, Culture & Society* 19(1): 45–63.

Turner, F. (2009) 'Burning Man at Google: A cultural infrastructure for new media production', *New Media & Society* 11(1): 73–94.

Turner, V. (1987) 'Carnival, ritual and play in Rio de Janeiro'. in A. Falassi (ed.) *Time Out of Time: Essays on the Festival*, pp. 74–90. Albuquerque: University of New Mexico Press.

Urry, J. (2002a) 'The global complexities of September 11th', *Theory, Culture & Society* 19(4): 57–69.

Urry, J. (2002b) *The Tourist Gaze* (2nd edition). London: Sage.

US Government Accountability Office (2010) *Media Report*. Washington DC: GAO.

Vallely, P. (1985) 'Bureaucrats take note', *The Times*, 24.07.1985.

Van Luijk, N. (2010) 'The 2010 Winter Olympic Games: (Re) framing protest', Faculty of Graduate Studies, University of British Columbia, Vancouver.

Walvin, J. (1975) *The People's Game: A Social History of British Football*. London: Allen & Unwin.

Warner, J. (2010) 'The charitable-giving divide', *New York Times*, 22.08.2010.

Waterman, S. (1998) 'Carnivals for elites? The cultural politics of arts festivals', *Progress in Human Geography* 22(1): 54–74.

Waxman, H. (2006) 'A memo to the Democratic Member of the House of Government Reform Committee regarding new information about Katrina contracts'; at: http://oversight.house.

Weber, M. (1978) *Economy and Society*, volumes 1 and 2. Berkley: University of California Press.

Weightman, B. (1980) 'Gay bars as private spaces', *Landscape* 24(1): 9–16.

Weightman, B. (1981) 'Commentary: Towards a geography of the gay community', *Journal of Cultural Geography* 1: 106–12.

Wellmer, A. (1992) *The Persistence of Modernity*. Cambridge, MA: MIT Press.

West, C. (2011) 'Cornell West Says Occupy is critique of oligarchy'; at: www.bbc.co.uk/news/world.

Whitson, D. and Horne, J. (2006) 'Underestimated costs and overestimated benefits? Comparing the outcomes of sports mega-events in Canada and Japan', *Sociological Review* 54: 71–89.

Wilensky, H. (1960) 'Work, careers and social integration', *International Social Science Journal* 12: 145–60.

Willener, A. (1970) *The Action-Image of Society*. London: Tavistock.

Williams, M. and Bowdin, G. (2007) 'Festival evaluation: An exploration of seven UK arts festivals', *Leisure Management* 12(2): 187–203.

Wood, E. (2009) 'Evaluating event marketing', *Journal of Promotion Management* 15(1): 247–68.

World Bank (2007) www.worldbank/org

Yeoman, I., Robertson, M., Ali-Knight, J., Drummond, S. and McMahon Beattie, U. (2004) *Festival and Events Management*. Oxford: Elsevier.

Yrjola, R. (2009) 'The invisible violence of celebrity humanitarianism', *World Political Science Review* 5(1): 279–92.

Zagal, J.P. and Bruckman, A.S. (2005) 'From samba schools to computer clubhouses', *Convergence* 11: 88–105.

AUTHOR INDEX

SUBJECT INDEX